BUNSHAFT

FORM THROUGH TECHNICS

NICOLÁS SICA PALERMO

ORO Editions
Publishers of Architecture, Art, and Design
Gordon Goff: Publisher

www.oroeditions.com
info@oroeditions.com

Published by ORO Editions

Author: Nicolás Sica Palermo
Book Design: Nicolás Sica Palermo
Project Manager: Jake Anderson

10 9 8 7 6 5 4 3 2 1 First Edition

ISBN: 978-1-961856-91-2

Prepress and Print work by ORO Editions Inc.

Printed in China

ORO Editions makes a continuous effort to minimize the overall carbon footprint of its publications. As part of this goal, ORO, in association with Global ReLeaf, arranges to plant trees to replace those used in the manufacturing of the paper produced for its books. Global ReLeaf is an international campaign run by American Forests, one of the world's oldest nonprofit conservation organizations. Global ReLeaf is American Forests' education and action program that helps individuals, organizations, agencies, and corporations improve the local and global environment by planting and caring for trees.

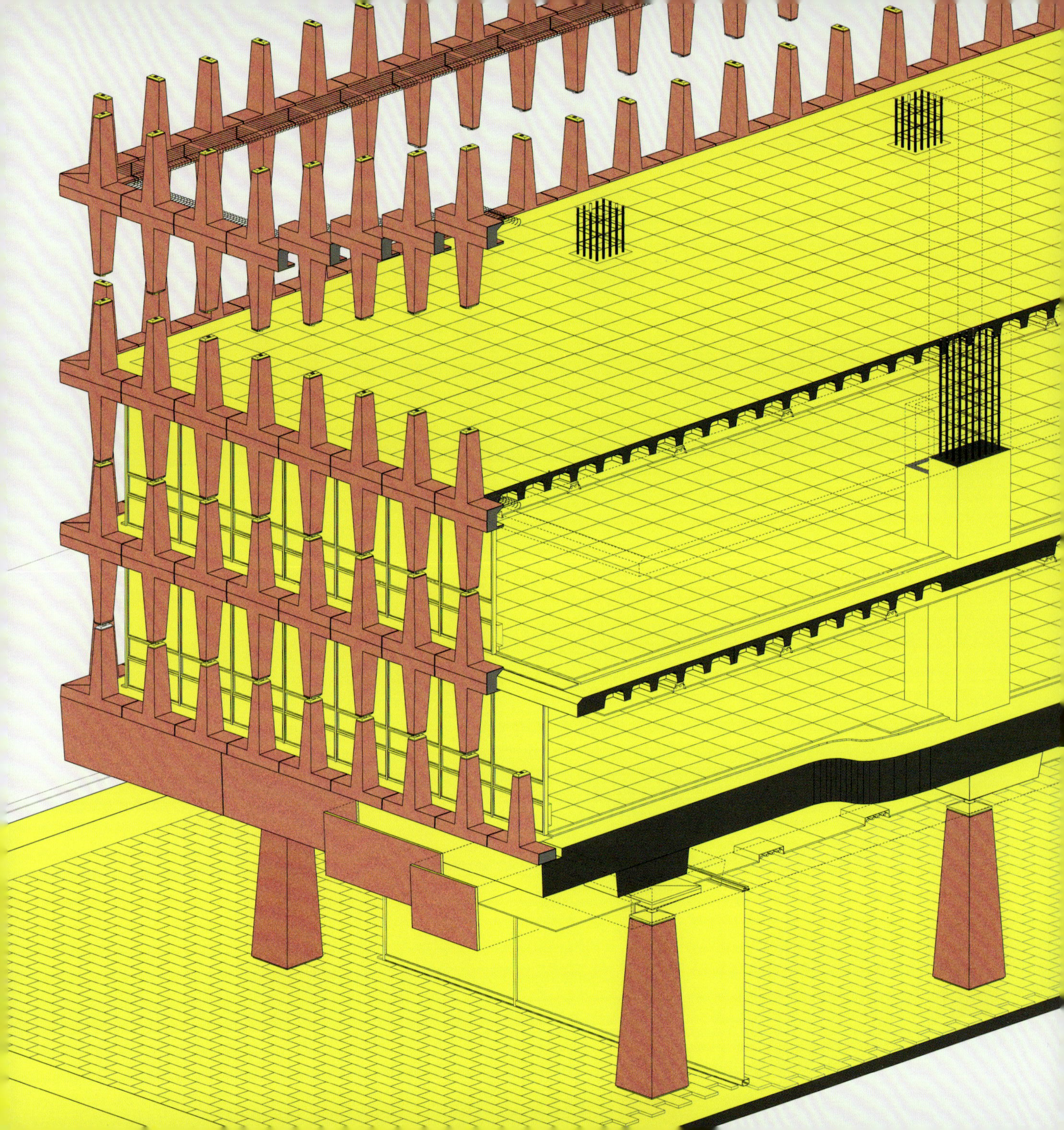

Contents

Acknowledgments

Many people were by my side during the long journey of writing the doctoral thesis that gave rise to this book and they deserve, at the very least, my most sincere thanks.

To my thesis director an friend Cristina Gastón, for her tireless help and clarity of thought.

To Teresa Rovira, who gave me perhaps the best professional development opportunity I have ever had, teaching me so much throughout those years in Barcelona.

To my group and doctoral classmates Inês, Eunice and Edu, with whom I have shared during this last year and a half the successes and mistakes of doing a doctoral thesis.

To the ETSAB/UPC staff, mainly Luz Soro, Consuelo Jurado and Sílvia Feliu, for their help during those years.

From the U.S., to architect Roger Duffy and archives manager Wendy Chang, both from S.O.M., for having received me at the company's offices in New York, giving me support in obtaining fundamental materials for the research.

To Prof. Kenneth Frampton, who agreed to be my tutor during my stay at Columbia University in New York, giving his opinion about the work and opening important doors for me at S.O.M.

To Prof. Carol Krinsky, who cordially attended me in her office at NYU, making herself available for anything within her reach.

To Engineer Matthys Levy, who kindly hosted me for a fruitful and very interesting discussion at the Manhattan offices of Weidlinger and Associates.

To Pamela Shaw, one of the managers and secretaries of the Property Management Group, the company that owns the former John Hancock

Building in New Orleans, and Mr. Sydney Besthoff, the current owner of the property, who kindly welcomed me to the building for a tour, giving me permission to obtain original plans and project documents.

To Sam Bollen and Mary Durand, officers of the American Enterprise Group, for allowing me to visit and receive executive plans of the former American Republic Insurance Company building in Des Moines.

From Brussels, to Christian Dugardyn and Robin Hill, architects of ING Bank, for hosting me while renovations were being made to the former Bank Lambert building.

The transformation of the thesis into a book is the realization of a dream for me. A joy that I believe to be unique. So I would also like to thank the staff of ORO Editions. To Gordon Goff, founder, and Federica Ewing, manager, for betting on the book and very kindly leading its realization until this moment. And also to Jake Anderson, editor, for his usual efficiency, patience and friendliness.

I owe a special thanks to my family. In them I find the basis, encouragement and motivation to try to pursue all the worthwhile things in life.

To my mother, Stella, to my sisters Paty and Pia and to my nephew Pedro, for supporting me and understanding my absence during so many years and important moments.

To my old man, Humberto, who would appreciate this book, since he was an engineer and liked logic and structure. Perhaps that is the origin of it all.

To my precious kids Nina and Franco, who fill my days with truth and joy.

And finally to the love of my life Pati, for whom I have no words to describe my gratitude.

I hope you like it.

Introduction

On the left:

Examples of the buildings studied in the thesis that originated the book.

Photos by the author.

The book proposes a precise and at the same time light review on the life and work of the architect Gordon Bunshaft, one of the most influential architects of the 20th century. The aim is to allow typical architectural graphic materials, in other words, photos and drawings, represent the character of his work, making clear what his vision was on forms, construction, art and, most definitely, architecture.

The works of Gordon Bunshaft, developed while working for the multinational architectural firm SOM – Skidmore, Owings & Merrill – put together a number of concrete and abstract elements that fully reflect the modern movement during the years of its maximum artistic expression.

In the early fifties, the Lever House attracted fame and commissions, becoming a paradigm for new modern office building projects. The evolution of SOM's design and construction processes generated a wide variety of formal solutions during the '50s. Fundamental to this process, the work organization of the firm was based on three basic aspects: modern architecture, American organizational methods and expertise, and the development of techniques and industrialized building materials. Toward the sixties, SOM projects started to have more expressive and technically refined structures, which enhanced formal attributes and gained more functions than usual.

Bunshaft's career showed that his professional profile depended on two basic functions: designing buildings and managing the fundamental decisions of a team dedicated to carrying out large architectural commissions. His temperament and objectivity to direct efforts towards specific goals allowed him to earn a leading role in the company, and also in his professional environment. The prestige in New York society, and throughout the United States, was not the result of his ability to sell, nor the consequence of his good relationships with important figures in New York society, but rather, of his skills as a designer, which, added to a great leadership capacity, opened a wide field of work possibilities. Added to that, the triad of SOM – modern architecture, North American organizational methods and the mastery and development of available industrialized construction techniques and materials – fully supported him.

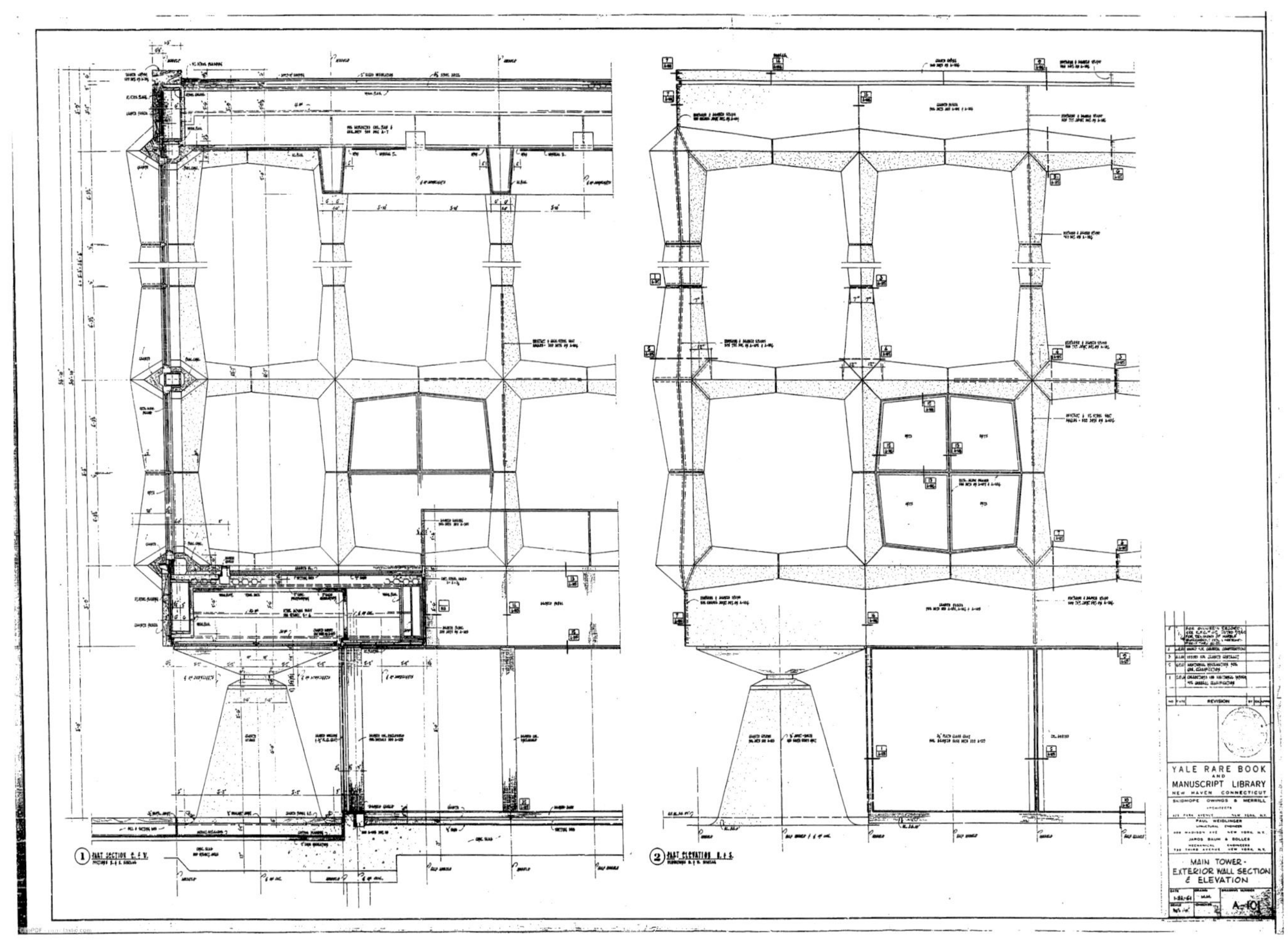

Plan number A-101, part of the Beinecke Rare Book and Manuscript Library executive project.

Modern art decisively influenced Bunshaft's projects. Commissions from large companies with generous budgets gave him the opportunity to include renowned artists in projects. Art was incorporated both abstractly, serving as a subjective reference when designing the buildings, and concretely in the works, when materialized in sculptures, paintings and tapestries, which always assumed spatial prominence. In works such as the Manufacturers Trust, built in Manhattan, or the Beinecke Library at Yale University, it is evident that the cooperation between artist and architect is based on a two-way relationship, in which the artistic work and the receptacle were conceived as a unity: one being generated in the light (or influence) of the other.

The variety of architectural solutions managed by the architect, his team and some collaborators is remarkable. Throughout his career, he designed buildings for rural sites and urban skyscrapers with steel structures and curtain walls; institutional buildings with concrete finishes, as well as factories, museums and hotels. Over four decades, his production accompanied technological advances, the state-of-the art and some cultural and social changes in the US, which are revealed in the presence of materials, construction systems and spatial configurations. However, Gordon Bunshaft never abandoned architectural modernity as the formal matrix for his projects.

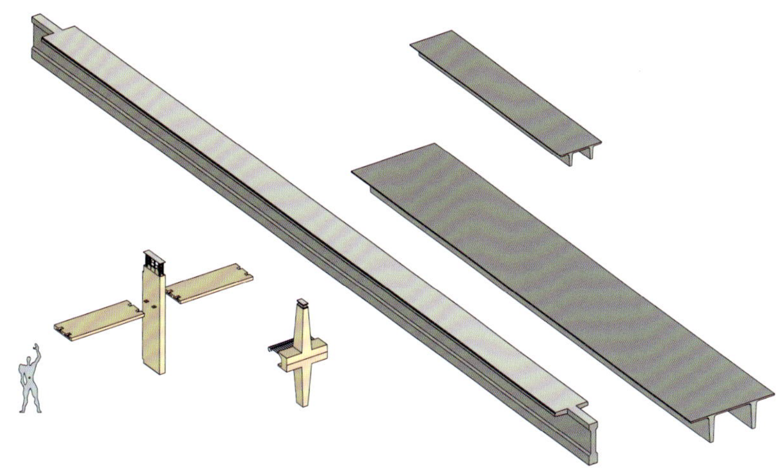

Precast concrete elements for works of Gordon Bunshaft.

Drawing by the author.

4 3/4"
5 1/2"
actual size for Book.

Gordon Bunshaft

On the left:

Gordon and Nina Bunshaft at the construction of their home in East Hampton, New York. The photograph has dimensions handwritten by Bunshaft himself, which served to indicate where the print should be cut to be placed in his biography, authored by Carol Krinsky.

Photo by Hans Namuth.

Gordon Bunshaft (1909-1990) was born in the city of Buffalo, State of New York. The son of Yetta and David Bunshaft, who had immigrated from Russia a year earlier, he lived in his hometown until the age of nineteen. Entering MIT in 1928, Bunshaft obtained a Bachelor's degree in 1933 and a Master's degree in 1935. With a travel scholarship of US$ 3,000, he managed to spend eighteen months in Europe from 1935 to spring 1937. In the fall of that year, he joined the architectural firm founded by Louis Skidmore and Nathaniel Owings, that had just opened an office in New York. He started in the company as a designer, becoming a partner in 1946 and, a few years later, head of the New York office. His most valuable contribution for the company was, undoubtedly, the direction of the architectural projects commissioned to SOM, mainly those destined for the office in New York.

Formative years at MIT and entry into Skidmore, Owings & Merrill (SOM)

Some aspects of Bunshaft's academic and professional training, accomplished before his integration into the SOM team, are important in order to clarify his characteristics as a working architect in subsequent years within the company. Research carried out by professor Carol H. Krinsky and professor Nicholas Adams, as well as some texts published in magazines during the first years in which Bunshaft worked at SOM, endorse this perspective.

MIT's institutional methods were based on the aesthetic and organizational theories of the French classicist school. The studies emphasized historic architecture and the importance of efficient circulation, with an emphasis on a clear differentiation between spaces according to their function. Thus, modern architecture was not part of the degree curriculum with which the students, motivated by young emerging architects of that time, searched for information on new ideas in books, magazines and recently erected modern buildings. The first books of Le Corbusier were of great interest to Bunshaft: "They [Le Corbusier's books] became the alphabet of young architects all over the world."[1]

At that time there were not many texts in English on Mies, and Bunshaft was not able to read German publications. Already on the Master's course,

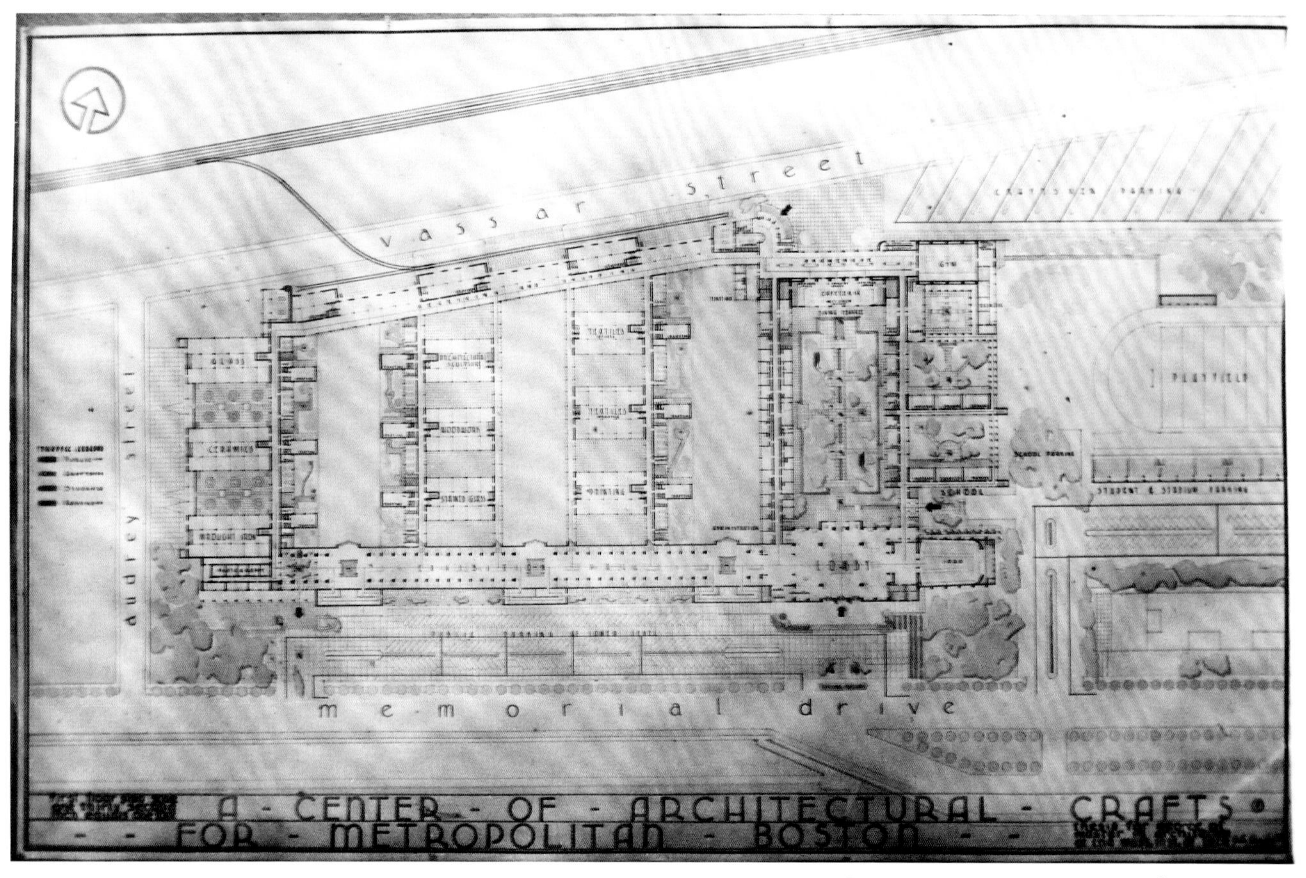

General plan of Gordon Bunshaft's final project for his Master's degree at MIT, 1935.

he had classes with a young professor named Lawrence B. Anderson, later dean of MIT, who developed students' interest in modern architecture. Likewise, the ideas of the students were not yet clear and most of the projects were close to the architecture of Auguste Perret from the 1920s.[2]

After finishing his studies, Bunshaft began working in an office in Boston. A few months later, he registered to participate in the Rotch Traveling Fellowship, a university scholarship that would cover travel expenses, conceived as an award through a competition of architectural projects. The US$ 3,000.00 obtained for the first prize in the competition gave Bunshaft the opportunity to travel around Europe, visiting buildings such as the Van Nelle factory in Rotterdam and the Swiss Pavilion, work of Le Corbusier, in the university city of Paris. Bunshaft confessed that he did not really understand those buildings at first due to his not being sufficiently knowledgeable about modern architecture at that time.

In the spring of 1937, on return from Buffalo after the long trip to Europe, Bunshaft decided to try to get a job in New York. After a few unsuccessful attempts, he began working with Edward Durell Stone. Shortly after, Stone was forced to dismiss his team and Bunshaft had an opportunity to work with the industrial designer Raymond Loewy.

Dissatisfied with the job, Bunshaft asked Stone to recommend him to Louis Skidmore, who had been in partnership with Nathaniel Owings since 1935. Owings was in charge of the Chicago office, while Skidmore was just opening the New York office; the decision was made because one of the company's clients needed architects in the city. Besides that, the 1939 New York World's Fair would offer him good job opportunities. When Skidmore, an experienced exhibition designer, was invited to participate, Bunshaft had his first opportunity to work at SOM as an architect in charge, leading the Venezuelan Pavilion project for the Fair. It was the beginning of a career that would last until 1979.[3]

It should be noted that from the time he began working with Skidmore and Owings in 1937 until 1950, Bunshaft was absent for three years. After completing the second building for which he was the responsible designer – the Hostess House, at the Great Lakes Naval Training Center, Illinois – Bunshaft, who was a reserve officer in the US Army, was promoted to captain. In 1944, During World War II, he was sent to London and Paris to work with emergency medical facilities and field hospitals, being part of the Corps of Engineers.

After being released from his duties with the army, in 1947, Bunshaft was still in the plans of the partners of SOM; thus, he was to join the Chicago office. After remonstrating with Owings, he managed to join the New York team, and after a month became partial partner and chief designer of the

Sketch of San Lorenzo del Escorial, Spain, made by Bunshaft during his study trip with the Rotch scholarship, 1935.

The Hostess House at the Great Lakes Naval Training Center, Illinois.

Manhattan office. Finally, at a company meeting in 1949, Bunshaft applied with five other partial partners (including Merrill) to become a full partner. The great expansion of the company at that time allowed Skidmore and Owings to grant him what they themselves wanted[4].

According to Prof. Carol Krinsky, the first months in the New York office triggered in Bunshaft mixed feelings. His quick ascension to head of the office gave him more responsibilities than he had ever experienced. The nature of the company demanded from its partners certain aptitudes for personnel management, as well as for attracting commissions; social relationships with important figures in New York society, such as politicians and business owners, were considered highly important and desired. He was no club man, nor aspired to be one, and certainly not a society man; his main desire was to work on the firm's projects.

The Venezuelan pavilion at the 1939 World Fair in New York.

Plan of the Venezuelan pavilion at the World Fair in New York.

On the left

Gordon Bunshaft and some Connecticut General Life Insurance Company executives during a project presentation for the headquarters, later built in Bloomfield, Connecticut. Early 1950s.

Bunshaft and SOM partners

Gordon Bunshaft's personality and his particular way of working were quite different from any of the other three SOM partners, whose surnames give the name to the firm. Louis Skidmore, a founding partner, had a special talent for finding the right professionals to fill the jobs within the organization. He had a strong personality and great sales skills. Nathaniel Owings was an aggressive and argumentative person, becoming rude at times. He had a behavior defined by Bunshaft as that of a "playboy," and was energetic and persuasive in making presentations to clients. More outgoing than Skidmore, Owings was the most effective of all in getting commissions for the company.

The last of the three to join as a partner, John Ogden Merrill, was an architectural engineer. When he arrived at the company, his partners expected him to bring many commissions, but over time he showed that he had more skills working internally in the company than selling projects and getting new projects.[5]

Gordon Bunshaft was a young architect, clearly influenced by what appealed to him visually, with little practice in project management and almost no experience in the business world. His main baggage were the studies carried out up to that moment and an illusion fed by the architecture that he had academically learned and seen. The triumphant career through the university, crowned with the Rotch award and travel scholarship, demonstrate his sparkling interest for architectural projects, indicating less willingness to deal with the bureaucratic issues of the profession which came along with the duties of a partner in a large company structure.

The following years showed that Bunshaft's professional profile leaned toward his personal projecting practice, which was constantly tied to the management of a team dedicated to carrying out important architectural commissions. His strong personality and objectivity when directing efforts toward specific goals, many of which transformed into acts of excessive vehemence and arrogance to colleagues, allowed him to earn a leading place in the company, and also within his professional environment.[6]

His prestige in New York society, and even in the United States generally, was not the result of sales abilities or good relations with important figures. His skills as a designer, added to great impetuosity and leadership capacity, opened up a wide field of work possibilities. It seems that Bunshaft had a special ability for making the things that he loved, including modern architecture and art, become part of his work universe, his daily routine, which, ultimately, would shape his life.

On the left

From left to right: Bunshaft, White, Mies, Nervi, Merril and Sert, gathered in the 1960s to judge an architectural competition in Chicago.

Page 369 of the report "Man-Made America," from *Architectural Review* british magazine, December 1950.

periphery to shore

MAN MADE AMERICA

38 39 40 The week-end exodus by motor car, even if only for the day or an afternoon, has become a summertime ritual for the average inhabitant of a large American city, and space for car-parks a major problem for city and other authorities possessing amenities likely to attract the car owner.

41 Leaving the city in search of the seaside, the motorist passes again through the kind of suburb that was once a small town in its own right. Food, sex and drink are the most heavily advertised American commodities. Billboards may be found anywhere, from the tops of skyscrapers to the roofs of these little suburban stores. **42** Along the main street the shops, in valiant competition, have 'modernized' the late nineteenth century structures in which they are still housed. 'The Castle,' once a private house in the style known as Richardsonian Romanesque, which dotted the East until 1900, has succumbed to the inevitable and become a restaurant. **43** On this eminence, city dwellers find the summer temperature ten degrees cooler than in town and will drive out here for dinner after the office is closed.

369

Bunshaft in America

The post-war American social and economic context has been the study subject of various investigations, and different authors have engaged to analyze this important phase of transformation in the country's culture. The architecture and, in short, the built cities were important "mirrors" of this process: they reflected the artistic modernity that was expanding and also the economic and technological growth of the country's industries between the forties and fifties.

The special issue of the British magazine *Architectural Review* (AR) published in December of 1950, was devoted entirely to the existent architectural panorama in the USA. Under the title of "Man-Made America," the English magazine presented an important investigation that discussed the economic and social context of the country, relating it directly to the situation of architecture and urbanism in those years and trying to point out the existing perspectives for the following decades.

Seven years later, in 1957, the magazine published another special issue, which can be considered a sequel of "Man-Made America." Not coincidentally titled "Machine-Made America," it was published analogously to that of 1950, and was authored by the same English editorial team and some invited American scholars. In both cases, the basic elements of argument were the typical images of the country, taken and collected in situ by the writing team.

"Machine-Made America,"[7] from 1957, outlined a systematic analysis of the evolution in modern architecture of the '50s in the US. The issue presented a preface and three chapters – Syntax, Genetrix and Matrix – and related a triad composed of modern architecture built in the territory up to 1957, leading architectural firms in the country and the changes occurring in North American culture, promoted by technological innovations.

Syntax presented the curtain wall as being the representative element of the modern architecture of those years. A sort of icon that conglomerated the main characteristics, gathering in a work, at the same time, a high level of constructive systematization, the standardization of the elements available in the market and the acceptance and dissemination by architects and clients; Genetrix displayed an extensive inventory of American architects who, according to the magazine, had creatively evolved, supported by the growth of industrialization in North America; and finally, Matrix projected the individual and collective achievements of US architects onto the double background – metaphorized in the chapter title as a web, a matrix, made up of international modernism, and American culture.

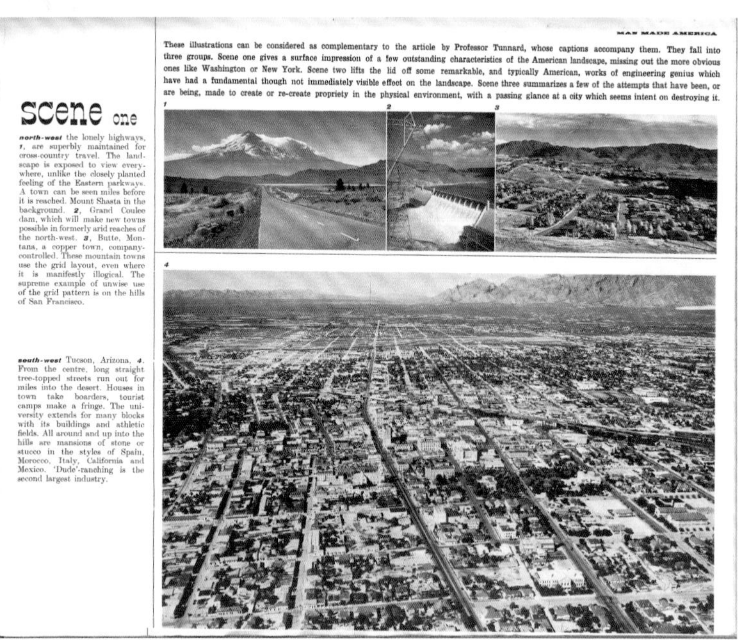

MAN MADE AMERICA

These illustrations can be considered as complementary to the article by Professor Tunnard, whose captions accompany them. They fall into three groups. Scene one gives a surface impression of a few outstanding characteristics of the American landscape, missing out the more obvious ones like Washington or New York. Scene two lifts the lid off some remarkable, and typically American, works of engineering genius which have had a fundamental though not immediately visible effect on the landscape. Scene three summarizes a few of the attempts that have been, or are being, made to create or re-create propriety in the physical environment, with a passing glance at a city which seems intent on destroying it.

scene one

north-west the lonely highways, 1, are superbly maintained for cross-country travel. The landscape is exposed to view everywhere, unlike the closely planted feeling of the Eastern parkways. A town can be seen miles before it is reached. Mount Shasta in the background. 2, Grand Coulee dam, which will make new towns possible in formerly arid reaches of the north-west. 3, Butte, Montana, a copper town, company-controlled. These mountain towns use the grid layout, even where it is manifestly illogical. The supreme example of unwise use of the grid pattern is on the hills of San Francisco.

south-west Tucson, Arizona, 4. From the centre, long straight tree-topped streets run out for miles into the desert. Houses in town take boarders, tourist camps make a fringe. The university extends for many blocks with its buildings and athletic fields. All around and up into the hills are mansions of stone or stucco in the styles of Spain, Morocco, Italy, California and Mexico. 'Dude'-ranching is the second largest industry.

1 2 3 4

entrance

21 22 23

21 The motorist is heading for the centre, but to get there he will probably pass through other centres which have been absorbed into the city. This was once a village street, but it has become a shopping centre for what is now a suburban district. **22** A suburban residential street—this one in a south-eastern city. Note the glassed-in front porches which are joined to form a terrace at ground-floor level, while individuality rears its head above in the monumental dormers, a pair to each house and each pair different. **23** An older residential district of frame houses built between 1900 and 1910 in the north-eastern town chosen for this study. They overlook a little park of American elms, so different in formal character from their English counterparts, and beautiful even in the depths of winter. **24** This is one of the more fortunate New England cities; it was built around a green in 1638, and the green is still there. Most of the houses which formerly surrounded it have gone, to make way for commercial buildings, but some of these are interesting enough. The central building in this picture is the City Hall, one of the earliest examples of Ruskinian gothic in America; the central portion with the tower was built in 1861 by the architect Henry Austin. Its scale is ruined by the tall office building

366

Pages from the report "Man-Made America," from *Architectural Review* magazine, December 1950.

Genetrix

Genetrix tried to identify and collect the history of those characters who were contributing in a practical way to the establishment of modern architecture in the US during the 1950s. The section is an important record of those architects in the late fifties who were actually planning and building works of architecture and urbanism throughout the country. It is a valuable record, which, beyond emphasizing personal trajectories, collected some of the fundamental ideas behind the works of this outstanding group of architects.

According to *Architectural Review,*

> *it attempts to trace each contribution to its source in a man's background, training, the vicissitudes of his career, his heroes, his outlook and his inner convictions. It is specially designed to give architects outside America a more rounded picture of the American architectural scene.*[8]

The magazine claimed that young European architects knew many of their American professional colleagues, some of whom were famous and firmly established in their minds; but with so many young architects in North America, it was often difficult to attach their names to buildings. According to the AR editors, a good way to clarify these aspects was to bring to the surface the personalities behind the conceptions of the buildings.

Thus, the magazine asked American architects to fill out questionnaires previously prepared by the editors. The answers to those questions, accompanied by photographs of their most recent works (and an occasional reminder of earlier ones), were published with the architects listed by age – from oldest to youngest (Frank Lloyd Wright requested that his work must be omitted).

The list of architects presented by Genetrix, with names preceded by ages in 1957, is as follows:

71 Mies van der Rohe
65 Richard Neutra
61 Wlliam Wurster
61 William Lescaze
57 Pietro Belluschi
56 Louis Kahn
55 Mario Corbett
55 Edward Stone
54 Marcel Breuer
53 Victor Gruen
53 Paul Schweiklter
52 Bruce Goff
50 Philip Johnson
49 Robert Alexander
49 Raphael Soriano
49 Vernon DeMars
48 Gordon Bunshaft
48 John Rex
46 Eero Saarinen
46 Eliot Noyes
46 Whitney Smith
45 Ernest Kump
45 Hugh Stubbins
44 Minoru Yamasaki
44 Carl Koch
44 T.A.C. (average age)
44 A. Quincy Jones
42 Ralph Rapson
42 Edward L. Barnes
41 Harry Weese
41 John Johansen
40 I.M. Pei
39 King Lui-Wu
38 Paul Rudolph
37 Roger Lee
37 Peter Blake
36 Ulrich Franzen
34 Reginald C. Knight
33 Thornton Ladd
32 Pierre Koenig

Cover of the special issue of the British magazine *Architectural Review,* May 1957, entitled "Machine-Made America."

The number of prominent architects presented, and also the number of works designed by them, is remarkable. As can be verified in the list, in 1957 almost half of the architects featured were between the ages of 35 and 40, which can be considered an immature age range for an architect's career.

Taking the ordering criteria of the list, which puts the oldest at the top, the architect presented in the first place was Mies van der Rohe. Even if the cataloging had begun with the most influential and important professional in activity at that time instead of starting with the oldest, the German master would still be the first to appear. The article indirectly hinted at that idea in the last paragraph of Mies's presentation:

> *Europe could not have fulfilled his promise; he [Mies van der Rohe] has perhaps gained more from and given more to the US than any other emigre outside the realm of atomic physics. He has produced a lyricism of two constituent US psychological facts – unlimited space and unmitigated technology – in a form that is neither provincial nor crude, and can be held up to the rest of the world as an example of a convincing machine-age architecture. The rest of the world has taken note and, wherever*

architectural thought is on the move, the influence of Mies – American Mies – can be felt. Indeed, he ranks with Le Corbusier, Nervi and Candela as one of the fundamental form-givers of the fifties, and of no other American architect can this be said.[9]

The echo of Mies's practice at that time was also pointed out in "Machine-Made America," and two of the architects presented later ended up being named in the section dedicated to the German architect:

Though Mies's achievement could hardly be more personal, the superficial appearance of the buildings in which that achievement is embodied has facilitated the visual acceptance of a repetitive, endless, grid façade, while the work of two architects most ready to admit his influence, Eero Saarinen and Gordon Bunshaft, has effectively bridged the gap between one man's vision and an industrial product.[10]

The page and a half dedicated to Gordon Bunshaft presented his personal history and briefly commented on some of the most important buildings designed by the architect up to that time: the United States Air Force Academy, Connecticut General Life Insurance, Manufacturers Trust Bank and skyscraper projects, one for Union Carbide Company and the other for Chase Manhattan Bank. Besides that, the section on Bunshaft quoted the architect himself giving his opinion regarding Mies:

Although a German by birth, his recent buildings represent the truly great urban architecture of our country. In contrast to the foreign use of reinforced concrete, we employ steel framing as a basic structural system for most urban buildings. Mies van der Rohe's work truly expresses this fact.[11]

Personal references aside, Bunshaft declared to AR that stylistic discrepancies in contemporary American architecture are more evident between different types of buildings than between buildings in different geographic regions, confirming that there was already conventional architecture in the country, and it should be promoted by the hands of the main and most influential architecture firms.

In a discussion between Bunshaft, Saarinen and Philip Johnson, described by Mrs. Saarinen, Bunshaft "defended the need for a common style, the necessity of a vernacular, and in the work for which he has been directly responsible – Lever House, the Manufacturers Trust and Connecticut General Life Insurance buildings – he has done as much as anyone in America to promote an architectural vernacular of today.[12]

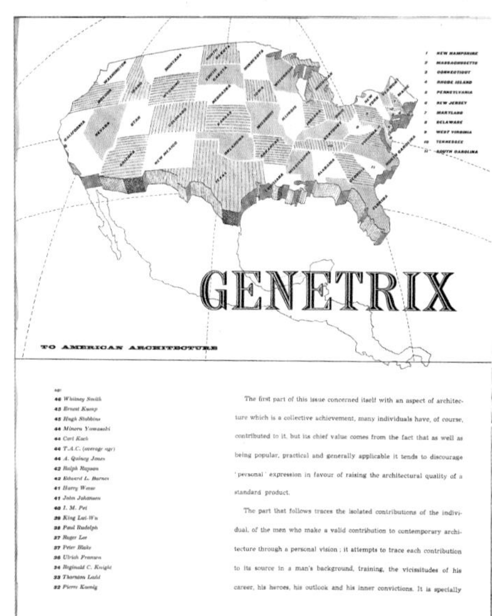

GENETRIX

TO AMERICAN ARCHITECTURE

46 Whitney Smith
45 Ernest Kump
45 Hugh Stubbins
44 Minoru Yamasaki
44 Carl Koch
44 T.A.C. (average age)
44 A. Quincy Jones
42 Ralph Rapson
42 Edward L. Barnes
41 Harry Weese
41 John Johansen
40 I. M. Pei
39 King Lui-Wu
38 Paul Rudolph
37 Roger Lee
37 Peter Blake
36 Ulrich Franzen
34 Reginald C. Knight
33 Thornton Ladd
32 Pierre Koenig

The first part of this issue concerned itself with an aspect of architecture which is a collective achievement, many individuals have, of course, contributed to it, but its chief value comes from the fact that as well as being popular, practical and generally applicable it tends to discourage 'personal' expression in favour of raising the architectural quality of a standard product.

The part that follows traces the isolated contributions of the individual, of the men who make a valid contribution to contemporary architecture through a personal vision; it attempts to trace each contribution to its source in a man's background, training, the vicissitudes of his career, his heroes, his outlook and his inner convictions. It is specially

Page 337 of the chapter Genetrix, from "Machine-Made America."

The conception of "vernacular" architecture referred to by Bunshaft necessarily involved the application of typical structural systems and materials found in the US, or rather, found in the US construction industry. Among these materials and construction elements produced through standardized methods by the industry exclusively for architecture, curtain walls were the first and most representative, being applied to buildings of different types throughout the United States.

Pages 358 and 359 of the chapter Genetrix, from "Machine-Made America," featuring Gordon Bunshaft, then 45 years old.

49

Berkeley, California

Vernon De Mars, born in San Francisco in 1908, is rare among US architects in having more or less the turn of mind and the reputation that a European housing-specialist might have. He arrived at this by entering Government service (after some years of variously directed activity preceded by study at the University of California) to design emergency camps and temporary accommodation for migratory labour in the *Grapes of Wrath* epoch in California. The upshot was a resolve to rectify the complete absence of any American contribution to either the architecture or the sociology of housing, and its realization were the adobe-walled row-houses at Chandler, Arizona, that have found their way into every text-book, and the collective subconscious of the Modern Movement. Much of De Mars' work since then has also been in public finance housing, but he and his office also design rental housing, and have made inroads into the merchant-building housing field, as well as community planning work. He is fairly heavily committed to a preference for row-houses as against land-wasting detached units, and was also involved—with Koch, Kennedy, Rapson and Brown—in the design of the very English-looking *Eastgate Apartments* scheme of flats in Boston. By way of contrast, his own private house at Berkeley, California, where he now teaches, is free-standing and admittedly Japanese in extraction. But he does not rate Japan as a primary influence on his work—European sources account for most of that, though not for the projecting party-walls at Chandler—nor among his professed current admirations, which are directed towards Le Corbusier, Aalto, less towards Mies—and therefore a little worried by the most recent work of Arne Jacobsen, whom he otherwise admires—Nervi, Picasso, Portinari and Leger.

Below Chandler Farms, Arizona, a community farming project of 1938 for immigrant families. Each terrace comprises eight four-room apartments; construction is of native adobe and cost per unit was $2,097, including garage. Below, De Mars' own house, built in 1951 at Berkeley, California. The frame is wood, with a module of 8 ft. by 4 ft.; external walls are redwood boards and cedar.

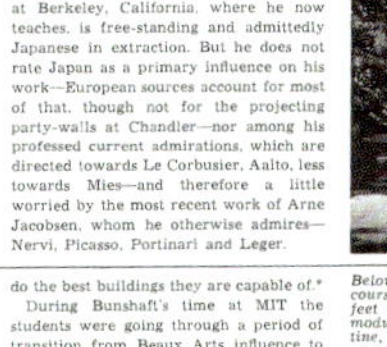

48

New York City

Gordon Bunshaft was born in Buffalo, New York, in 1909, and lived there until he was nineteen. As many children do he made drawings of houses, but the family doctor thought them so good he suggested that Bunshaft should be an architect. His violin teacher had two sons who were engineering students at MIT, and he decided then that he would go to MIT to study architecture. Entering MIT in 1928, he obtained a Bachelor's Degree in 1933 and the Master's Degree in 1935. On a Rotch Travelling Fellowship of $3,000 he spent eighteen months in Europe from 1935 until the Spring of 1937, and, in the autumn of that year, he joined the firm of Skidmore and Owings—Skidmore had just opened an office in New York and Owings was running a small office in Chicago. He started in the firm as a designer and, for the past twenty years, it is to design that he has devoted most of his time. He was made a partner in 1946.

In 1937, the main concern of the office was to build up a practice, and the atmosphere was extremely businesslike; this is still the order of the day, but running through it all is a determination on the part of all the members of the firm to do the best buildings they are capable of.*

During Bunshaft's time at MIT the students were going through a period of transition from Beaux Arts influence to the modern movement, the chief mentor, as in so many other schools at the time, being Le Corbusier. Gordon Bunshaft now considers Mies van der Rohe one of the greatest living architects. 'Although a German by birth, his recent buildings represent the truly great urban architecture of our country. In contrast to the foreign use of reinforced concrete, we employ steel framing as a basic structural system for most urban buildings. Mies van der Rohe's work truly expresses this fact.' Bunshaft's most admired painters are Leger, Miro, Picasso, Ben Nicholson and Mondriaan, and, for contrast, Dubuffet. Among sculptors he singles out Brancusi, Picasso and Giacometti, with Chadwick and Noguchi as close runners-up. Artists who have done work, or are in the process of doing it, for buildings by Skidmore, Owings and Merrill are: Calder, Miro, Steinberg, Seymour Lipton, Lippold, Bertoia, Noguchi and Stuart Davis.

Bunshaft answered, along with a number of other American architects when they were asked the same question, that stylistic cleavages in contemporary American architecture are more apparent between building types than between regions. In the domestic field he sees a certain differentiation from place to place, but he lays this at the door of certain strong personalities working in those regions, producing what he calls 'charm school' designs, as opposed to the more disciplined standards of the 'international' style.

In a discussion between Bunshaft, Saarinen and Philip Johnson, described by Mrs. Saarinen, Bunshaft 'defended the need for a common style, the necessity of a vernacular', and in the work for which he has been directly responsible—Lever House, the Manufacturers Trust and Connecticut General Life Insurance buildings—he has done as much as anyone in America to promote an architectural vernacular of today.

*Skidmore, Owings and Merrill have four offices—New York, Chicago, San Francisco and Portland, Oregon. There are twelve general partners, five in New York, four in Chicago and three in San Francisco. There are 17 associate partners, divided among the offices. The total staff is approximately 900. Also, in the New York, San Francisco and Portland offices they employ consulting structural and mechanical engineers as well as consultants in acoustics, lighting and other specialized fields. In the Chicago office there is a complete staff of structural and mechanical engineers. (For a description of the office organization see A.R., Feb., 1956.)

Below, model of final design for the US Air Force Academy, in course of construction, 7 miles north of Colorado Springs, 6,500 feet above sea level. The structure is based on a 3 ft. 6 in. module; facing materials will include marble, granite, travertine, and native stone. Bottom, Connecticut General Life Insurance offices, Bloomfield, Connecticut. The structure is exposed steel columns and the curtain wall heat- and glare-absorbent glass and porcelain enamel spandrels, all flush. Four large interior gardens are sunk into the main wing; areas within the building are divided by brightly coloured acoustical screens.

358

Bunshaft (cont.) *Above, the Manufacturers Trust Bank, New York. The first floor glass panels are 22 ft. by 9 ft. 8 in. Ceilings of thin corrugated plastic are supported on aluminium Ts under a field of cold cathode tubes; their flow eliminates the surface reflection of the curtain walls. Below, Harry Bertoia's gilded steel sculptural wall in the main counting hall. Right, projected 41-storey office block on Park Avenue for Union Carbide, due to be finished in 1958. Bottom, piazza and lower floors of the projected 60-floor Chase Manhattan Bank.*

48

Los Angeles, California

John Rex, of the firm of Honnold and Rex, was born in Los Angeles in 1909, and studied architecture at the University of Southern California from 1927-1932. The office has a total staff of eleven and does work of all kinds, ranging from a few thousand to a few million dollars. Rex's admirations are (painters) Rico Lebrun and the late Orozco of Mexico; (sculptors) Noguchi, Rosenthal and Bertoia. 'In my twenty-three years experience of architecture', Rex says, 'I have concluded the only really "organic" architecture is the cave—despite the exaltations of some architects. The tendency, since the first Egyptian architect accepted a commission, has been a progression towards standardization.'

Anderson house, Los Angeles; it is a steel frame structure with external facing of natural redwood.

Above, Westchester Junior High School, for 2,500 students, completed in 1952. Below, Robbins house, Beverly Hills, California, seen from the paved terrace outside the living area; it is of frame construction with redwood finish.

museum of modern art
bulletin
Skidmore, Owings & Merrill
architects, U.S.A.

First Experiences

During its first years of existence, SOM managed to have various commissions, being the buildings for the Century of Progress exhibition in Chicago (1933) and for the Universal Exhibition in New York (1939) in the most important work opportunities, which yielded long contracts and attracted clients, permitting recruitment of more specialized and qualified personnel. The Century of Progress was the starting point for the creation of the company, while The Universal Exhibition in New York established a turning point in the firm's trajectory. Bunshaft, the main project manager in the commission, designed the Venezuela pavilion, his first building as architect in charge at SOM, which finally became the true propaganda "stand" for the company.

THE MoMA BULLETIN (autumn of 1950)

The printed bulletin of the New York museum, in its Volume XVIII, No. 1, autumn of 1950, collects the materials presented at the exhibition – photos of works and models, plans – and also brief explanations about the firm and its intentions toward architecture.

As the directors of MoMa declared in the presentation text: "They work together animated by two disciplines which they all share – the discipline of modern architecture and the discipline of American organizational methods."[13] The description, together with the projects' presentation, establishes an important testimony about the little-known and, even less, studied practice of SOM from that time.

The beginnings of the company

During its first years of existence, SOM managed to have various commissions, being the buildings for the Century of Progress exhibition in Chicago (1933) and for the Universal Exhibition in New York (1939) in the most important work opportunities, which yielded long contracts and attracted clients, permitting recruitment of more specialized and qualified personnel. The Century of Progress was the starting point for the creation of the company, while the Universal Exhibition in New York established a turning point in the firm's trajectory. Bunshaft, the main project manager in the commission, designed

On the left

MoMA bulletin cover, Volume XVIII, No. 1, Fall 1950, featuring materials presented at the "Exhibition of Recent Buildings by Skidmore, Owings and Merrill."

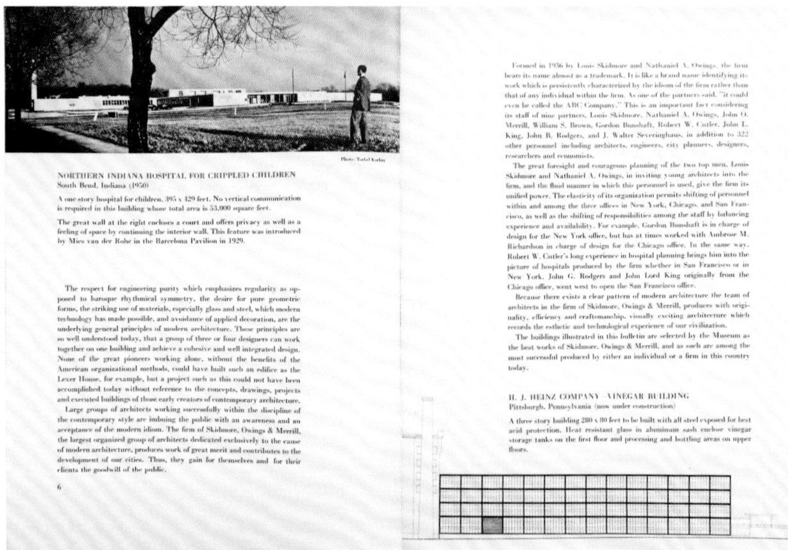
NORTHERN INDIANA HOSPITAL FOR CRIPPLED CHILDREN
South Bend, Indiana (1950)

A one story hospital for children, 395 x 129 feet. No vertical communication is required in this building whose total area is 53,000 square feet.

The great wall at the right encloses a court and offers privacy as well as a feeling of space by continuing the interior wall. This feature was introduced by Mies van der Rohe in the Barcelona Pavilion in 1929.

The respect for engineering purity which emphasizes regularity as opposed to baroque rhythmical symmetry, the desire for pure geometric forms, the striking use of materials, especially glass and steel, which modern technology has made possible, and avoidance of applied decoration, are the underlying general principles of modern architecture. These principles are so well understood today, that a group of three or four designers can work together on one building and achieve a cohesive and well integrated design. None of the great pioneers working alone, without the benefits of the American organizational methods, could have built such an edifice as the Lever House, for example, but a project such as this could not have been accomplished today without reference to the concepts, drawings, projects and executed buildings of those early creators of contemporary architecture.

Large groups of architects working successfully within the discipline of the contemporary style are imbuing the public with an awareness and an acceptance of the modern idiom. The firm of Skidmore, Owings & Merrill, the largest organized group of architects dedicated exclusively to the cause of modern architecture, produces work of great merit and contributes to the development of our cities. Thus, they gain for themselves and for their clients the goodwill of the public.

6

Formed in 1936 by Louis Skidmore and Nathaniel A. Owings, the firm bears its name almost as a trademark. It is like a brand name identifying its work which is persistently characterized by the idiom of the firm rather than that of any individual within the firm. As one of the partners said, "it could even be called the ABC Company." This is an important fact considering its staff of nine partners, Louis Skidmore, Nathaniel A. Owings, John O. Merrill, William S. Brown, Gordon Bunshaft, Robert W. Cutler, John L. King, John B. Rodgers, and J. Walter Severinghaus, in addition to 322 other personnel including architects, engineers, city planners, designers, researchers and economists.

The great foresight and courageous planning of the two top men, Louis Skidmore and Nathaniel A. Owings, in inviting young architects into the firm, and the fluid manner in which this personnel is used, give the firm its unified power. The elasticity of its organization permits shifting of personnel within and among the three offices in New York, Chicago, and San Francisco, as well as the shifting of responsibilities among the staff by balancing experience and availability. For example, Gordon Bunshaft is in charge of design for the New York office, but has at times worked with Ambrose M. Richardson in charge of design for the Chicago office. In the same way, Robert W. Cutler's long experience in hospital planning brings him into the picture of hospitals produced by the firm whether in San Francisco or in New York. John G. Rodgers and John Lord King originally from the Chicago office, went west to open the San Francisco office.

Because there exists a clear pattern of modern architecture the team of architects in the firm of Skidmore, Owings & Merrill, produces with originality, efficiency and craftsmanship, visually exciting architecture which records the esthetic and technological experience of our civilization.

The buildings illustrated in this bulletin are selected by the Museum as the best works of Skidmore, Owings & Merrill, and as such are among the most successful produced by either an individual or a firm in this country today.

H. J. HEINZ COMPANY—VINEGAR BUILDING
Pittsburgh, Pennsylvania (now under construction)

A three story building 280 x 80 feet to be built with all steel exposed for best acid protection. Heat resistant glass in aluminum sash enclose vinegar storage tanks on the first floor and processing and bottling areas on upper floors.

Double page spread from the MoMA Bulletin, Volume XVIII, No. 1, fall 1950.

Presented on these pages are a hospital project for crippled children and the vinegar factory and warehouse for H.J. Heinz.

the Venezuela pavilion, his first building as architect in charge at SOM, which finally became the true propaganda "stand" for the company.

In the years that followed, the Chicago office had some important government commissions underway for the construction of residential complexes. The project that brought prestige was the Hostess House at the Great Lakes Naval Training Center, IL, finished in 1942. However, the most valuable project for the company after the two great exhibitions was, without a doubt, the city of Oak Ridge, built at the request of the US Army in the state of Tennessee.

In 1943, the project for 42,000 inhabitants consisted of buildings for housing, a school, a commercial complex and a church. The following year the project changed and the proposal was expanded, reaching a capacity for 75,000 inhabitants. The project was secretly conceived and built, with an atomic bomb[14] having been designed and produced there, something that really demonstrates the importance of the urban complex for the North American army. As Henry Russell Hitchcock states,

> *Moreover, the experience it provided, with the necessary expansion of the office force (finally up to some 450 men), laid the organizational foundation for undertaking the extensive and varied private commissions that came their way in increasing numbers when the building curve turned upward two or three years after the War was over.*[15]

The company's expansion also took place toward the west coast of the country, and the San Francisco office grew considerably. But what proved to be a truly relevant transformation for the company was the opening of the New York office. According to Prof. Nicholas Adams, the team assembled by Skidmore, consisting of Robert W. Cutler (specialist in hospitals), J. Walter Severinghaus (who ended up specializing in the residential sector), William S. Brown (expert in prefabricated residential buildings), and Gordon Bunshaft, the designer par excellence – added to his good relations with important men such as Robert Moses (president of the New York State Parks Council and the Long Island State Park Commission), and some publicity action gave the company the possibility of having important commissions and, more importantly, of carrying out high-quality work.[16]

Double page spread from the MoMA Bulletin, Volume XVIII, No. 1, fall 1950, featuring the Lake Meadows housing project in Chicago.

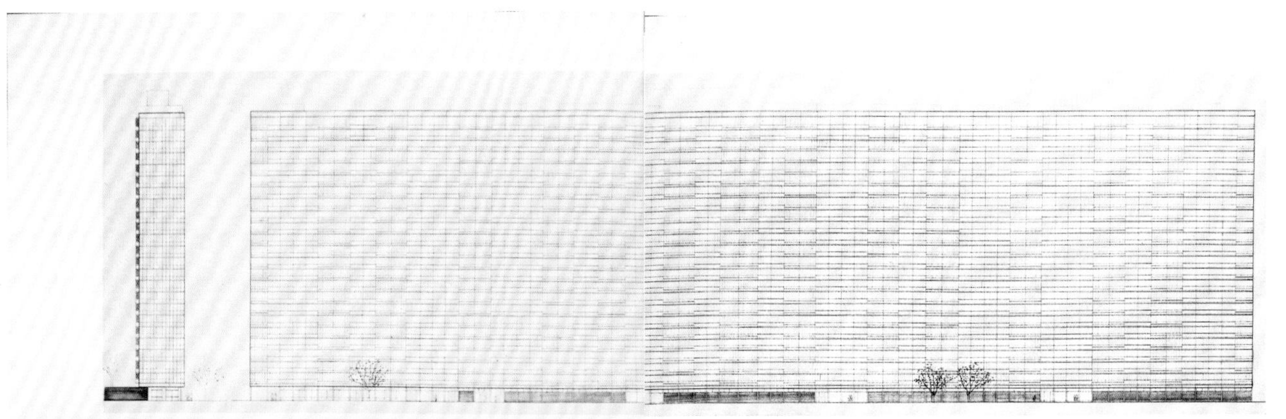

Photo: Chicago Aerial Survey Company

LAKE MEADOWS—CHICAGO
(See page 16)

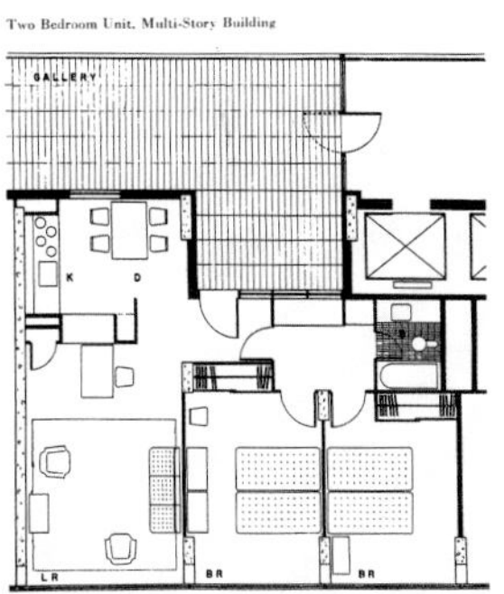

For the year 1940, the volume of the construction cost of SOM had risen again, and by 1941 it almost doubled the value of the previous year. Some hospital complexes increased the portfolio of commissions during those years. In the state of New York, we can name the Bellevue Medical Center of the University of New York and the Hospital for the Veterans' Administration of Brooklyn, the latter designed and built under the responsibility of Gordon Bunshaft.

Double page spread from the MoMA Bulletin featuring the Bellevue Medical Center in Manhattan.

NEW YORK UNIVERSITY—BELLEVUE MEDICAL CENTER
New York, N. Y.

This Medical Center will contain the College of Medicine and Post Graduate Medical School; the Institute of Physical Medicine and Rehabilitation, and University Clinic; Hall of Residence; University Hospital and Alumni Hall. The Center covers approximately 11 acres, from 30th to 34th Streets and from 1st Avenue to the East River in New York City. The University Hospital will be 20 stories high and contain 600 beds; the Hall of Residence will house 300 people; there will be a medical library for 150,000 volumes. One unit is now under construction.

This asymmetric arrangement of functionally disparate units which is spread over four city blocks is a precedent-creating plan. The open areas and separate buildings will do away with the tedium of the gridiron pattern of stone and brick.

In the concern for the geometric shape and in relating these functionally separated units to the New York City scene, the architects have made a practical contribution as well as a contribution to the dream of all modern architects to change the monotony of the 19th century city pattern.

Photo: Ezra Stoller, Pictor

16

Photo: Ezra Stoller, Pictor

BROOKLYN VETERAN'S ADMINISTRATION HOSPITAL
Brooklyn, New York (1950)

The site of this 1000 bed general hospital is approximately 17 acres at the southern end of Brooklyn. This provides an ocean view on the southern exposure. The elongated main structure which is 506 feet takes full advantage of sun and view. There are 2 nursing units of 40 beds each on each floor, which locates 95% of the beds in rooms with southern exposure. The Hospital portion is 17 stories high.

Photo: Ezra Stoller, Pictor

Double page spread from the MoMA Bulletin featuring the Brooklyn Veteran's Administration Hospital.

The MoMA exhibition bulletin summarizes the history of the group together with a description of the internal organization and modus-operandi of the team:

> *The great foresight and courageous planning of the two top men, Louis Skidmore and Nathaniel A. Owings, in inviting young architects into the firm, and the fluid manner in which this personnel is used, give the firm its unified power. The elasticity of its organization permits shifting of personnel within and among the three offices in New York, Chicago and San Francisco, as well as the shifting of responsibilities among the staff by balancing experience and availability. For example, Gordon Bunshaft is in charge of design for the New York office, but has at times worked with Ambrose M. Richardson in charge of design for the Chicago office. In the same way, Robert W. Cutler's long experience in hospital planning brings him into the picture of hospitals produced by the firm whether in San Francisco or in New York. John G. Rodgers and John Lord King, originally from the Chicago office, went west to open the San Francisco office.*[17]

The works and projects presented in the exhibition were selected by MoMA. The Museum had Philip L. Goodwin as president and Philip C. Johnson as director of the Department of Architecture and Design that year.

In total, 10 works were selected, which were presented through photos, drawings and brief project memories. It is important to say that they were shown unevenly, with some of them having more prominence than others:

- Northern Indiana Hospital for Crippled Children - South Bend, Indiana
- H. J. Heinz Company – Vinegar Building – Pittsburgh, Pennsylvania (at that moment under construction)
- Lever House. Office Building for Lever Brothers Company – New York, NY (at that moment under construction)
- Lake Meadows – Chicago
- Central Staff Offices for the Ford Motor Company – Dearborn, Michigan
- Del Monte Shopping Center – Del Monte, California
- New York University – Bellevue Medical Center - New York, N.Y.
- Garden Apartments – Oak Ridge, Tennessee (1950)
- Oil Refining Town – Amuay Bay, Venezuela
- Brooklyn Veteran's Administration Hospital – Brooklyn, New York (1950)

The set reflects the strict vision of the institution towards modern architecture. For SOM, the exhibition was an important showcase for society and potential clients.

On the Left

Dave Hughes, Charlie Hughes and Gordon Bunshaft, in May 1950, finishing the model of the project for the Ford Motor Company Headquarters - Dearborn, Michigan.

SOM: works and projects toward 1950

It was not until the end of the '40s that architecture began to show off the technological advances mentioned by studies such as "Man-Made America," from 1950. The North American industry had not yet managed to significantly influence civil construction in the country, nor had the architects and ordinary clients.

"Man-Made America" shows that the industrialization carried out by the war industry – as well as by the manufacture of commercial goods such as cars, household appliances, furniture, etc. – had already established itself in the country and was rapidly changing the habits of the inhabitants. Modern architecture was still moving slowly in the direction of systematization and construction through industry, and a few prototype projects for small-scale prefabricated structures were just starting to emerge. Despite this, some architects already stood out for exploiting formal alternatives from steel construction systems in their works and projects, including Gordon Bunshaft.

While Mies van der Rohe was presented by the report as being the greatest reference among North American professionals – either in the technical field, using the available technologies, or in the project field, holding a prominent position in matters of the formalization of modern architecture in the US – SOM was barely mentioned.[18]

This was most likely due to the fact that two of the buildings that could demonstrate the high technical and design level of the firm's architects – Lever House and H. J. Heinz Vinegar Factory and Warehouse – were still projects. However, the work presented at the MoMA exhibition in the fall of 1950 already included SOM's projects, indicating the great potential of the group to absorb new technologies through its own architectural projects, something that would be developed in the following years. In fact, the company was going to be the one that managed to fulfill the American promises elucidated by "Man-Made America".

The buildings that were to become the most representative of SOM in the 1940s were those built with steel structures, almost always covered with concrete for fire protection. The structural configurations – in plan and in section – were regular grids, but in most cases this arrangement was not visually reflected on the exterior of the buildings. Apart from bearing loads, the main internal function of the structure was to guide the placement of internal partitions and main façade elements, such as mullions and parapets.

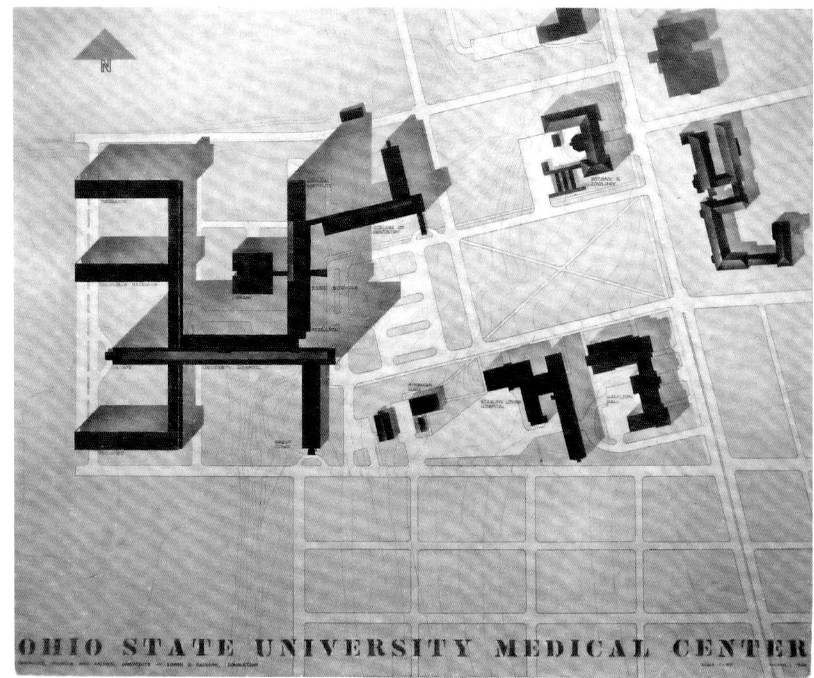

The project for the Ohio State University Medical Centre, by SOM (1946), noted by H. R. Hitchcock as one of the new and remarcable modern complexes of the 1940s in the USA.

The initial version of the Lake Meadows complex featured in the catalog, and was about to be built in Chicago bears out these ideas. The project had two large 23-story buildings facing each other, creating a long interstitial open space, and another 11 two-story buildings arranged around the main two. The materials presented in the catalog on this project are not abundant. In a façade drawing of the large blocks, published on a double page, a big façade panel with large horizontal openings from side to side can be seen. An enlarged plan of a typical house shows the columns, apparently made of reinforced concrete, and confirms that the two façades would have cantilever slabs. On one side, a wide corridor, called "gallery," with a large cantilever of about 2.5 m; and on the other, the walls of the bedrooms and living rooms, with small cantilever projections of approximately half a meter.

The hospitals on display, New York University Bellevue Medical Center and the Brooklyn Veterans Administration Hospital, feature steel structures encased in concrete. On the façades, the parapets of the windows are arranged continuously throughout the entire length of the buildings, attenuating the presence of the columns and creating continuous windows. For the Brooklyn hospital, Bunshaft – responsible for the project – also adopted continuous horizontal concrete sun shades over the windows. It is interesting to com-

Brookling Hospital with the newly completed structure (March, 1948) and later, completely finished.

pare the analogous images, taken from the same viewpoint, of the recently finished structure with the completed building. The visually powerful steel frame of the hospital ends up being totally hidden by slabs, windows and interior and exterior walls, demonstrating Bunshaft's early tendency to follow modern architecture with Corbuserian attributes. In fact, the photo presented in the catalog is precisely that of the main block of the Brooklyn hospital.

ONE
668

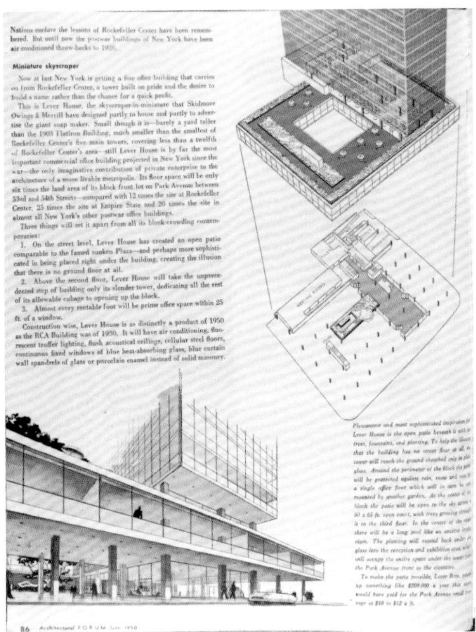

Nations enclave the lessons of Rockefeller Center have been remembered. But until now the postwar buildings of New York have been air conditioned throw-backs to 1926.

Miniature skyscraper

Now at last New York is getting a fine office building that carries on from Rockefeller Center, a tower built on pride and the desire to build a name rather than the chance for a quick profit.

This is Lever House, the skyscraper-in-miniature that Skidmore Owings & Merrill have designed partly to house and partly to advertise the giant soap maker. Small though it is—barely a yard taller than the 1903 Flatiron Building, much smaller than the smallest of Rockefeller Center's five main towers, covering less than a twelfth of Rockefeller Center's area—still Lever House is by far the most important commercial office building projected in New York since the war—the only imaginative contribution of private enterprise to the architecture of a more livable metropolis. Its floor space will be only six times the land area of its block front lot on Park Avenue between 53rd and 54th Streets—compared with 12 times the site at Rockefeller Center, 25 times the site at Empire State and 20 times the site in almost all New York's other postwar office buildings.

Three things will set it apart from all its block-crowding contemporaries:

1. On the street level, Lever House has created an open patio comparable to the famed sunken Plaza—and perhaps more sophisticated in being placed right under the building, creating the illusion that there is no ground floor at all.

2. Above the second floor, Lever House will take the unprecedented step of building only its slender tower, dedicating all the rest of its allowable cubage to opening up the block.

3. Almost every rentable foot will be prime office space within 25 ft. of a window.

Construction wise, Lever House is as distinctly a product of 1950 as the RCA Building was of 1930. It will have air conditioning, fluorescent troffer lighting, flush acoustical ceilings, cellular steel floors, continuous fixed windows of blue heat-absorbing glass, blue curtain wall spandrels of glass or porcelain enamel instead of solid masonry.

86 Architectural FORUM June 1950

Architectural Forum page from June 1950, in which the project for the Lever House is presented.

On the left

Photo of the Lever House from the Seagram Building

Photo by the author, 2010.

The Lever House (1949-1950)[19]

The Lever House is different from the projects with steel structure designed by the company until the late 1940s. The glazed curtain wall façade allows a glimpse of the interior elements, but the columns cannot be clearly perceived, except on the first level of the base. The irregularities in the arrangement of columns in typical floor plans are not reflected in the volumetric purity of the building. The dimensional difference between the two structural spans of the shorter façades is visually masked behind the curtain wall. Compared with Mies van der Rohe's Seagram Building – built soon after, just on the other side of Park Avenue – it can be said that the structural system of the Lever House is not strongly expressed in the built form.

On the other hand, the rigorous structural grid stipulated by Mies unites the whole building, guiding the entire complex both structurally and visually. Even so, it is undeniable that the construction of the Lever House established a before and after in the trajectory of the firm. From a business point of view, some new technical resources applied mainly to the cladding of the building gave SOM the status of a leading company both nationally and internationally. From an architectural point of view, the building inaugurated a long process of formal and constructive developments in the conception of high-rise office buildings.

The June 1950 issue of the *Architectural Forum* magazine featured an article entitled "Miniature Skyscraper of blue glass and metal challenges postwar craze for over-building city lots" in which the project for Lever House is presented before its construction had been completed: "Lever House must be studied as a model of contemporary design and up-to-the-minute construction techniques."[20]

The structural system seems to have been later adapted to the formal conception. The arrangement of columns responds to the positioning and basic dimensions of the fundamental elements for the composition, such as the location of the internal courtyard of the base and the basic dimensions of the office block. Regarding the latter, there are two different structural spans regarding the smaller façade, something that seems to have been defined after the general configurations of the typical floor plan.

The general structural spans of the Lever House are equivalent to 28' (8.53 m) and 21' (6.45 m). Only the larger structural span fits perfectly with the modulation of the curtain wall. It is due to the fact that the structure is set back to respect the façade perimeter, which has a cantilever equivalent

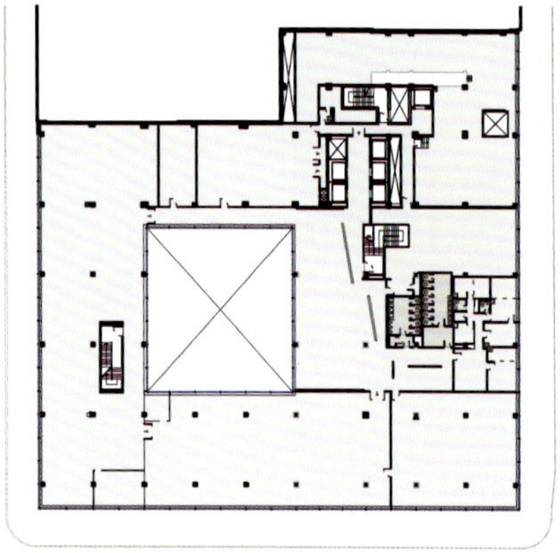

53RD STREET

54RD STREET

PARK AVENUE

First Floor

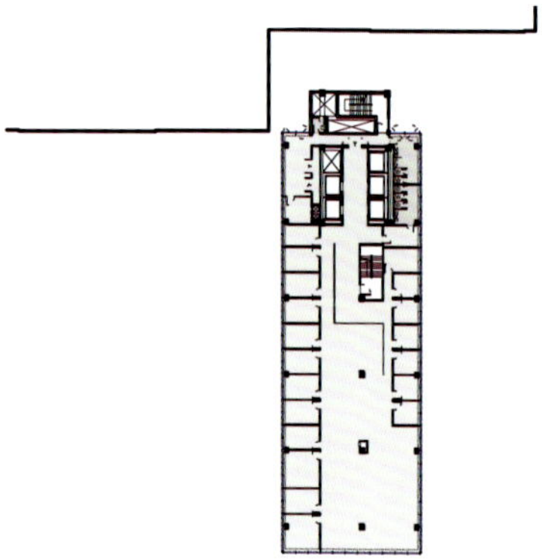

Typical Floor

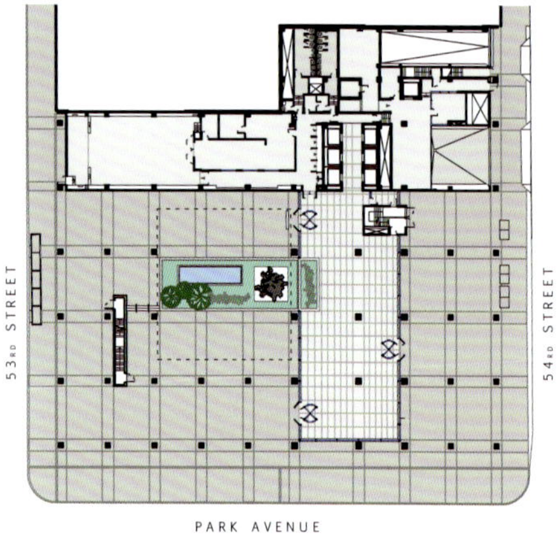

Ground Floor

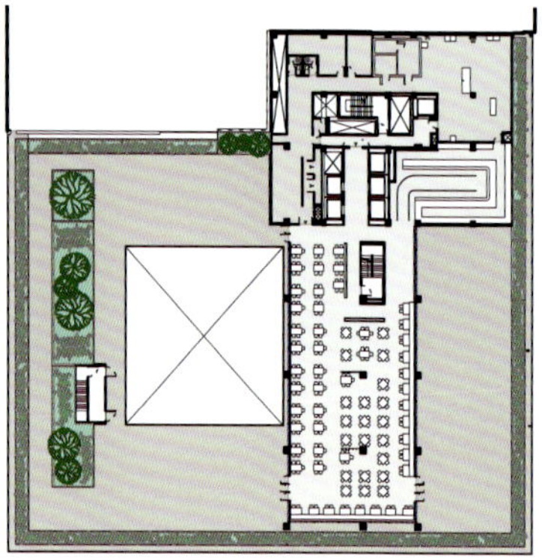

Second Floor

LEVER HOUSE

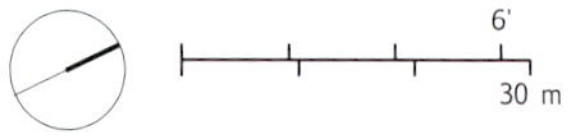

6' 30 m SCALE 1/1250

to two modules of the curtain wall only in the largest dimension of the typical floor plan. In the smaller façade (facing Park Avenue) there is not enough distance between the columns and the perimeter of the building in order to generate corner modules or submodules in the façade. Despite the lack of rigor in the dimensional relationships between structure and interior elements such as partitions and ceilings, all the four façades are seen from the outside as a uniform grid, generating formal balance.

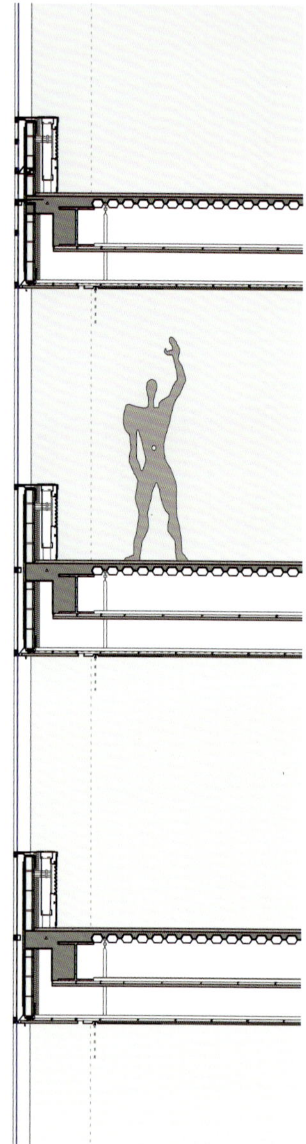

Typical Façade Section

6' 2 m SCALE 1/75

Detail of the façade of the Lever House.

Photo by the author, 2010.

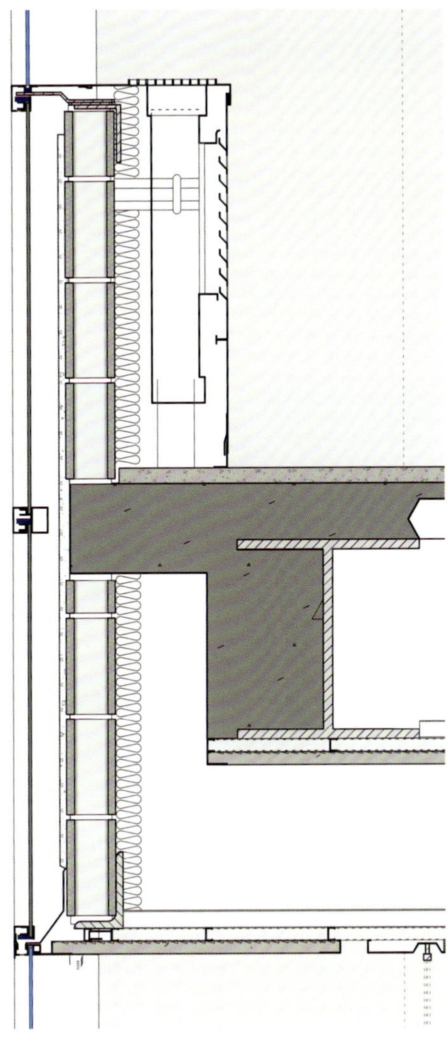

Detail

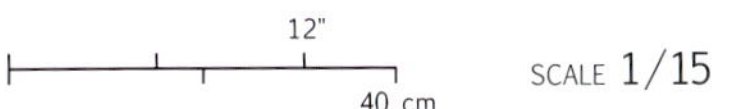

SCALE 1/15

The structural configuration makes clear the importance given to the construction of a volumetrically pure block, whose external surfaces should be as smooth and visually clean as possible. Such a characteristic is enhanced by visual attenuation of mullions and transoms on the curtain wall and by the full cladding of the façade with glass and acrylic panels. *Architectural Forum's* article cited above establishes a brief comparison between the curtain walls of the Lever House and the Building for the UN, finished shortly before in New York:

> *Flush exterior, contrary to the United Nations Secretariat practice, where the framing around the exterior glass is made 4 in. deep to cast shadows and accentuate the pattern, the stainless-steel frame on the glass or porcelain enamel on Lever House will project by only 1 in. The mullion will be 2 1/2 in. wide. There will be one broad 14 in. horizontal band at the window head, a narrow 2 1/2 in. band at the sill line.*[21]

It is also interesting to note the care and importance with which the incorporation of the curtain wall to the building was treated at that time, transcending constructive and architectural aspects. *Architectural Forum* also reported on the scaffolding for exterior cleaning of the glass that would be installed on the façade, further highlighting the prominence that the building's gleaming curtain wall would assume.

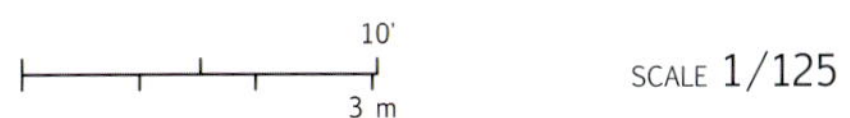

SCALE 1/125

On the left

Photo and façade section of the H.J. Heinz Company Vinegar Plant and Warehouse.

Drawing by author.

H. J. Heinz Company Vinegar Plant and Warehouse (1948-1950)[22]

Another work designed during those years and presented in the MoMA catalog also reflects Bunshaft's concerns on the search for better ways of conceiving building façades, mainly with regard to the relationships between structure and frames.

The H. J. Heinz Company vinegar plant and warehouse, briefly but objectively presented in the catalog through a concise text and a façade drawing, can serve to explain the intentions of the architect toward the formal exploitation of the structure, something that cannot be fully appreciated at Lever House. In that sense, the elevations of the building expose some of the most important visual aspects of the project. The factory was more than 300' long and about a third as wide, with 100,000 square feet (9,290.3 square meters) of interior space divided among three stories.[23] The structural grid of slab edges and columns appears painted black from the outside and establishes the outer limits of the building.

From the inside to the outside, the main beams are supported by the façade columns, but the secondary beams, which support the slabs and provide horizontal stability, are set back in relation to the perimeter. The horizontal steel members that can be seen from the outside attached to the façade columns are actually covering the edges of the reinforced concrete slabs. On the ground floor, the space is double height and these horizontal profiles do not receive any slab or other type of vertical load.

Site plan of the H.J. Heinz Complex, Pittsburgh, Pennsylvania.

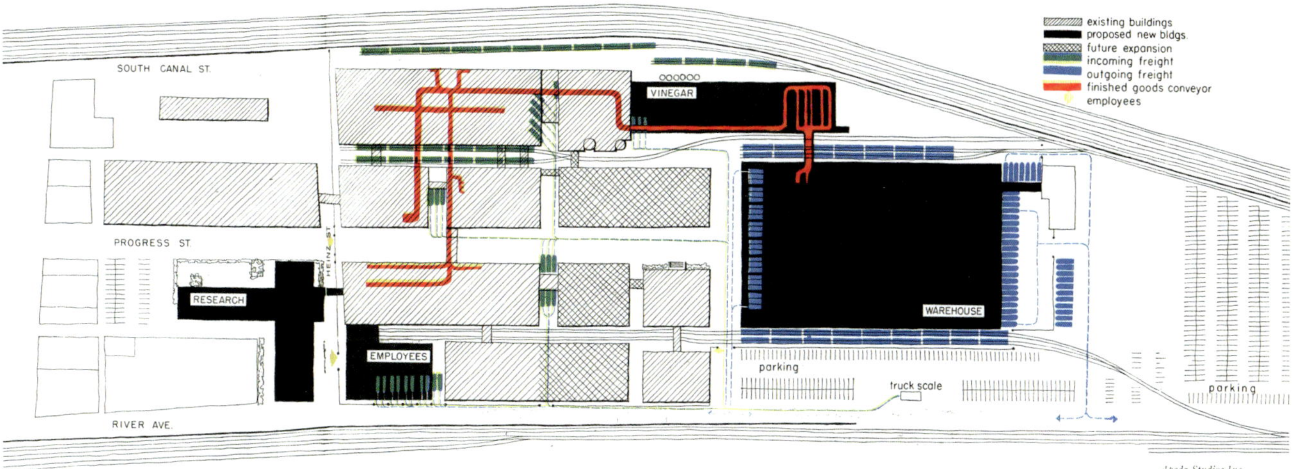

Professor Carol H. Krinsky explains some interesting features on the building's façade:

> *The refinement typical of Bunshaft's work from his early maturity can be seen in the factory's pattern of slender, shiny aluminum mullions, muntins and ventilation sash. It provides a delicate counterpoint on the larger floor-and-bay divisions of the steel frame, and a shiny grayish white contrast to the rich blue glass and black steel, a contrast reinforced by the bright red door. Aluminum offered functional advantages too: it is resistant to vinegar and it is light, allowing metal parts to be attached to the frame from the interior so that work could proceed quickly even in bad weather.*
>
> And adds:
>
> *The interior's open spaces are filled with vinegar vats and machines. Some areas have floors, others only grillwork catwalks. The glass that looks blue on the exterior appears milky white from the interior. While it reduces summertime heat, it offers no protection against winter cold, making heaters necessary. The interior is steel covered by a rubber-based paint that counters the effects of acetic acid; its white color coordinates with that of the windows panes.*[24]

Internally, this structural configuration gave the building spatial flexibility, making it possible to place or remove slabs and floors, creating areas with single or double heights. Externally, careful work with the structural system was carried out, in which the dimensions and positions of its elements define the elemental form of the building; the work with colors makes clear the intention of the architect to visually exploit proportions and geometry set by supporting elements.

Among the projects presented in the autumn of 1950 MoMA Bulletin, the H. J. Heinz vinegar factory and warehouse was the work that best exploited

Detailed façade section of the H. J. Heinz vinegar factory.

Drawing by author.

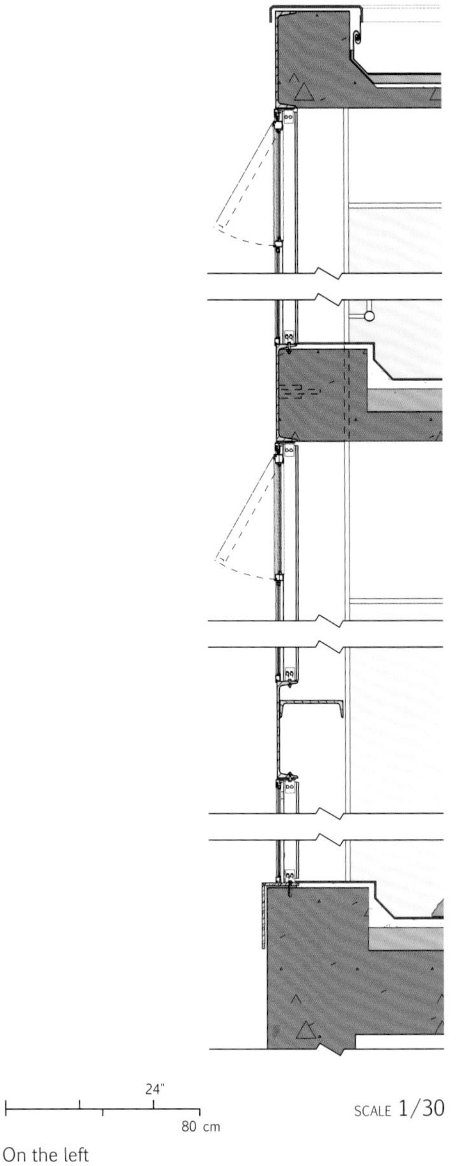

On the left

Aerial view of the H.J. Heinz vinegar factory and warehouse.

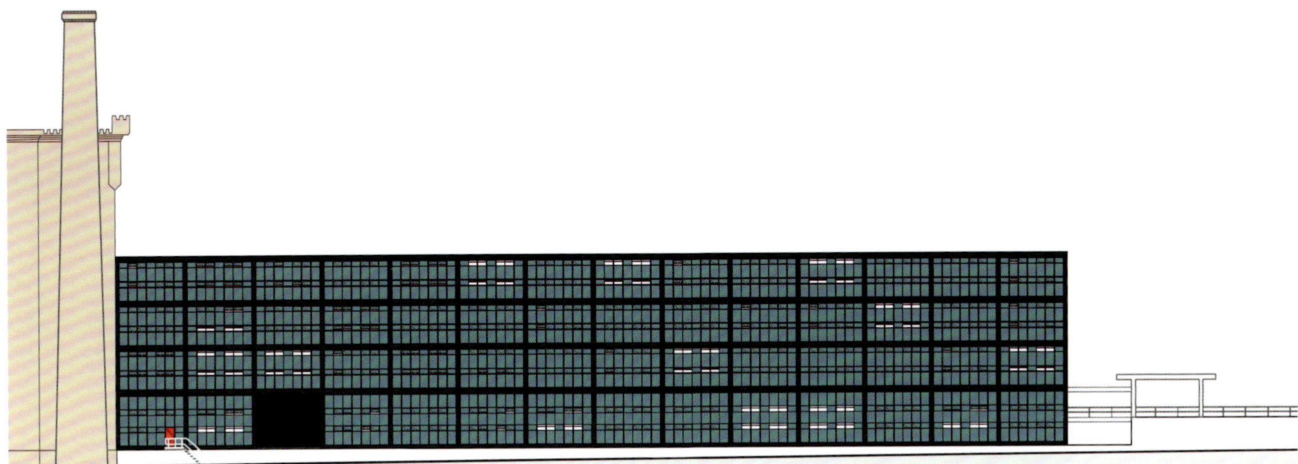

Vinegar factory façade.

Drawing by author.

the formal possibilities of its supporting structure. The Lever House brought fame and commissions to SOM and it became one of the paradigms for the conception of modern office buildings. However, the evolution of SOM in terms of design and construction processes is reflected in the wide variety of buildings built in the ‘50s. The subsequent use of new materials and construction techniques, such as precast concrete, resulted in the company being able to innovate repeatedly along the 10 years that followed without abdicating the modern architecture in which its trademark was established.

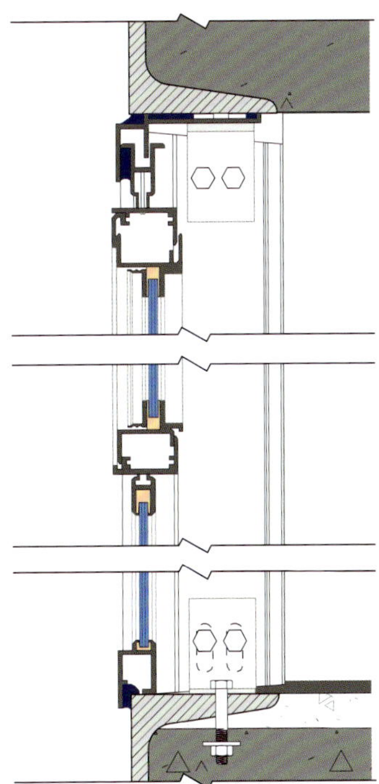

On the right

Façade detail (upper edge and center) of the H. J. Heinz vinegar factory.

Drawing by author.

SCALE 1/5

On the left

Façade detail (lower edge and center) of the H. J. Heinz vinegar factory.

Drawing by author.

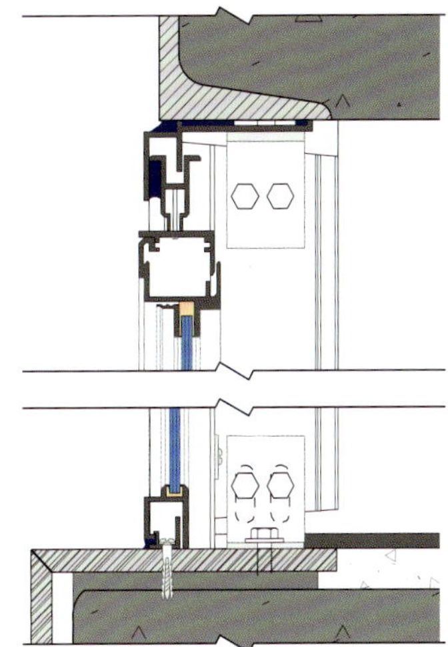

Historical Examples

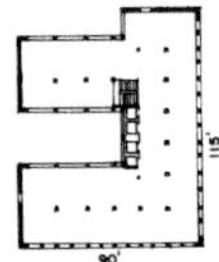

1. Guaranty Building, Buffalo, New York/ Completed 1895/ Adler & Sullivan, Architects

2. Reliance Building, Chicago, Illinois/ Completed 1895/ Burnham & Root, Archilects

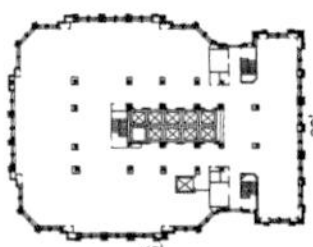

3. Tribune Tower, Chicago, Illinois/ Completed 1925/ Raymond Hood and John Mead Howells Architects

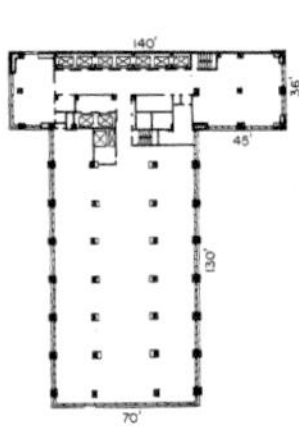

4. Philadelphia Saving Fund Society Building/ Philadelphia, Pennsylvania/ Completed 1932/ Howe, I. Lescaze, Architects

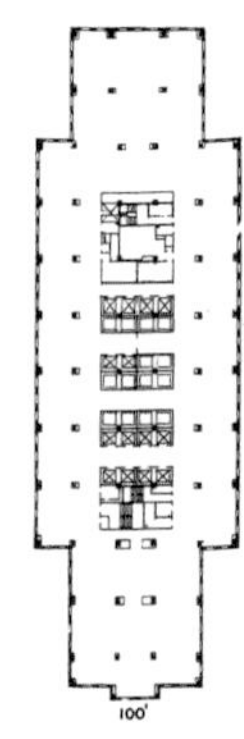

5. R.C.A. Building, Rockefeller Center, New York/ Completed 1932/ Reinhard I. Hofmeister; Corbett, Harrison and MacMurray; Hood & Fouilhoux, Associated Architects

Curtain Walls

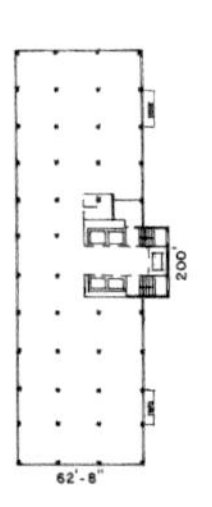

6. Equitable Savings & Loan Association Building, Portland, Oregon/ Completed 1948/ Pietro Belluschi, Architect

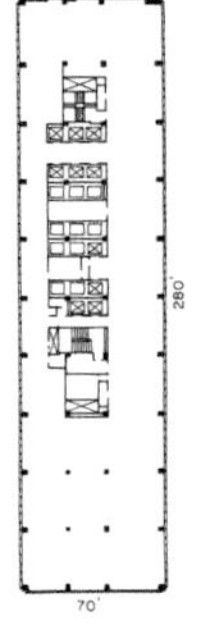

7. United Nations Secretariat Building, New York, New York/ Completed 1950/ UN Headquarters Planning Commission; Wallace K. Harrison, Director of Planning

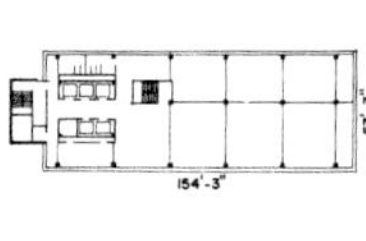

8. Lever House, New York, New York/ Completed 1952/ Skidmore, Owings & Merrill, Architects

9. Seagram Building, New York, New York/ Completed 1958/ Ludwig Mies van der Rohe and Philip Johnson, Architects; Kahn & Jacobs, Associated Archrtects

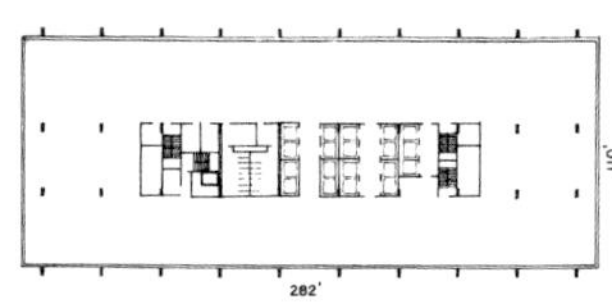

10. Chase Manhattan Bank, New York, New York/ Completed 1961/ Skidmore, Owings & Merrill Architects

Form, Technics And Construction

Between 1955 and 1965, the development and establishment of modern American architecture received significant contributions from SOM and Gordon Bunshaft. Within this temporary cut, a technological background was set, encompassing the operation of companies and factories which promoted the incorporation of prefabrication into architecture. Through the clarification of this context, the consolidation of some construction techniques is revealed, which, when put into practice, generated new types of structures and architectural forms. Part of these innovations ended up being incorporated into the practices of Bunshaft and his advisers, who could be, in addition to architects, civil, mechanical and structural engineers.

Steel Pacesetters

The evolution of steel structures anticipates and prepares the ground for developments in industrialized concrete. As architects Iñaki Abalos and Juan Herreros point out in their book *Technique and Architecture in the Contemporary City – 1950-2000*:

> *The reticular structure had been for modern architects a constructive paradigm univocally linked to the skyscraper and to isotropic space. However, this structural typology will be put into crisis from 1950 when considering the balance conditions of a vertical solid from the topological perspectives opened by experimentation with spatial structures and the analysis of scale problems and proportion in skyscrapers. The primacy of horizontal actions gives rise to a work program carried out in the sixties – to reduce the wind penalty – which translates into new optimized provisions of the structural mass.*[25]

On the left

Typical floor plans of the North American office buildings taken from Robert P. Sitzenstock's study "Evolution of the High-Rise Office Building" and presented chronologically.

Pages 148 and 149 of the September 1963 issue of *Progressive Architecture* magazine.

The article "Evolution of the High-Rise Office Building", by Robert P. Sitzenstock, published in *Progressive Architecture* magazine in 1963, stated that the size of structural spans in early steel-framed buildings was generally about 15' x 20' (4.6 x 6.1 m), the size of a standard office space. When flexible workspace planning was introduced, the need for large spans became apparent, with dimensions of approximately 25' x 25' (7.6 x 7.6 m) – or the equivalent in usable areas – being quite common throughout the 1940s and

Diverse Concepts

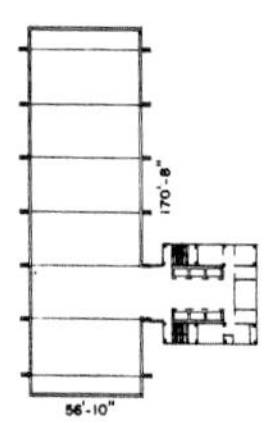

11. Inland Steel Building, Chicago, Illinois/ Completed 1958/ Skidmore, Owings & Merrill, Architects

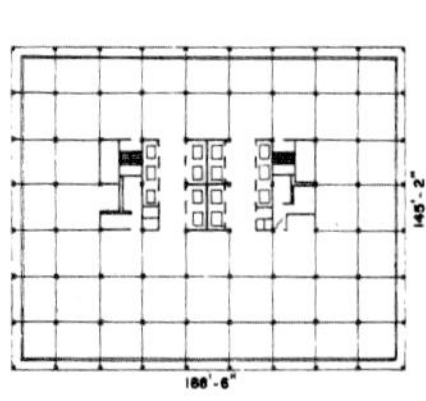

12. Hartford Building, Chicago, Illinois/ Completed 1961/ Skidmore, Owings & Merrill, Architects

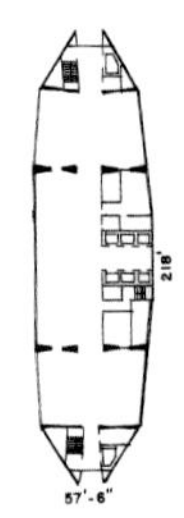

13. Pirelli Building, Milan, Italy/ Completed 1960/ Gio Ponti and Alberto Rosselli, Architects

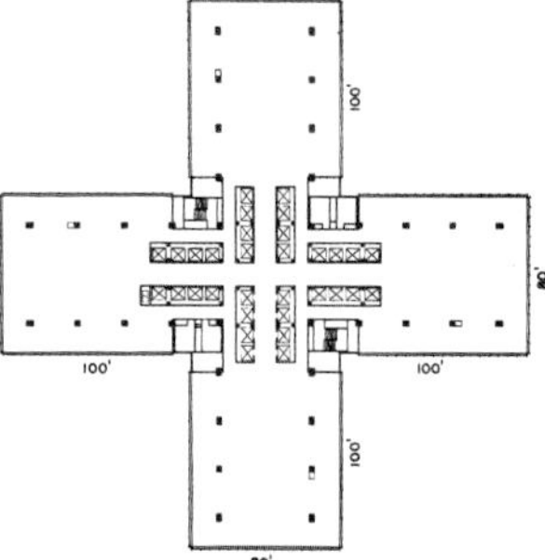

14. Royal Bank of Canada Building, Place Ville Marie, Montreal, Canada/ Completed 1962/ I. M. Pei & Associates, Architects

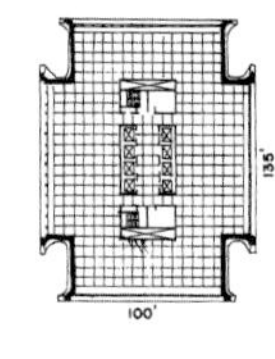

15. Metropolitan Tower, Honolulu, Hawaii/ Unrealized project, designed 1960/1. M. Pei & Associates, Architects

Long Spans

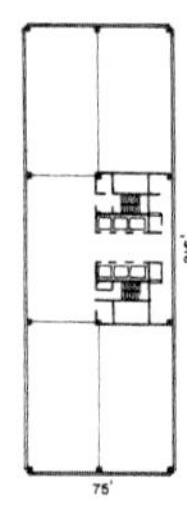

16. Norton Building, Seattle, Washington/ Completed 1960/Bindon & Wright, Architects; Skidmore, Owings & Merrill, Consulting Architects

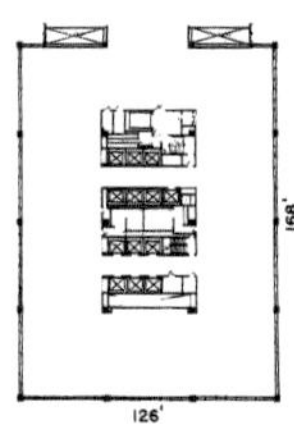

17. Continental Center, Chicago, Illinois/ Completed 1963/ C. F. Murphy Associates, Architects

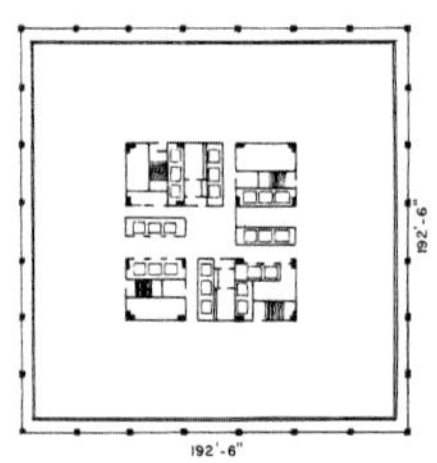

18. Tennessee Gas Building, Houston, Texas/ Completed 1963/ Skidmore, Owings & Merrill, Architects

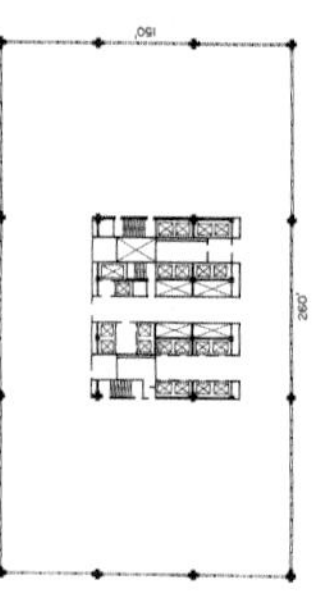

19. Chicago Civic Center, Chicago, Illinois/ Under construction/ C. F. Murphy Associates, Architects; Skidmore, Owings & Merrill and Loebl, Schlossman & Bennett, Associate Architects

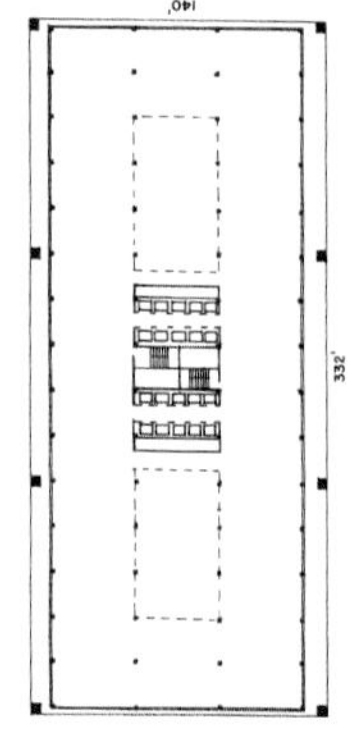

20. Concrete Office Building/ Master's Thesis, I.I.T., 1948/ Myron Goldsmith, Architect

Bearing Walls

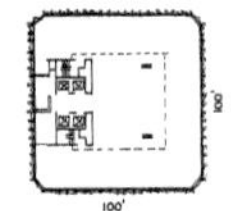

21. Blue Cross Building, Boston, Massachusetts/ Completed 1960/ Paul Rudolph and Anderson, Beckwith & Haible, Architects

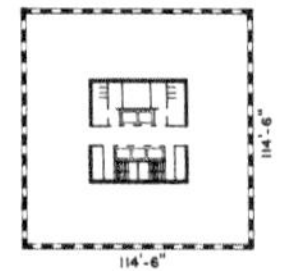

22. John Hancock Building, San Francisco, California/ Completed 1960/ Skidmore, Owings & Merrill, Architects

23. IBM Building, Pittsburgh, Pennsylvania/ To be completed 1963/ Curtis & Davis, Architects

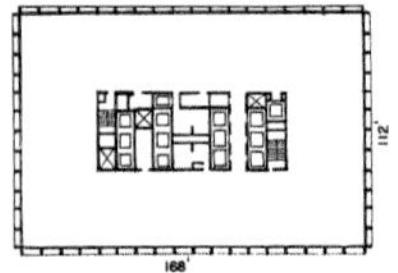

24. Brunswick Building, Chicago, Illinois/ To be completed 1964/ Skidmore, Owings & Merrill, Architects

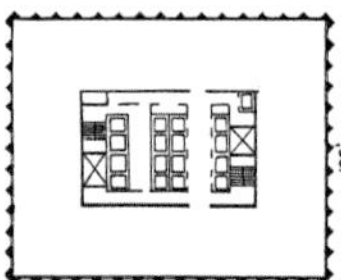

25. CBS Building, New York, New York/ To be completed 1964/ Eero Saarinen & Associates, Architects

1950s. Sitzenstock's study also discusses the advances made in the design of typical floor plants:

> *The interior layout of the typical early high-rise office building consisted of individual offices of approximately 320 sq ft ranged along double-loaded corridors, all of them on exterior walls with operable windows. Flexible office floors, which could be laid out to suit the tenant, were introduced in 1930 in the RCA Building (New York; Reinhard & Hofmeister; Corbett, Harrison & MacMurray; Hood & Fouilhoux, Associated Architects; [...] In the Lever House (New York, 1952), Skidmore, Owings & Merrill began their development of the movable metal-and-glass partition, which was perfected in their buildings for Union Carbide (1960) and Chase Manhattan (1961; 10) in New York. The co-ordination of movable partitions, lighting, and air conditioning has been achieved through the use of modular planning. The size of the office building module depends on many factors: high or low rents, structural system, size of individual offices, and special use requirements. The module may range from 3'-5", as in the Equitable Building (New York, 1961, SOM) to 6'-0", as in the United AirLines Executive Offices (Chicago, 1962, SOM). The typical module for buildings built in the past few years or now under construction ranges from 4'-7" to 5'-0".*[26]

On the one hand, the aspirations of clients and architects pointed toward more diaphanous plants, more flexible internal partition systems and more efficient lighting and air conditioning systems. On the other hand, the development of elements and components for construction by the industry, architects and engineers indicated the application of new construction systems and materials. SOM finished up being one of the main agents of this process.

A quick examination of the set of works that Gordon Bunshaft was in charge of makes it clear that during the first 20 years of his career, almost all of the buildings were erected with metal structures. The Lever House marked a paradigm; nevertheless, two basic architectural demands emerged in new commissions for office buildings: open-plan spaces, free of barriers or supports that did not allow flexibility in their physical occupation; and work spaces with optimized and integrated installations and building systems (electrical, hydraulic, HVAC and lighting). The evolution is shown through a series of compared plants and sections. Through the series, it is possible to perceive some constructive and formal aspects originating from buildings with steel structures that became extreme in buildings with industrialized concrete components.

On the left

Typical floor plans of the North American office buildings taken from Robert P. Sitzenstock's study "Evolution of the High-Rise Office Building" and presented chronologically.

Pages 148 and 149 of the September 1963 issue of *Progressive Architecture* magazine.

Metal Frames and Structures

By the mid-fifties, some circumstances had changed, and the way of tackling the design of steel and glass skyscrapers within the SOM offices was no longer the same as when Lever House was projected. Its structure is masked behind the uniform and shiny glass curtain wall. The framework of beams and columns is behind the glazed façade and is not easily visible from the outside. The main intention of the architect is clear: basically to group the services and vertical circulations in a core, extending a grid of supports with varied structural bays until completing the previously stipulated perimeter of the plant. The eccentricity of the core and the irregularity of the structural modules are established due to the previously designed functional organization of the plant and certain configurations that respond to the conditions of the site.

Later projects sort to increase the internal areas free of obstacles, and the architect strove to remove the columns from the middle of the spaces. The vertical supports moved toward the perimeter until they manifested themselves on the outside. The physical presence of the structure in the interior tends to progressively dilute at the same time that it gains visual presence from the outside. The organizational discipline of the supporting elements is accompanied by calculation criteria in which a logic of structural eccentricity is sought. The precise ordering of the components and the unification of the structural spans make it possible to have a smaller variety of elements, mainly beams.

Between 1956 and 1958 the building for the Inland Steel Company was erected in Chicago. The skyscraper – which had Gordon Bunshaft as a consulting architect – has two connected bodies, one for services, technical installations and vertical circulation, and the other for office floors. The structural system of the main volume – which has 19 levels – is made up of two rows of columns in each of the long façades. The columns are placed on the perimeter of the slabs, outside the building envelope. The conception required certain strategies to achieve a good degree of integration between the structural system and the complementary subsystems.

The large glass surfaces that cover the four façades and the heat generated internally due to the lighting system generated large thermal loads inside the floors. Consequently, the linear length of HVAC ducts and the sizes of their section had to be increased. Regarding the structure, to eliminate vertical supports within the typical plan spaces, beams of considerable height were needed. Due to this, the web of each of these steel beams has a considerable number of openings to accommodate ducts and other installations. The supply of hot and cold air is given through diffusers in the ceiling and also through supply ducts with diffusers next to the façade. The return air is taken by ceiling grilles.

In 1961, the construction of the Chase Manhattan Bank, another skyscraper in which important structural developments were implemented, was completed. The structural approach is similar to that of the Inland Steel, but the project for Chase acquired many more complexities due to its large scale: 60 floors and almost 2,300,000 Sq Ft (213,677 m2).

The columns of the Chase Manhattan are exteriorized with respect to the building envelope, suggesting that the tower is supported only on the longest façades. The short façades are cantilevered, further highlighting these features. The configuration reduces the visual weight of the skyscraper, which is located in the middle of the network of narrow streets of Lower Manhattan.

The structure has three rows of modular bays. The central modules are practically square, measuring 32' (9.75 m) in both directions. The two lateral rows have the same dimension of 32' (9.75 m) in the direction of the long façades and different dimensions in the shorter ones: 30' (9.144 m) along the south side of the tower and 40' (12.192 m) along the north.

The spacing between the columns in the short façades was limited by the height of the cross beams, which had to be reasonably low, given the height of the skyscraper. If it weren't for that, the architect could possibly have freed the center of the plan from vertical supports, bearing the tower only on the outer columns. It should be said that a sub-module of 1.47 m (4.8') commands the entire structure.[27]

Almost simultaneously, between 1957 and 1960, the headquarters of the Union Carbide Company was built on Manhattan Island. The complex is made up of two connected volumes – a high-rise tower and a lower body – which are structurally arranged with a conventional framework of beams, columns and slabs.

The Union Carbide structural frame is evenly distributed in both plan directions and also in height. The floor plan of the tower has a practically square geometry, with the core of services and vertical circulation in the center encompassing the internal columns. Structurally, modules have, in plan, approximately 20' x 40' (6.1 x 12.2 m) and the framework of beams and columns configure the volume of the building. It is clad in stainless steel sheets painted black on the outside, which visually reinforces the expression

Metal Frames And Structures
Series of Typical Floor Plans

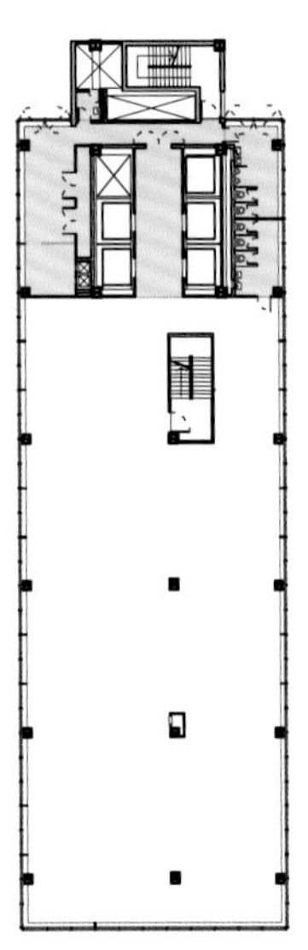

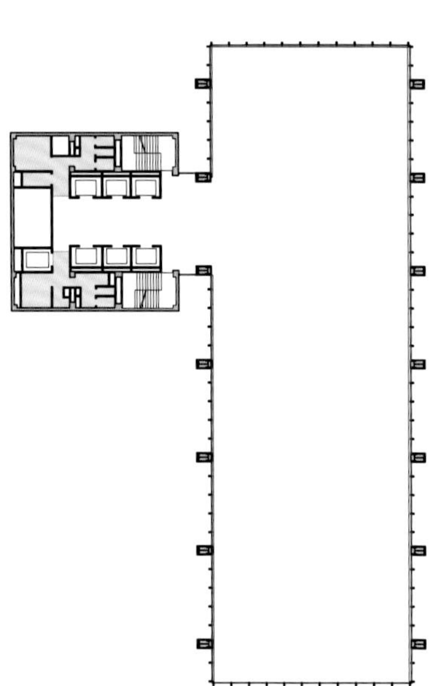

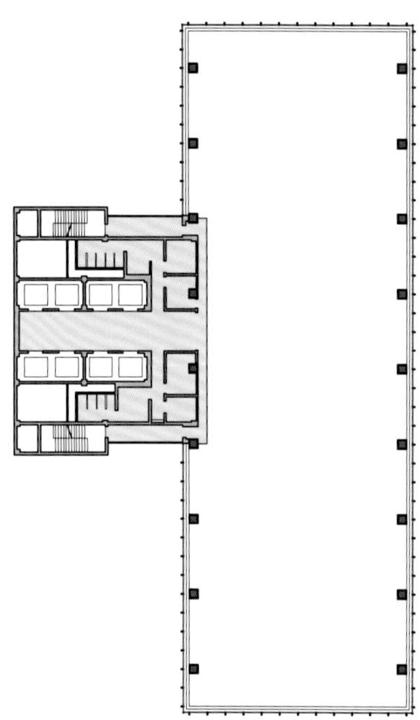

LEVER HOUSE

1952

INLAND STEEL*

1958

CROWN ZELLERBACH*

1959

60'

20 m

SCALE 1/750

* Works for which Bunshaft was not the chief designer or partner in charge.

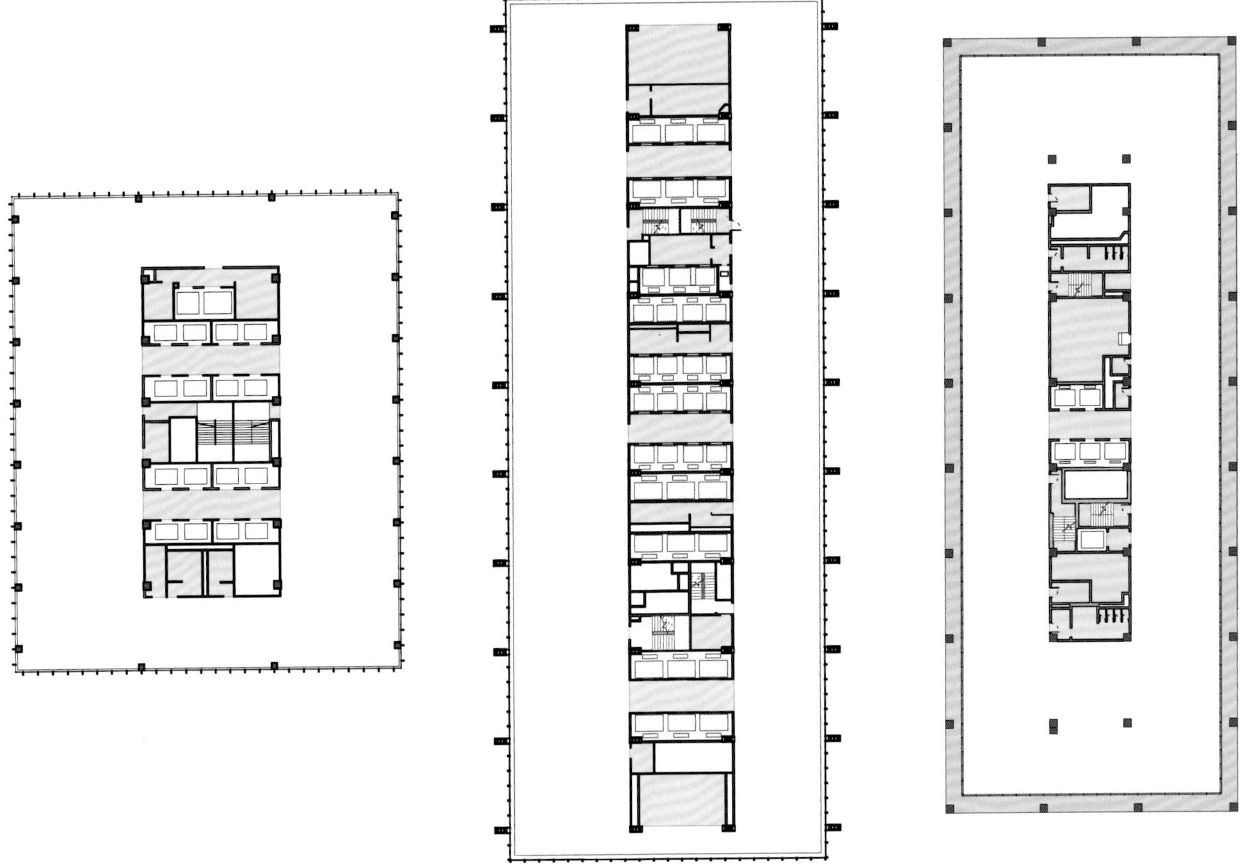

UNION CARBIDE

1960

CHASE MANHATTAN

FIRST CITY BANK

1961

of the structure on the outside. Vertical stainless-steel mullions run the entire height of the building, uniting all the façades and accentuating the verticality of the tower. Mullions dimensionally define the glass panes of the façade; its length of 5' (1.52 m) is equivalent to the measurement defined for the internal distribution modulation, and is a multiple of the 20' (6.1 m) that rules the structural distribution.

Some technical solutions were devised to optimize and make the use of spaces flexible through a high level of systems integration. The basic idea was to solve within the space between the slab and false ceiling the integration of air conditioning, sound control and lighting systems; while having the false ceiling visually appreciated as a total plane of light. This configuration contemplated the suppression of HVAC diffusers or opaque panels to compose ceilings. In addition, the design provided modular arrangement and the placement of the interior partitions of the offices. The integration of these systems was taken to an extreme that had never been achieved by SOM until the completion of the building.[28]

The false ceiling panels are framed by a grid of profiles of two different sections, placed along the two directions of the plant. Those of type "A" have a larger section area and serve as extractors and diffusers for air conditioning. The air is withdrawn and reaches the false ceiling profiles through narrow ducts placed above them. The "tee" type has a simpler section, and only receives the interior partitions and the reflective metal vaults that make up the lighting system. It should be noted that, based on a desire of the owners, the design of the false ceiling elements was thought out in such a way that company officials themselves would be able to change the distribution of partitions within the office spaces during the night, without it being necessary to go up to the roof or use specialized labor to make adjustments in installations or acoustic insulation.[29]

For the first time in the First City National Bank, built in Houston between 1959 and 1961, the perimeter structure was completely separated from the glass windows, remaining set back from the edge of the slab. The structure no longer admits internal adjustments, dissimulations; the projection of slabs and columns draws the apparent profile of the building and everything is visible from the exterior. Increasing structural bays results in increasing the edge of the border beams, hindering, as a consequence, the form of installation systems throughout the building.

The building is composed of three volumes – a 32-story office tower, a bank office and a parking lot. The office tower has a rectangular typical floor measuring 252' x 99' (77 x 30.4 m). The structural framework of steel beams and columns is covered in concrete and cladding with marble panels. As mentioned earlier, for the First City, Gordon Bunshaft placed the windows of the office block with dark gray tinted glass, approximately 5'7" (1.70 m) away from the outer limit of the building. From a bioclimatic point of view, the solution can be compared to that applied to the Reynolds Metals Company (a project to be discussed later), a building for which Bunshaft incorporated external slab extensions as horizontal sun shades between which were placed vertical brise-soleils. The First City solution is clearly more austere as there are no vertical elements for sun protection.

The structure is visually powerful. The contrast between the marble cladding and the dark gray windows adds even more visual weight to the building skeleton. Finally, the same solution is repeated on the four façades, accentuating the visual elementality of the block.

On the typical floors, the architect brought together core services and vertical circulations. Two rows of seven internal columns break the rhythm established by the perimeter supports and are misaligned in relation to the axes of the two central columns of the shorter façades. In addition, two of the four detached central columns in the office space are not aligned with the corresponding transversal structural axes, being closer to the core. This means that the structural rhythms on the outside of the building are maintained, but inside, the structure was adapted to the spatial configuration that generated work spaces free of columns or other immovable obstacles.

It is necessary to clarify that when the First National Bank of Houston was built, the urban context was quite open in terms of neighboring buildings, a condition that may have influenced the design decisions regarding the external formalization of the structure. In dense areas, such as the island of Manhattan, the architect also designed skyscrapers with the structure exposed to the outside, but with a slightly lighter visual appearance: in both the Union Carbide and the Chase Manhattan, the glass is not behind nor distant from the perimeter columns, resulting in the structural frame not standing out so much in the built-up mass.

Metal Frames And Structures
Series of Photographs

LEVER HOUSE

1952

INLAND STEEL*

1958

CROWN ZELLERBACH*

1959

* Works for which Bunshaft was not the chief designer or partner in charge.

UNION CARBIDE

1960

CHASE MANHATTAN

FIRST CITY BANK

1961

Structures with Industrialized Concrete Components

The innovations presented in the fifties and sixties by the North American construction industry, whether materials or construction systems, almost always represented stimulation for design, bringing formal alternatives for the new commissions taken by SOM. The large number of works handled by the different headquarters of the company forced in a certain way the production of an important variety of formal solutions, and the use of new constructive elements stimulated the production of a greater diversity of visual solutions.

In the search for open spaces, the placement of vertical supports on the perimeter and center of the building floors becomes extreme, dispensing with the isotropy of the structural grid as a technical paradigm.

A good example of this kind of situation occurred after the construction of San Francisco's John Hancock Company headquarters building, carried out between 1958 and 1959. For the 14-story tower, the accomplishment of the free plan through a perimeter structure was accomplished by building external bearing walls in concrete cast in situ. The typical floor plan measures 116' x 116' (35.5 x 35.5 m), and there is a central core which installations and vertical circulations run. It was found that the building producing an echo in the other offices of SOM during a meeting of partners in December 1957 in Colorado Springs, provoking reactions in Bunshaft and Walter Netsch.[30] Some of the solutions presented by the project ended up being incorporated into other commissions carried out in other parts of the country. Among all the offices of SOM, San Francisco's branch was the one that explored reinforced concrete the most in its projects during those years.

Within SOM, the New York group approached its commissions with special attention to these aspects, and the incorporation of these "novelties" achieved with concrete structures by other offices of the firm were carefully observed and debated, and lead to new achievements in the development of concepts directed, for example, with the use of supporting steel elements, a registered trademark of the New York headquarters in the field of construction. Such knowledge exchange was based on the work of the multidisciplinary team, which endorsing or not the market novelties, applied the expertise in the works through the formal criteria already implicit in the practice of the group.

The use of reinforced in situ concrete lead by the office of SOM in San Francisco can be compared to what the New York office developed in matters of structures with precast concrete elements. Bunshaft and his colleagues began to introduce, even for commissions that could be carried out with steel or in situ cast concrete, the technique and the material, working with it in a more direct way than the other offices.[31] The use of the material toward the middle of the fifties occurred predominantly in buildings such as large factories and warehouses. Already in 1956, the number of manufacturers of structural concrete elements for civil construction grew remarkably.

Between 1956 and 1965, Gordon Bunshaft and his team carried out two projects with supporting perimeter frames made up of precast concrete elements, which the British concrete engineer and researcher A.E.J. Morris described as external structural screens, which resulted in the establishment of some basic parameters for the construction technique. Similar to the developments with steel structures, the outer perimeter structure is separated from the glazed windows, set back from the edge of the slab. In buildings with precast concrete elements, the perimeter frame outlines the exposed profile of the building, and the whole structure is visible.

The *Architectural Forum* magazine of May 1959 published SOM's preliminary project for the Banque Lambert, a nine-story office building to be erected in Brussels. The subtitle of the article "SOM puts the bones outside the skin," written by Peter Blake six years before the building was completed, is revealing: "The U.S. architects who helped perfect the smooth glass-and--metal skin will now put it behind an emphatic structure of precast concrete, creating a double wall system for a new bank in Brussels."[32]

On the typical floor plans, the vertical structure of the Banque Lambert is made up of a perimeter frame composed of precast concrete crosses and a central core. The slabs are bidirectional and reticular, in concrete cast in situ. On the ground floor the structure is different: in addition to the core, reinforced concrete columns support the loads from the upper plants.

During the same period, another remarkable project was carried out by Bunshaft exploiting the same structural concept. The eight-story building for the John Hancock Company in New Orleans was completed in 1962, ratifying the effectiveness and formal result of the structural type. Slightly different from the Brussels bank, the supporting perimeter frame of John Hancock is made up of columns and prefabricated horizontal panels.

Structures with Concrete Components
Series of Ground Floor and Typical Floor Plans

Typical Floor Plans

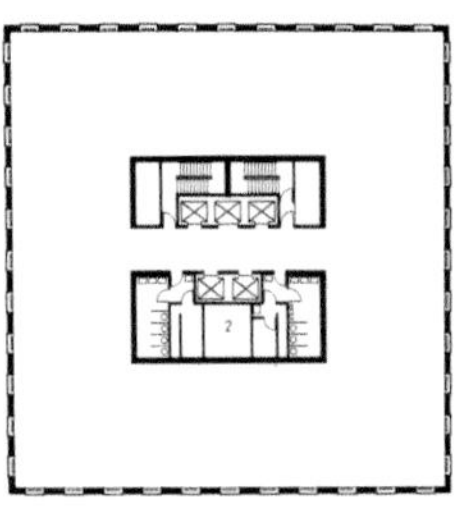

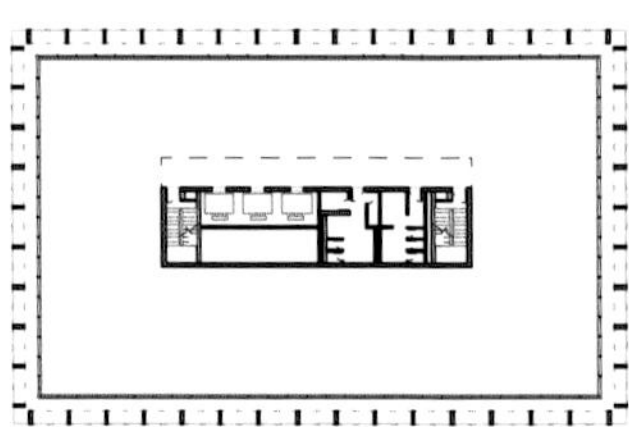

Ground Floor Plans

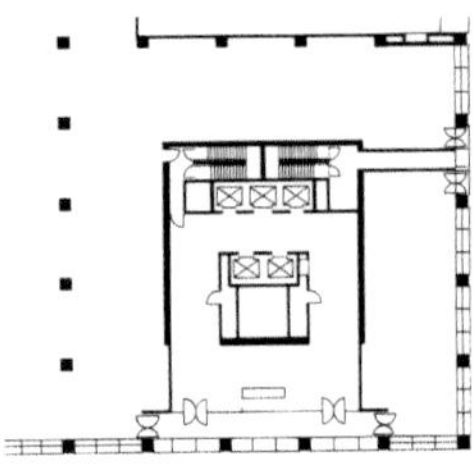

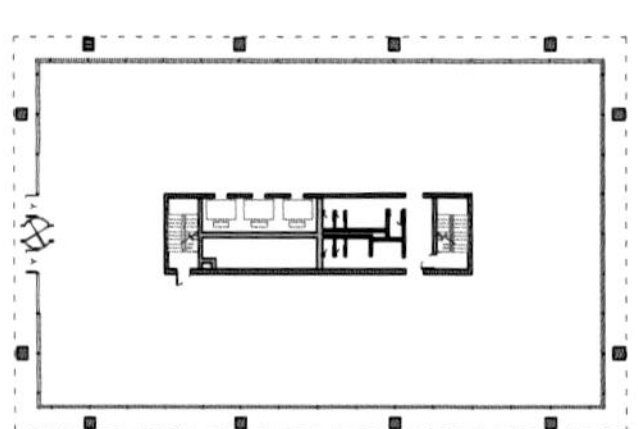

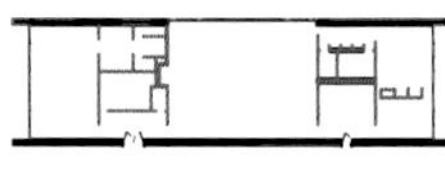

JOHN HANCOCK (S. FRANCISCO)*

1959

JOHN HANCOCK (N. ORLEANS)

1962

BUNSHAFT HOUSE

1963

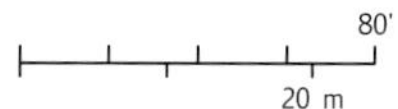

SCALE 1/1000

* Works for which Bunshaft was not the chief designer or partner in charge.

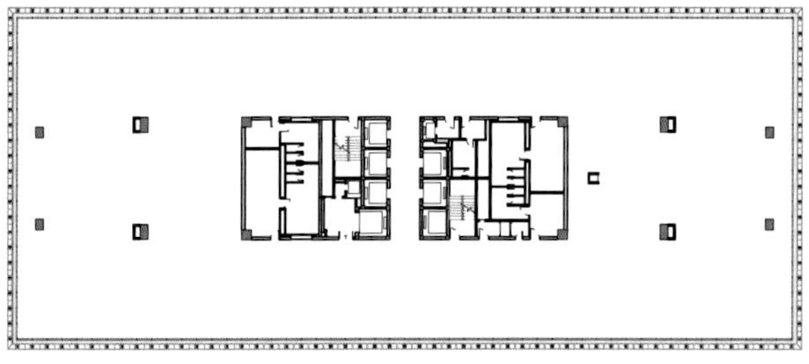

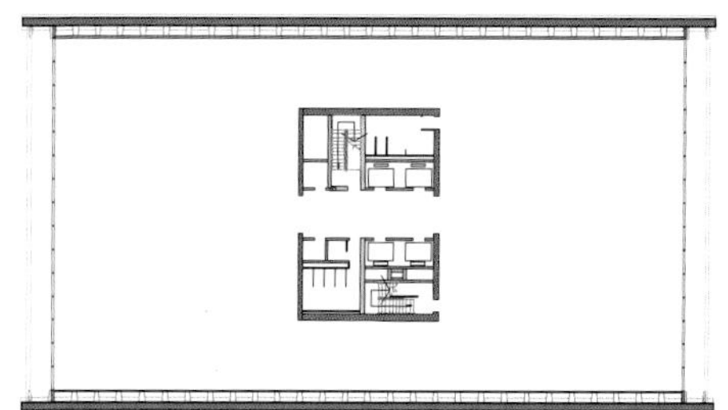

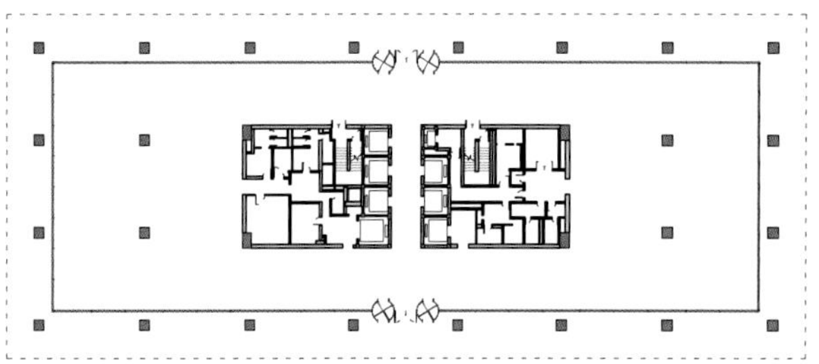

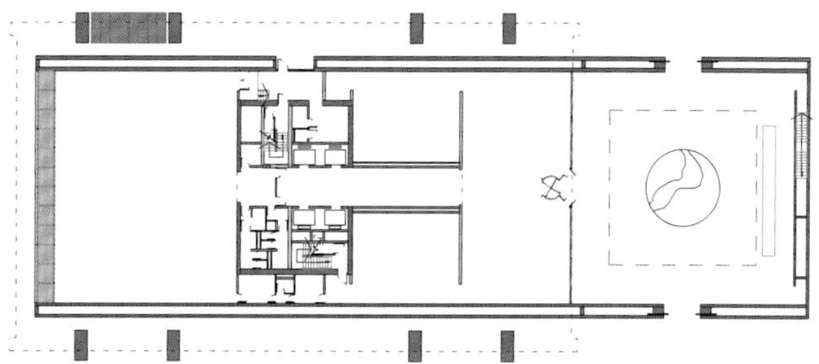

BANQUE LAMBERT

AMERICAN REPUBLIC INSURANCE COMPANY

1965

Structures with Concrete Components

Series of Photographs

JOHN HANCOCK (S. FRANCISCO)*

1959

JOHN HANCOCK (N. ORLEANS)

1962

BUNSHAFT HOUSE

1963

* Works for which Bunshaft was not the chief designer or partner in charge.

BANQUE LAMBERT

AMERICAN REPUBLIC INSURANCE COMPANY

1965

Steel and Concrete Long-Span Office Buildings

In the mid-1960s, many American corporations began to move their headquarters from dense urban centers to new buildings on the periphery of medium and small scales wealthy towns. This change was basically driven by the growth of the staff numbers, added to the fact that construction costs (whether labor or land area) in these areas were low compared to those found in the centers of large cities. In these cases, plot areas were large enough to not impose restrictions on the extension of building plans, stimulating the conception of work spaces with large spans. Perhaps the most significant example of this type of practice up to the late 1950s was the construction of the Connecticut General Life Insurance Company headquarters in Bloomfield, Connecticut. The development of the project lasted around four years, and the client enabled Bunshaft and his team to experience technical innovations that were to appear in many of the firm's subsequent works.

The offices of the Connecticut General Life Insurance Company had always been in Hartford, a small town known as "insurance city," located about 6 miles (10 km) from the site where the new headquarters was built. In 1957, the year the building was completed, Hartford was home to 41 insurance companies, employing around 22.000 people.[33]

The 280-acre site where the complex stands was former farmland, with a rich natural environment. The project included an urban plan and buildings with numerous facilities, including a full-service cafeteria and areas for after-hours activities. The idea of providing a very civilized and satisfying office environment for all employees was truly innovative at the time, and the result accurately reflected those intentions. The complex had three basic volumes: a four-story administrative and directors' office building measuring 72' x 216' (21.95 x 65.84 m) in plan, a large three-story building with 324' x 468' (98.76 x 142.65 m) and four regular internal courtyards, and a single-story cafeteria with a square plan measuring 101' (30.78 m) in length. Under these three parts of the complex there was an underground area with parking, auxiliary spaces and a large auditorium.

In addition to the programmatic novelties built by the new Connecticut General headquarters, the complex established a new variant within the architectural type of office buildings. The project, conceived by a multidisciplinary working group, gave rise to some important spatial changes that only materialized due to the implementation of innovations in the field of construction. The work developed by different groups – clients, architects, contractors (Turner Construction Company) and professional consultants (including the furniture company Knoll), led by Gordon Bunshaft, lasted about four and a half years with more than 500 meetings to discuss proposals and technical issues related to the project.[34]

> *The buildings were constructed on a 6-foot module, more generous than the one at Lever House. Nevertheless, with adroit placement of furniture, the architects discovered that executive offices could be reduced to 12 x 12 or 12 x 18 feet, with a few major offices measuring 18 x 18 feet. A 5-foot module that SOM used elsewhere because it coordinated well with standard dimensions for acoustical ceiling materials would have constricted some major offices to only 15 feet or expanded them unnecessarily to 20 feet. Smaller offices seemed larger because windows stretched along their entire width. The architects made a quarter-inch scale model of the work areas to help the interior designers, Knoll Associates, determine colors and furniture arrangements.*[35]

The most important of the innovations presented was the structural system devised by Bunshaft and his collaborators. Two of the basic design requirements were that no one should sit more than 30' (9.14 m) from a courtyard or exterior window and that there should be spaces free of vertical structural members at least 60' (18.29 m) long. In an effort to clear typical floor interiors from columns, structural mullions spaced 12' (3.66 m), equivalent to two modules, apart were applied to the façade, which at the same time received the loads from upper beams and slabs and accommodate the building's curtain-wall elements. Basically, the system is supported vertically on these mullions of both the internal and external façades, and on the internal columns integrated with the vertical circulation and service cores, almost always 24' (7.32 m) apart from each other. The horizontal structure is a grid of lattice and conventional "I" section beams arranged in two directions, on which lies a steel deck slab.

On the ground floor, the structure is different due to the enlargement of bays at the limits of the building, which have dimensions equivalent to six modules, that is, 36' (10.97 m). The columns have larger sections and the glazed enclosures are set back in relation to them. The steel columns, clad with stainless steel sheets, allow for the internal limits to be cleared of physical barriers, leaving the ground floor diaphanous in its direct relationship with the exterior. From an outside perspective, the columns allow for the prism, composed of the upper floors, to be visually released from the ground plane.

Steel and Concrete Long-Span Office Buildings

Series of Ground Floor and Typical Floor Plans

Steel Structures

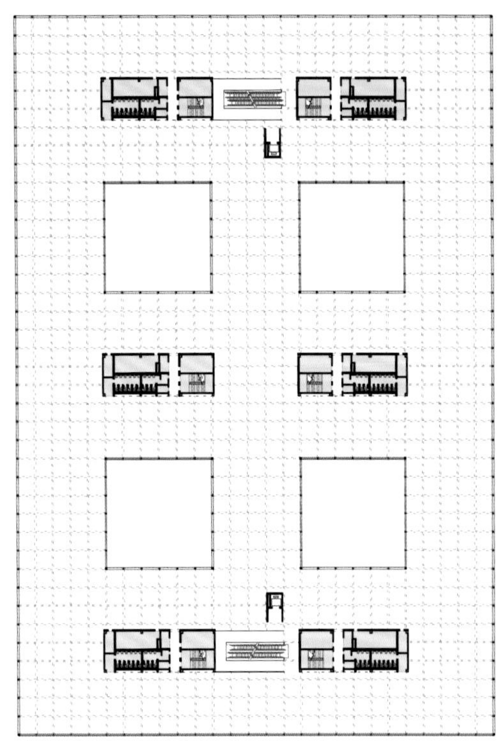

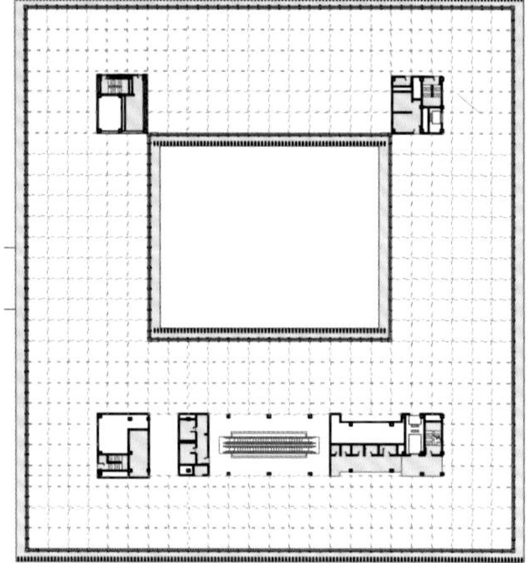

CONNECTICUT GENERAL COMPANY

1957

REYNOLDS METALS COMPANY

1958

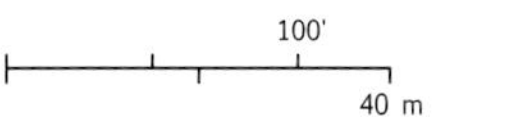

SCALE 1/1500

Concrete Structures

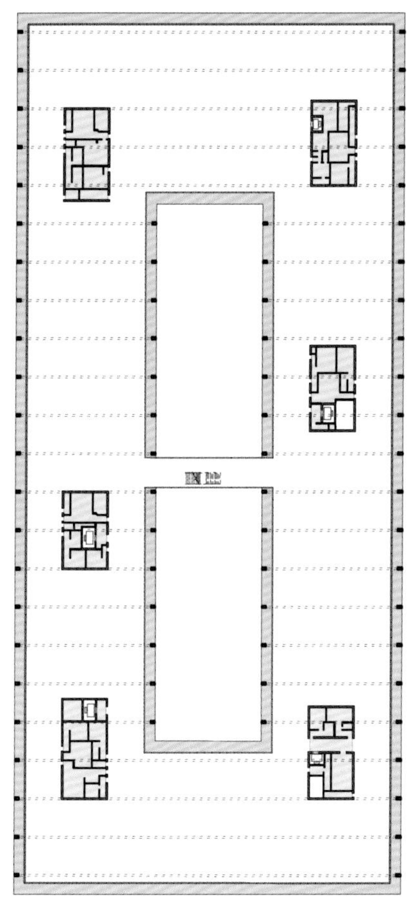

IBM CORPORATION

1964

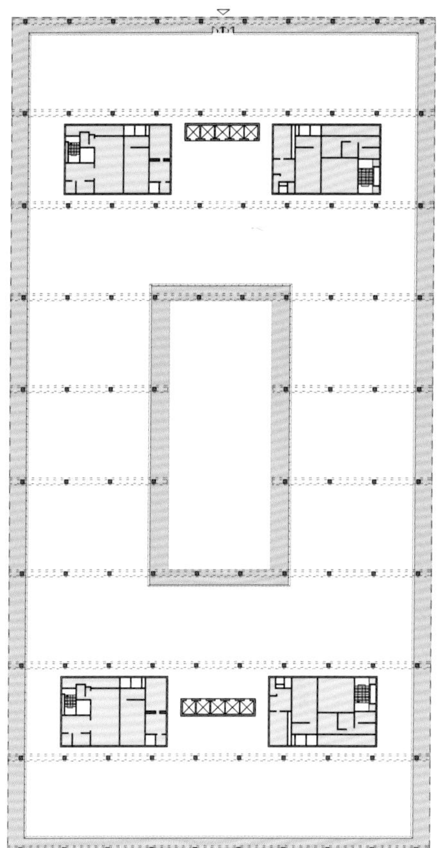

AMERICAN CAN COMPANY

1970

Such was the experimental nature of the project that the design team led by Gordon Bunshaft ordered the construction of a full-size "mock-up."

> *The 60-foot span was the maximum that could then be justified economically, and it fit the governing module. A full-size mock-up was made of a typical 60 x 70-foot working section, which the building committee could walk into to judge alternative materials and arrangements. It was also used by subcontractors preparing their bids.*[36]

Operations of this type would recur on other large projects, such as the Chase Manhattan Bank on Manhattan Island.

As can be seen in previous quotations, until those years, SOM's allusions to office buildings were for the most part, paradigmatic work, as in the Lever House. In this sense, constructive and visual correlations could be found between the structural façade modules of the Connecticut General and the base (ground and second floors) of the New York skyscraper. The ideas established in Connecticut were eventually ratified in another corporate building with a similar program but smaller in size, erected on a site with a large available area. The building for the Reynolds Metals Company, a major producer of aluminum elements, including the construction industry, finished in 1955 in Richmond, Virginia. The complex features a structural system very similar to that used at Connecticut General: the main building plant measures approximately 281' x 260' (85.75 x 79.45 m), and sits on a podium-like base.

At Reynolds Metals, the construction modulation used is different from that found in the Bloomfield building. The slabs finished up having a somewhat different formulation. The module became 5' 2" (1.57 m) and the aluminum-clad steel structural mullions of the façade are placed at that distance. The enclosure panels applied are different, consisting of fewer elements. A single glass panel spans the entire height of each floor; the slabs are covered on the façade by black-painted aluminum panels and there are no parapets. The floor slabs are made of steel lattice girders up to 3' 10" (1.17 m) high and are arranged in both directions of the floor plan. These floors are supported perimetrically on the structural steel mullions of the façade and internally on columns integrated into the circulation and service cores, the system being, in fact, very similar to that of the Connecticut General.

Apart from that, there is a kind of eave-like extension on each of the floor slabs that surrounds the entire external perimeter and the courtyard. These eaves not only reduce the direct solar incidence on the building but also support 880 vertical louvers placed on the east and west façades. In addition, they act as catwalks for repairs and washing of the windows. The louvers are 14' (4.27 m) high and 22" (56 cm) wide, and are operated by a program predetermined by a master clock, which anticipates the daily movements of the sun as the day progresses. Variations in the sun's position during the different seasons of the year also influence this adjustment automatically.

Based on these progresses, engineers, calculators and architects continued the search for larger structural spans, trying to achieve even more economical construction processes. By the mid-1960s, expressive results were reached with slabs composed of precast concrete slabs of "tee" and double "tee" sections. Between 1962 and 1965, Gordon Bunshaft and the New York office of SOM. carried out the project for the headquarters of the American Republic Life Insurance Company, a nine-story office building. The six upper floors form a raised volume supported vertically by two opaque in situ concrete walls. The floors of these floors are made of precast "tee" slabs placed side by side, spanning 99'4" (30.27 m) between the lateral load-bearing walls.

More than ten years later Bunshaft again used a precast concrete slab floor system very similar to that built for the American Republic. The headquarters for the American Can Company, completed in 1970, proved the efficiency of the slab system, which, unlike the American Republic, consisted of double "tee"-section slabs and not "tee" slabs. Apart from that, for the American Can Company, Bunshaft again used the formal solution employed in the Connecticut General and Reynolds Metals: two commissions completed more than ten years earlier in which large corporate buildings were designed for a large site with rich natural surroundings. Besides general features, such as the low height of the buildings and the presence of internal courtyards, these three complexes have structural similarities that reflect the intent of the architect and his clients to have open floor plans full of light and open visuals to the surroundings.

The American Can Company consists of two buildings on a base with five underground levels. The plan of the larger and main block measures 288' x 544'9" (166 x 88 m) and has a central courtyard measuring 175'3" x 69'12" (53 x 21 m).

Internal spaces are mostly collective work areas and the structure is composed of reinforced concrete portal frames cast in situ. Leaning on their girders are the double "tee" slabs that make up the two upper floors and the roof. Each precast slab spans 30' (18.3 m), this being one of the dimensions of the constructive module. In the other direction, the distance between the columns is 60' (9.15 m), a measurement proportional to the 10' (3.05 m) corresponding to the width of a double "tee" slab.

The American Can Company represents an efficient way of utilizing structural elements more commonly used in engineering works, from which great architectural advantage was taken, generating a very satisfactory formal solution.

Steel and Concrete Long-Span Office Buildings
Series of Photographs

Steel Structures

CONNECTICUT GENERAL COMPANY

1957

REYNOLDS METALS COMANY

1958

IBM CORPORATION

1964

AMERICAN CAN COMPANY

1970

Supporting Perimeter Frames Over 1st Floor Transfer Beams

The curtain wall of the Lever House is a milestone, and when it was published for the first time in the June 1950 issue of *Architectural Forum*, it was presumed, among other things, that the metal mullion of the window frame barely protruded from the glass. The solution set a minimum (protrusion distance?) and on subsequent occasions, the search did not go on to eliminate the mullion altogether but, on the contrary, to increase the relief of the curtain-wall profiles. Given the technical and formal transformations carried out in subsequent commissions, the structure on the perimeter gives relief to the contour. From the Lever House, where the mullions barely protrude from the glass to the outside, the structural elements take prominence on the perimeter, with the glazing being completely separated from the vertical supports. Even so, the columns descend from the typical floors and pass through the base, forming a continuity from the top to the ground.

At the end of the 1950s, Bunshaft began to apply perimeter structural grids made of industrialized elements in a series of buildings. In these cases, the structure is not only emphasized at the perimeter but also involves the adoption of structural bays of smaller dimensions than those found in the precedents with steel frame and curtain walls. For the works with perimeter grids, the use of load transfer structures on the first floor can be considered a key resource; understanding their meaning involves recognizing some of Bunshaft's formal predilections that ended up conditioning their use.

One of the recurring themes in his architecture is the treatment of the access floors to the buildings as large areas in which one can begin to experiment the internal spatiality and its frank integration with the environment. More than external access areas, they are platforms, given that in many cases they are elevated with respect to street level, and house in their internal functions parking areas, services, technical installations, etc. The treatment of these spaces contemplated the total urbanization of the site through the placement of sculptures, fountains, benches, lampposts, etc. The constructive modulations of the buildings extended directly to these contiguous spaces, defining the dimensions of the cladding, the cutting of paving stones, and even the positioning of the aforementioned urban planning elements.

In some works, these intentions are evident when one observes that the same travertine marble pavement, even with the same cutting, is used in the internal area of the ground floor and on the floor of the access platform. Therefore, the ground floor, where the internal parts are accessed, is visually connected with the exterior through large glazed windows and, in a sense, ends up becoming part of the platform. Finally, a basic condition for this to happen is due to the elevation of the body of the building, i.e. the volume shaped by the typical floors above this platform by a small number of columns, so that the internal space can be truly diaphanous.

Another of the recurring attributes of his buildings is perceived in their visual appreciation. By elevating the main body of the complexes from the access level, the architect increases the degree of visual independence of this in relation to the platforms, further increasing the perception of volumetric and formal purity already established by the uniform treatment of the façades.

Understanding these conditions can explain how some of the construction problems that permeated the conception of the projects were solved. As aforementioned, in buildings with perimeter supporting grids, the downward loads of the upper levels come from the exterior boundary and also from the core of the floors. Given the intention to free the ground floor, at the second-floor slab level it is necessary to redirect the perimeter loads to a reduced number of columns. This requires a transfer beam. In the center of the floors, the loads descend through the load-bearing core, which also includes vertical circulation and installation ducts.

These operations occurred predominantly in buildings with perimeter supporting grids made of precast concrete units. But there were other notable achievements in which the perimeter structures were built in steel or cast-in-place reinforced concrete, proving the effectiveness of the system. The perimeter structure of the Beinecke Library of Rare Books and Manuscripts, which will be discussed later, consists of large Vierendeel trusses formed by precast steel crosses welded in situ. The base members of these Vierendeel trusses operate as transfer beams as they transmit loads to four large ground-floor columns.

In the case of the American Republic Life Insurance Company, the two cast-in-place concrete screens rest on eight columns that free up the ground floor-platform and the collective spaces on the first floor.

In some buildings, including the Lambert Bank, American Republic Life Insurance Company and Beinecke Library, steel capitals or hinges were placed on the top of the ground-floor columns. In the case of the American Republic Life Insurance Company, it is interesting to note that these hinges, on the one hand, physically connect the columns and transfer beams by being welded to the steel reinforcement of both elements. In addition, they increase the resistance of the structure against lateral forces and absorb the

Supporting Perimeter Frames Over First Floor Transfer Beams

Detailed section series - steel buildings

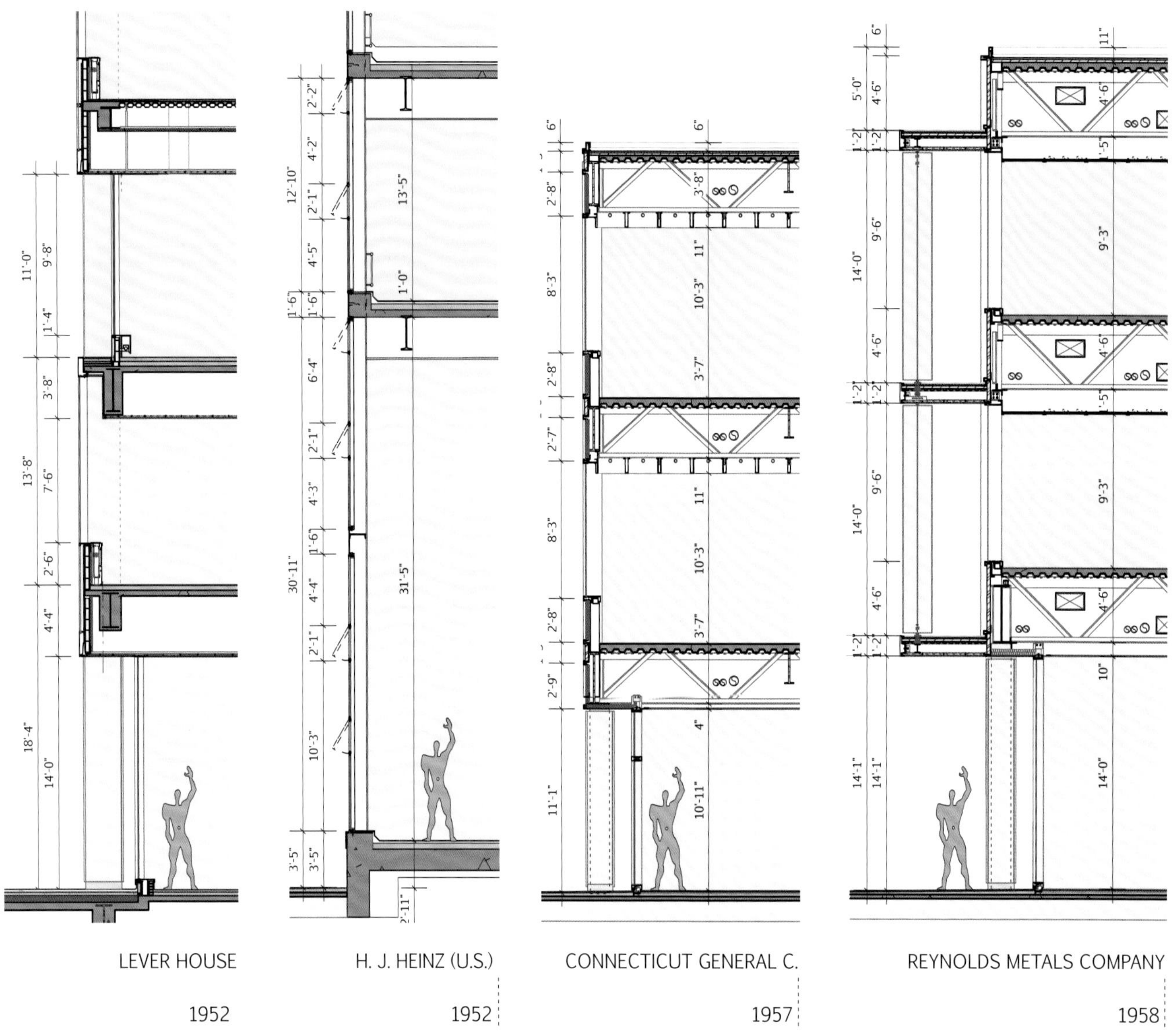

LEVER HOUSE

1952

H. J. HEINZ (U.S.)

1952

CONNECTICUT GENERAL C.

1957

REYNOLDS METALS COMPANY

1958

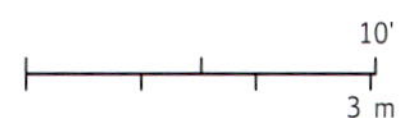

SCALE 1/125

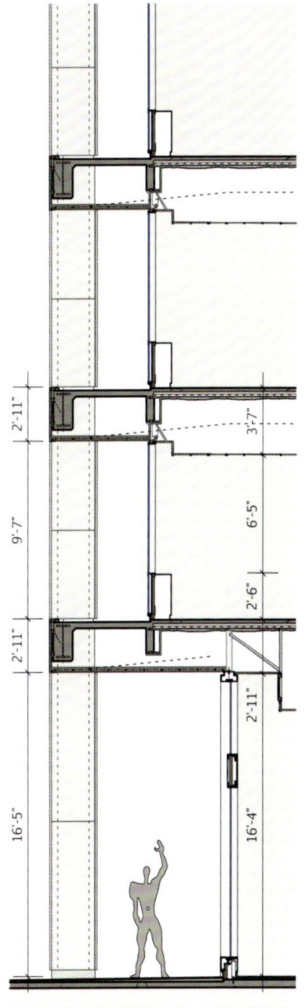

FIRST CITY NATIONAL BANK

1961

CHASE MANHATTAN BANK

1961

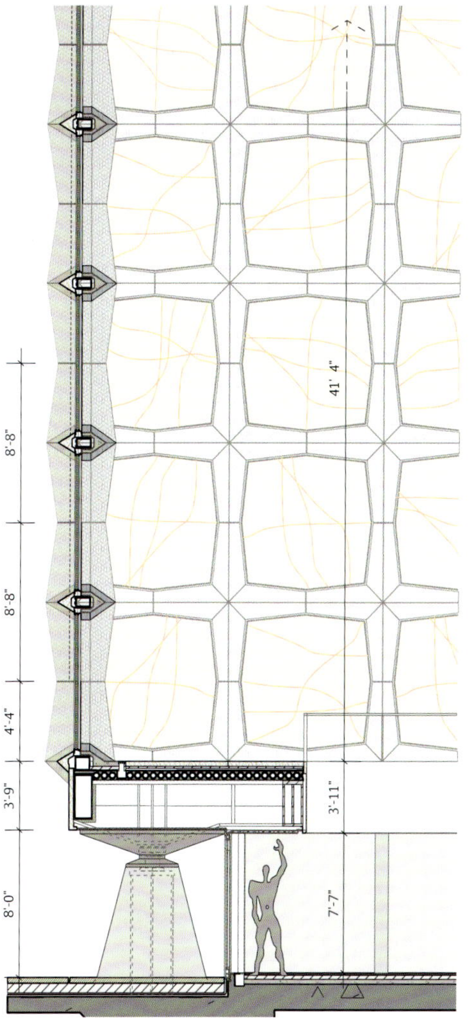

BEINECKE LIBRARY

1962

Supporting Perimeter Frames Over First Floor Transfer Beams

Detailed section series - concrete buildings

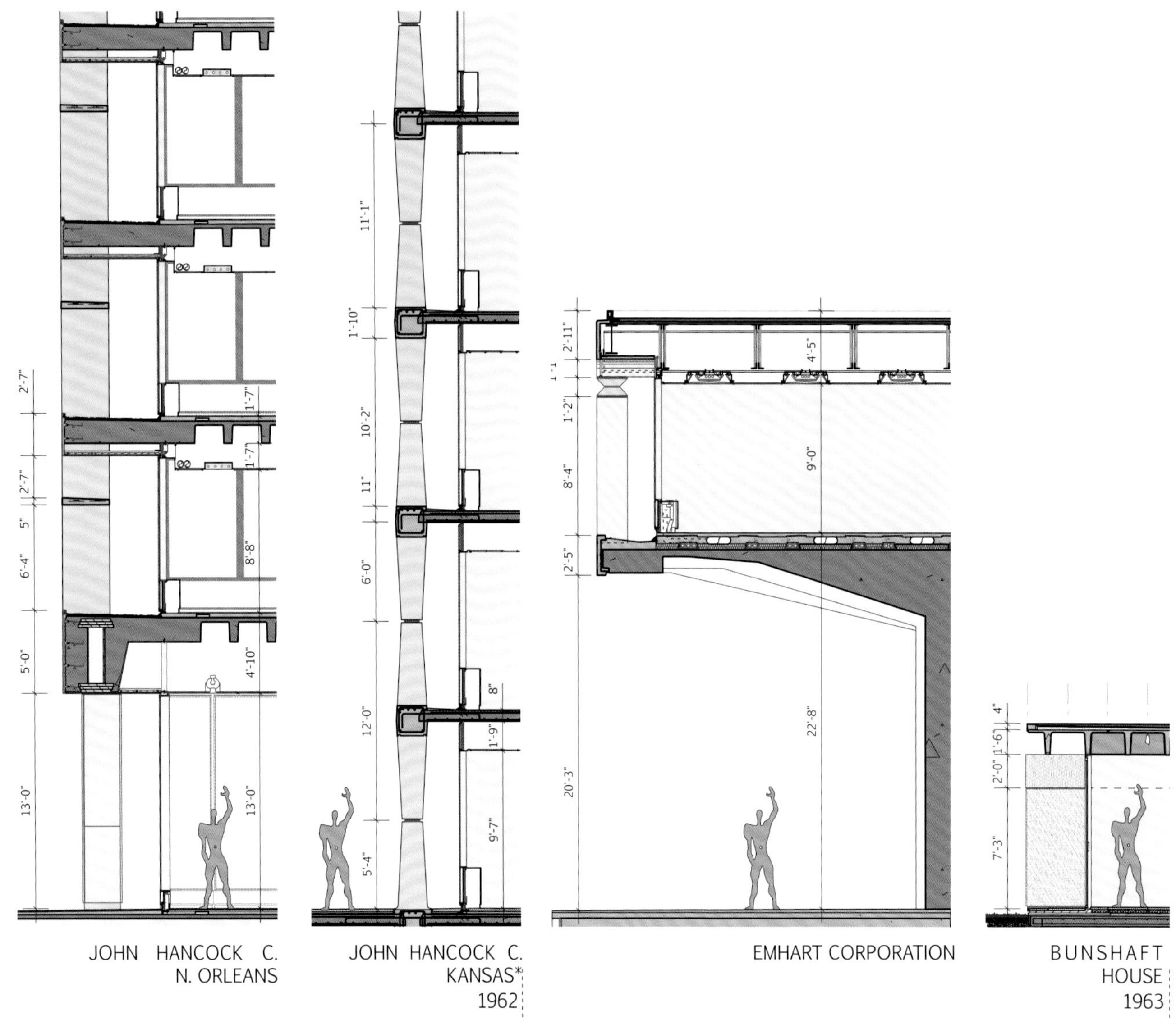

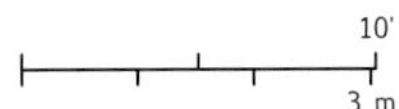

SCALE 1/125

* Works for which Bunshaft was not the chief designer or partner in charge.

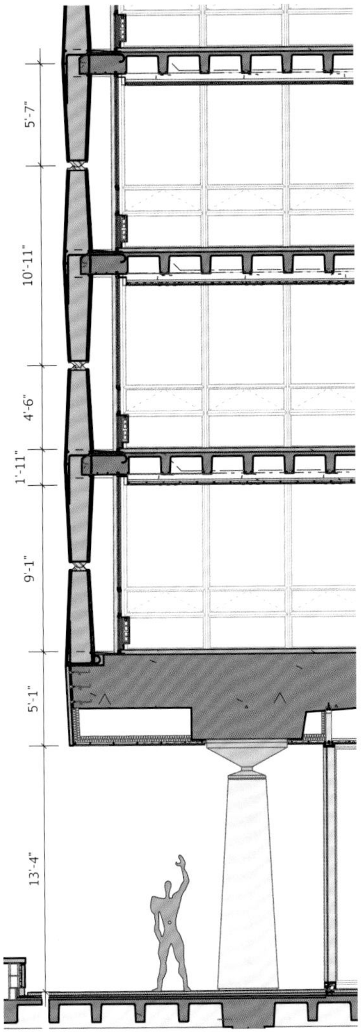

BANQUE LAMBERT

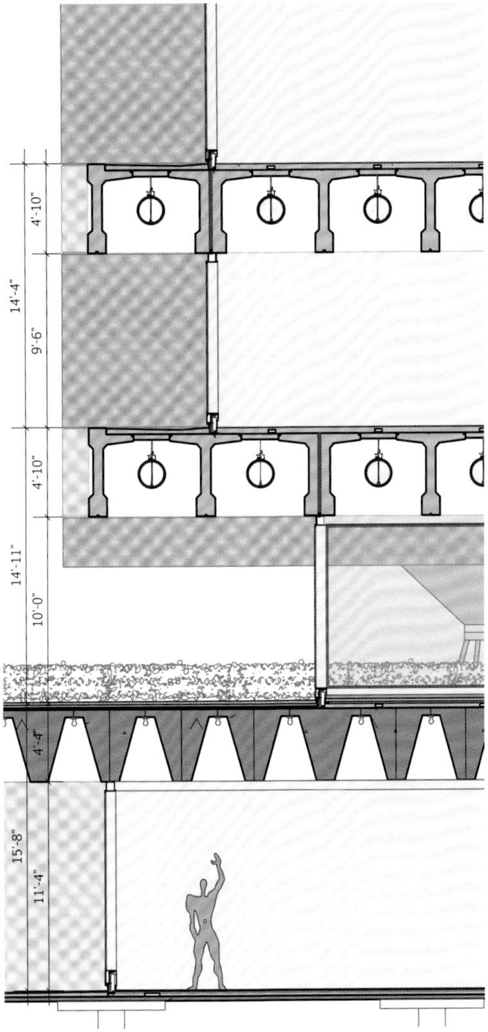

AMERICAN REPUBLIC LIFE INSURANCE COMPANY
1965

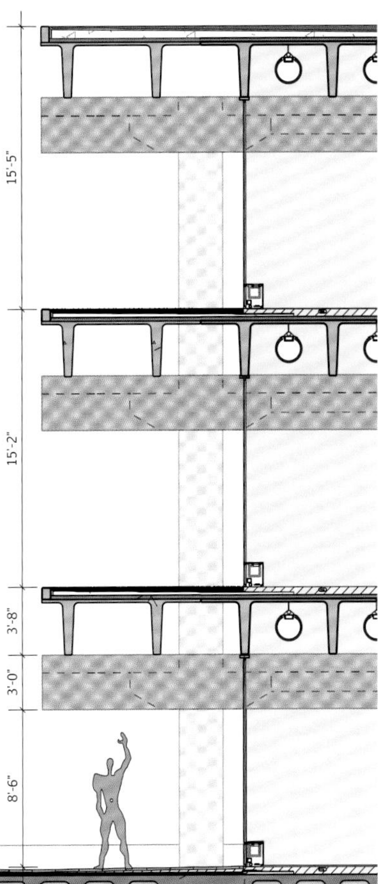

AMERICAN CAN COMPANY
1970

movement of the thermal variations of the 185'-long (56.39 m) concrete walls. On the other hand, the connectors help to increase the visual autonomy between the ground-floor columns and the concrete walls, and on a larger scale, between the ground-floor platform and the body of the building. This dual function of these connecting elements was achieved largely due to the design of the pieces. Broadly speaking, they always consist of two pyramidal parts that are joined at the apexes, the bases being welded to the surfaces of the elements to which they are attached. These are elements that translate one of the basic principles of Bunshaft's architecture: it is always worth trying to solve the greatest number of problems or variants through the adoption of just one solution or element.

Technical Ceilings

The construction of office buildings with large structural spans opened up numerous possibilities. Artificial air conditioning requires greater dedication on the part of the designer to integrate it into the architecture. The distribution of energy networks that feed the buildings increases the complexity, configuring a very important subsystem that is incorporated into the structural system and the distribution of work spaces.

Successive attempts at building long-span structures in combination with ventilation, air conditioning, lighting and electrical systems in high-rise skyscrapers, such as the Chase Manhattan Bank, were instrumental in enabling the architect and his team to design floors and ceilings of great technical efficiency and formal quality.

One of the first experiences in the conception of illuminated ceilings, in which these elements were conceived as planes of light, took place in the construction of the Manufacturers Hanover Trust Company. In this building, erected between 1953 and 1954 in Manhattan, the structure is conventional, i.e., it consists of steel columns and beams covered with concrete and reinforced concrete slabs.

In the year in which the Manufacturers Trust building had just been finished, construction began of the Connecticut General Life Insurance Company in Bloomfield. It is not fortuitous to find parallels between these buildings. Although in both projects the ideas of outlining the floor slabs, allowing it to be perceived from the outside, and covering the slabs by a false ceiling that aesthetically explores the lighting system are present, the Connecticut General building brings some significant novelties with regard to the integration of these elements with the supporting structure. While in the Manufacturers Trust the ceilings were detached from the slabs in order to disguise them and allow the air conditioning ducts to pass hidden above, in the Connecticut General building, the internal ceilings were directly composed of structural slab elements.

The structure of the Connecticut General building guided the placement of all the other systems, being also adapted to some technical demands stemming from them. As previously mentioned, the "I" section steel beams used in the Manufacturers Trust building became (due to the large structural spans established) trusses in the Connecticut General building. The latter inaugurated a new phase in the conception of supporting structures by Gordon Bunshaft and SOM.

Professor Carol Krinsky, based on her conversations with Bunshaft, describes in detail the technical ceiling system employed at the Connecticut General building. According to her, the ceilings were developed by the architects and not by the component manufacturers. In the words of Krinsky:

> *More than fifteen years later, the ceiling won approval for its excellence in creating 'a pleasing architectonic ambiance' and for its flexibility. Bunshaft himself thinks the system 'halfway solved the problems' of exposed services, and in later buildings he continued his search for even better solutions.*[37]

At the time the building was designed, there was considerable experimentation in the design of ceilings that concealed installation runs; grills hanging below ductwork and light fixtures which concealed the ducts, leaving them accessible; heating, lighting and ventilation systems were integrated. The Connecticut General building's overall ingenious system, widely imitated, represents SOM's first attempt to create exposed ceilings with integrated lighting, ventilation and acoustical systems while keeping energy consumption as low as possible.

The system also solved the problem of keeping the sprinklers unobstructed and properly positioned in a building that had no other fire protection installations or devices, and no conflicts with the air conditioning diffusers. Every 30 cm, white fluorescent tubes alternate with perforated steel acoustic panels. The lighting system integrated into the open ceiling grid was used in all spaces except the conference room, an employee entertainment area and the main lobby, where corrugated plastic ceilings were installed. Because the ceilings are normally viewed in perspective (not frontally), the presence of exposed fluorescent tubes are not irritating. The technical ceilings act as a sound absorber due to the fact that the acoustic panels were filled with fiberglass.

According to the September 1957 issue of *Architectural Forum* magazine,

> *Flexible partition system, custom-designed by SOM and tailor-made for the Connecticut General building has been put into mass production under the name C. G. Partition. The blinds and ceiling grid will also be repeated on a wide scale.*[38]

The same design and construction guidelines were followed for the Reynolds Metals Company building as for the Connecticut General building, and the slab solutions throughout the complex were very similar.

> *Suspended cellular aluminum ceiling panels diffuse both conditioned air and low-brightness fluorescent light into the offices below, and effectively conceal the ductwork, wiring, light fixtures, and steel trusses above. Fitted to the 2 foot 7 inch (79 cm) aluminum ceiling grid are rearrangeable aluminum partitions with honeycomb cores, aluminum posts, and baked*

enamel panels. Windows are shielded from the sun by the moving outside louvers, and by lightly-tinted gray glass.[39]

It is important to note that 2'7" (79 cm), the dimension of the ceiling grid module, equals half of the 5'2" (158 cm) of the structural façade module.

As happened with the vertical louvers placed on two of the building's façades, honeycomb perforated panels made of aluminum were designed due to a special request from the client.

The air conditioning system ducts and diffusers do not run next to the internal face of the windows as in the Connecticut General building. They are embedded in the slabs. The HVAC diffusers are placed in grilles on the floor, in addition to being in the technical ceilings in the internal spaces.

In both the Connecticut General building and the Reynolds Metals buildings, the height of the beams allowed for the crossing of all types of installations, such as wiring, piping and ducts, and were essential for the design of the entire floor system. The ceilings, on the other hand, are fully integrated into the basic modulations of the structure, and directly govern the placement of the internal partitions and walls on the working floors. The profiles of these partitions were specially designed to fit perfectly into the upper framework.

Instead of increasing costs and hindering the compatibility of installations and infrastructural subsystems, the changes imposed by the larger dimensions and measurements of the structural elements of the floor slabs were technically and formally exploited, and were fundamental for increasing the quality of the interiors.

Bunshaft's two projects in which the floor slabs are made of precast concrete units – the American Republic Life Insurance Company and the American Can Company – eventually established the continuity of the experiences carried out in the design of technical ceilings for the Connecticut General building and the Reynolds Metals Company buildings.

As for the American Can building, the double "tee" slabs that make up the floor slabs are fully exposed in the internal spaces. Along the vaults formed between their webs, circular cross-section ducts were placed to carry the heating and air conditioning systems. Fluorescent tubes were attached to these ducts to shed light on the vaults, which also function as perfect reflectors, creating ideal lighting for office work.

The exposure of the structure and the complementary systems was taken to the extreme. If on the one hand the structure itself defines the internal finishes and the essential design of the ceilings, i.e., the rhythm of vaults that are repeated throughout the spaces, on the other hand, the ducts had to be

Technical Ceilings

Sections

10'

3 m

SCALE 1/125

Steel Structure

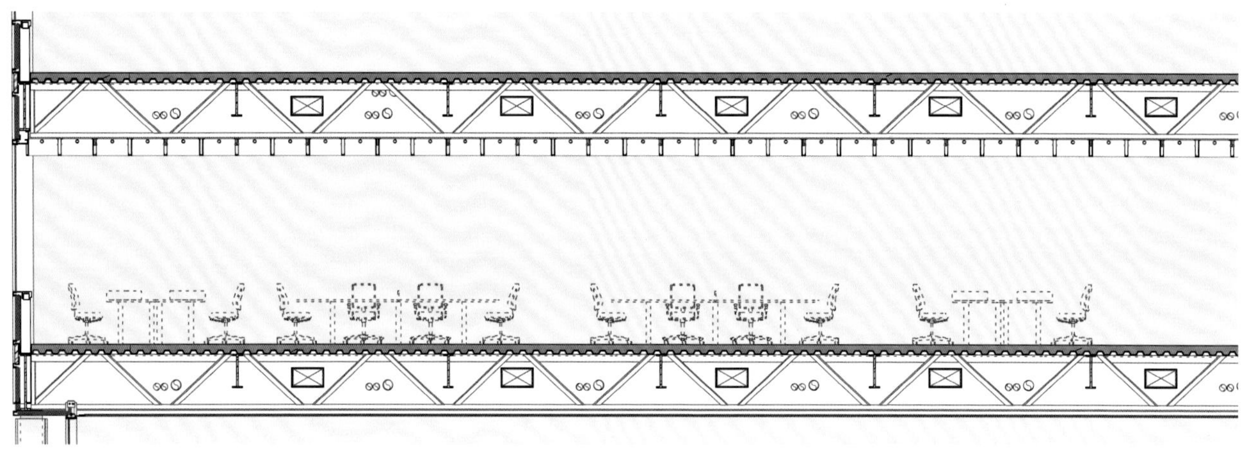

CONNECTICUT GENERAL COMPANY

1957

Concrete Structure

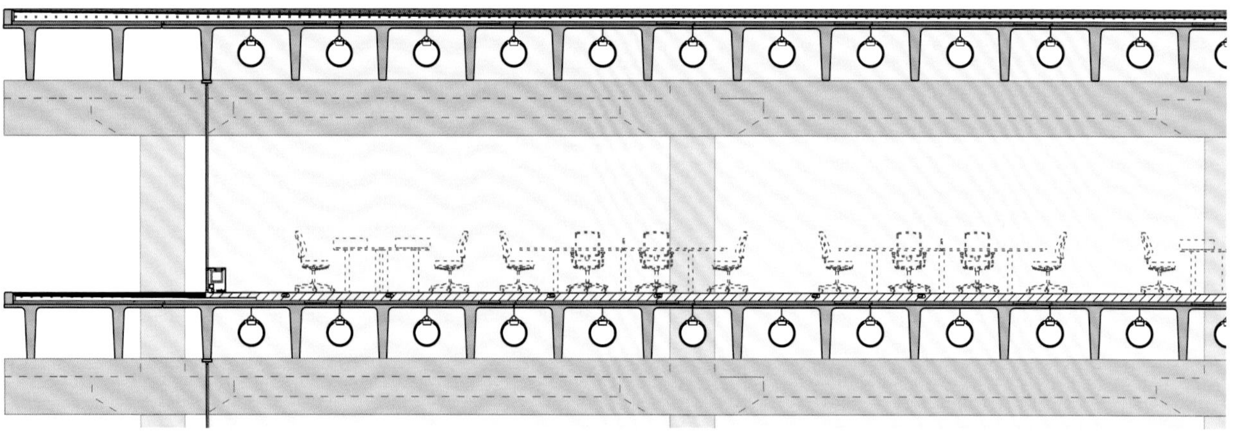

AMERICAN CAN COMPANY

1970

Interior photographs

designed and manufactured as pieces made exclusively for the building. Even so, both the circular ducts for heating and air conditioning and the fluorescent tubes for lighting were thought out in such a way that the materials, their production and assembly on site did not incur high costs.

Finally, it is important to emphasize that normally, during the years when the American Can Company and the American Republic Company were built, the “tees” and double “tees” were chosen from stocks of standard sections available from manufacturers, in accordance with structural determinants of clear span and overload, related to architectural considerations of deflection and warping. In England and the United States, standard precast and prestressed “tees” were generally available in lengths of 30 m or more, subject to transportation constraints, and longer spans could still be achieved by post-tensioning incremental T-beam sections. In both buildings, the units used were within this commercial frame, apparently not being specially designed for the construction, something that constituted an economic advantage for the use of these elements. In addition, by dispensing with accessories or complementary elements, such as false ceilings, insulation or interior cladding sheets, the system further increased the economy obtained.

Made of Steel

First City National Bank, 1959-1961
Houston, Texas

On the left:

The First City National Bank.

Photo by the author.

The First City National Bank, built in Houston between 1959 and 1961, consisted of three buildings – a 32-story office tower, an office pavilion dedicated to banking and a garage for parking. The complex was located in the Central Business District, and was one of the first skyscrapers in the area. It occupied the entire block defined by Main, McKinney, Fannin and Lamar Streets.

The nature of the site and the soil forced the development of an unusual solution in which the building assigned to parking spaces was located on the neighboring block, crossing the main site. To connect the separate parts, a subway tunnel was built.

The tower is rectangular in plan with overall dimensions of 252' x 99' (77 x 30.4 m). The air conditioning units occupy the top three floors. The first two floors were occupied by the bank's administration offices, and all the other floors were for rent or sale.

The bank office was an elegantly detailed glass pavilion that was linked to the tower lobby by two open-plan corridors flanking the office and secretarial areas. Its floor plan was 190' x 123' (57.91 x 37.5 m) with a floor-to-ceiling clear height of 30' (9.14 m). Its façade was composed of curtain walls of steel mullions covered with aluminum, emphasizing clearly its commercial function in which the enclosures functioned as a showcase. Its structure was formed by a succession of six porticos spaced every 27' 9" (8.46 m), which were composed of steel columns 114' 5" (34.87 m) apart and trusses 122' (37.18 m) long and 9' 6" (2.9 m) high.[40]

The distribution of the first floor, in which the two volumes of the complex were spatially connected, was given by three bands. The first was defined by the lobby of the office tower; the second by the connecting space between the bank and the tower, which comprised a delimited enclosure occupied by administrative staff; and the third by the bank office itself, with tellers and customer service desks.

The two main entrances to the complex were accessed from Main Street. One of them allowed access to the bank office and the other to the tower. McKinney and Lamar are streets of lesser hierarchy in the area's road network. In response to this condition, secondary accesses to the office were

On the left:

View of the First City National Bank from Lamar Street

Photo by the author.

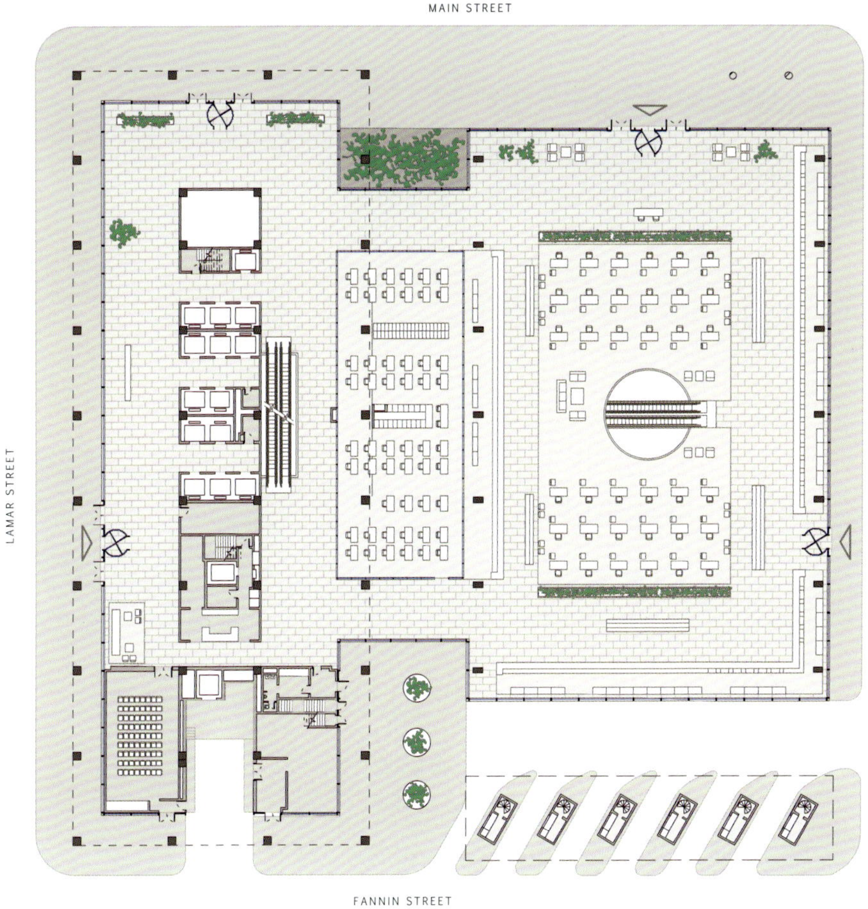

MAIN STREET

LAMAR STREET

MCKINNEY STREET

FANNIN STREET

Ground Floor

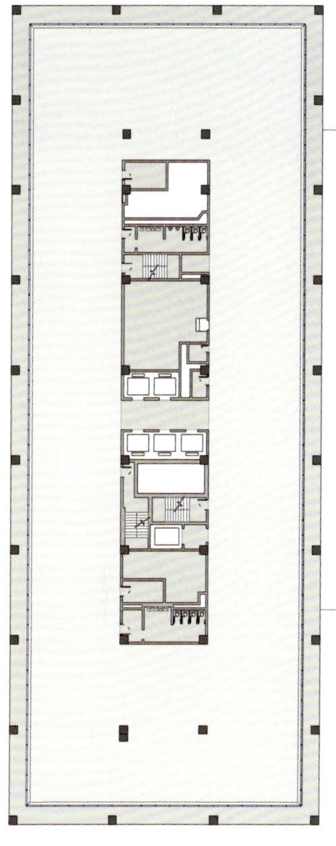

Typical Floor

placed on McKinney Street, and, to the tower, on Lamar Street. Road and service accesses were placed on Fannin Street. The banking office portion was occupied by six drive-through booths where customers did not get out of their vehicles. The façade of the office tower on this street is already destined for a dock and service entrance. Regarding the tower, it is interesting to note the way it was integrated into the surrounding sidewalks. The columns are at the edge of the building and reache the ground. All the enclosures, mostly glazed, were set back from the columns, creating a loggia-like gallery next to the public space. The height of the columns also contributed to the effective configuration of a gallery: while on the standard floors the clear height between the perimeter beams is 9' 6" (2.91 m), while on the first floor

it is 16' 5" (5 m).

The typical floors arewere structured around the service and circulation core, as the columns are located outside the glazed windows. The structure is composed of steel columns and beams covered with concrete and steel--deck concrete slabs. These elements were distributed using a grid system, with modular grids both in plan and elevation. In plan, the regularity of intercolumniation is noted on the perimeter, but not in the center. As already discussed, the columns inside the floor plan were arranged as close as possible to the circulation and installation cores in order to open up free space and flexibility for the layout of the office spaces. On the long façade there are nine intercolumns and the spans arewere 27' 9" (8.45 m). On the short façade there arewere 3 intercolumns and the spans are 32' 4" (9.86 m). In the internal part of the floor plan, between the external columns of the long façade and the columns immediately in the center, the distance is 35' 10"

View of the First City National Bank from Main Street.

(10.93 cm). The two center column lines arewere 25' 4" (7.72 m) apart at the short façade direction.

Bunshaft was not the designer of the garage building. The project was designed by the architects Wilson, Morris, Crain & Anderson, who arewere co-designersauthors of the other two parts of the complex. The 800-car parking lot consists of a series of seven overlapping, staggered floors. The 250 by 125 ft structure features an exposed concrete frame, which is coated with white vinyl. The staggered lines of the floors were concealed behind a perforated screen of charcoal gray tiles which recalls the gray glass of the office building. Infilling panels at street level are of the same Vermont White marble that sheatheds the tower.[41]

Details

The First City Bank was a pioneer in some technical and architectural aspects at the time it was finished.

> *Appropriately enough, considering its location, the owners can boast of several Texas-sized facts about their new bank: the largest 1/2 in. plate glass panels (9 x 23 ft) ever manufactured and installed in a building; the two tallest stainless steel flagpoles (they extend 100 ft above the sidewalk) rising anywhere; the biggest banking room (23,370 sq ft) designed to date by SOM; and (of course) the only illuminated ceiling anyone ever heard of that has its own elevator!*[42]

Interior of the elegant glass pavilion that housed the bank's office.

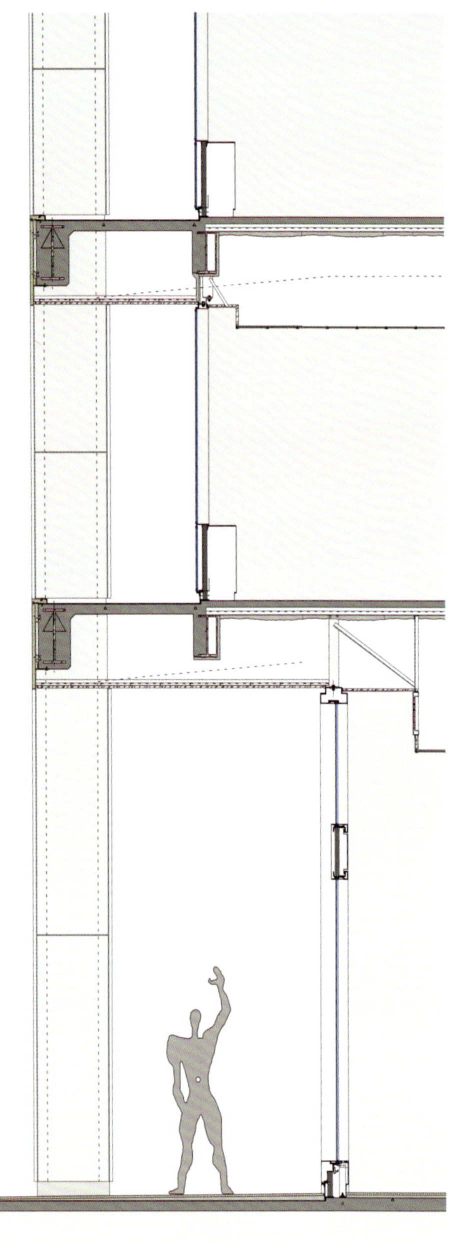

6'
2 m

SCALE 1/75

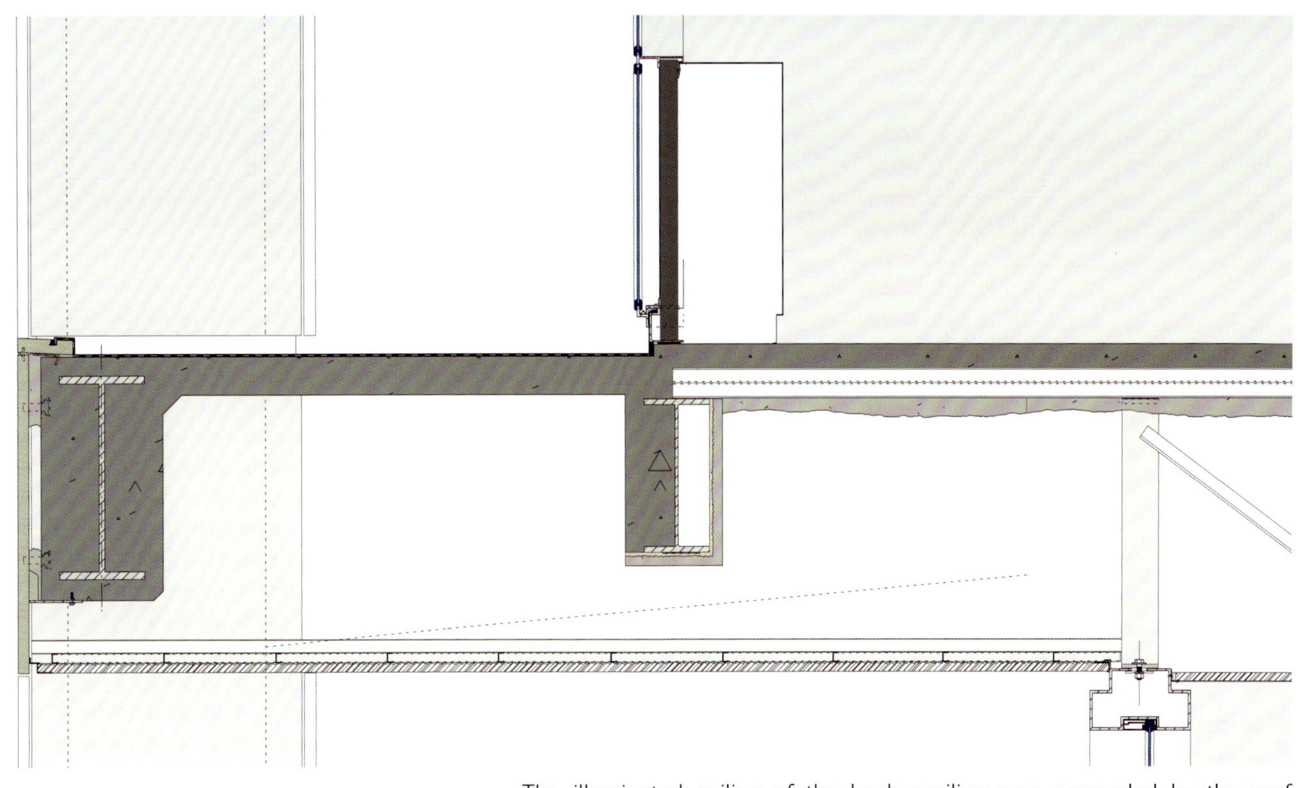

Detail showing structural elements configuring the external façade walkway.

Drawing by the author.

On the left:

Photo from Fannin Street and typical façade section.

Photo and drawing by the author.

The illuminated ceiling of the bank pavilion was suspended by the roof trusses. Its grid consisted of 4' 4 1/2" (1.33 cm) squares, within which 912 lighting fixtures were placed. A typical fixture consisted of a double pyramid of perforated aluminum and anodized gold, within which the light source was arranged to cast illumination both downward and on the ceiling itself. Air-conditioning equipment for the banking room could be located only above the ceiling. For maintenance, a telescoping hoist was installed in a two square opening near a corner of the pavilion. Catwalks were provided for equipment servicing.[43]

As previously described, in the office tower, the dark gray glazed windows were set back 5' (1.7 m) from the perimeter, forming an external walkway for cleaning and maintenance of the façades. In addition, this distance allowed the structure to function as a solar control element because of the way it was projected with respect to the windows. The steel beams and columns were clad with white Vermont marble cladding, and their contrasting colors with respect to the glazed enclosures made the building structure the most expressive formal element of the complex.

Chase Manhattan Bank, 1957-1961

New York, New York

On the left:

View of Chase Manhattan Bank from the west, from an upper floor of a building on Broadway.

The construction of the Chase Manhattan Bank took place between 1957 and 1961. It was, in many aspects, a complex and paradigmatic operation for the field of architecture and urban planning.

Although the bank already had its main facilities in buildings located on the site, and also in neighboring buildings, the decision to erect the skyscraper in southern Manhattan – a few meters from the New York Stock Exchange and the Federal Reserve, in the heart of the financial district – reflected the commitment of the directors and partners to the urban renewal of the area; the basic formal scheme adopted in the project fully confirms it.[44]

The urban strategy paid off, at least in the form of projects by Bunshaft and SOM. The pioneering Chase set the benchmark by inserting a public and accessible plaza with open connections to three different streets. To the northwest, it connects physically and visually to Broadway through the public pedestrian space that surrounds another Bunshaft-designed building, the Marine Midland Building (1961). Crossing the avenue, it follows the urban continuum through the blocks of buildings US Steel Plaza and One Liberty Plaza (1973), toward the site of the World Trade Center.

The Chase consists of a base, which is topped by the aforementioned civic plaza, and a 60-story rectangular plant building containing the bank's business offices and corporate space for lease. The base, excavated 90' (27 meters) underground, forms a sort of podium and contains a branch bank and cafeteria open to the public on its two upper internal levels, and garages, mechanical equipment and safes on the other levels. As a focal point for those entering the plaza from the steps that connect to the sidewalks on Nassau, Pine and William Streets, Bunshaft and his team proposed a large sculpture that was produced by the French artist Jean Dubuffet. *Group of Four Trees* was completed in 1972 and stands 43" (13 m) tall.

At 813' (247.8 meters) tall, the building was the sixth tallest skyscraper in the city and in the world when it was completed; its gross area is 2,239,530 square feet (approximately 208,059 square meters), costing USD 138 million at the time and being the largest banking structure built when it was inaugurated.[45]

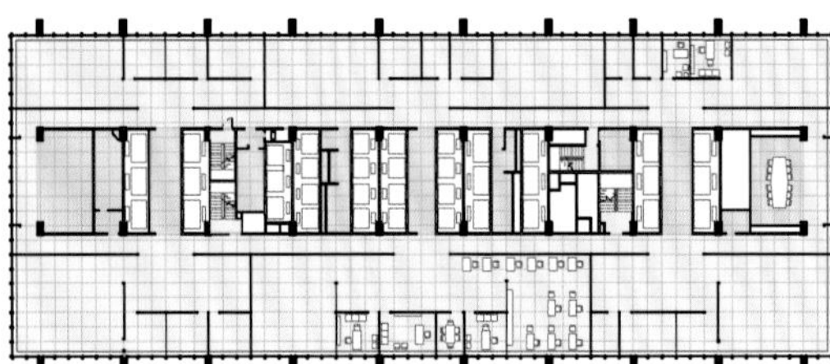

Typical Floor

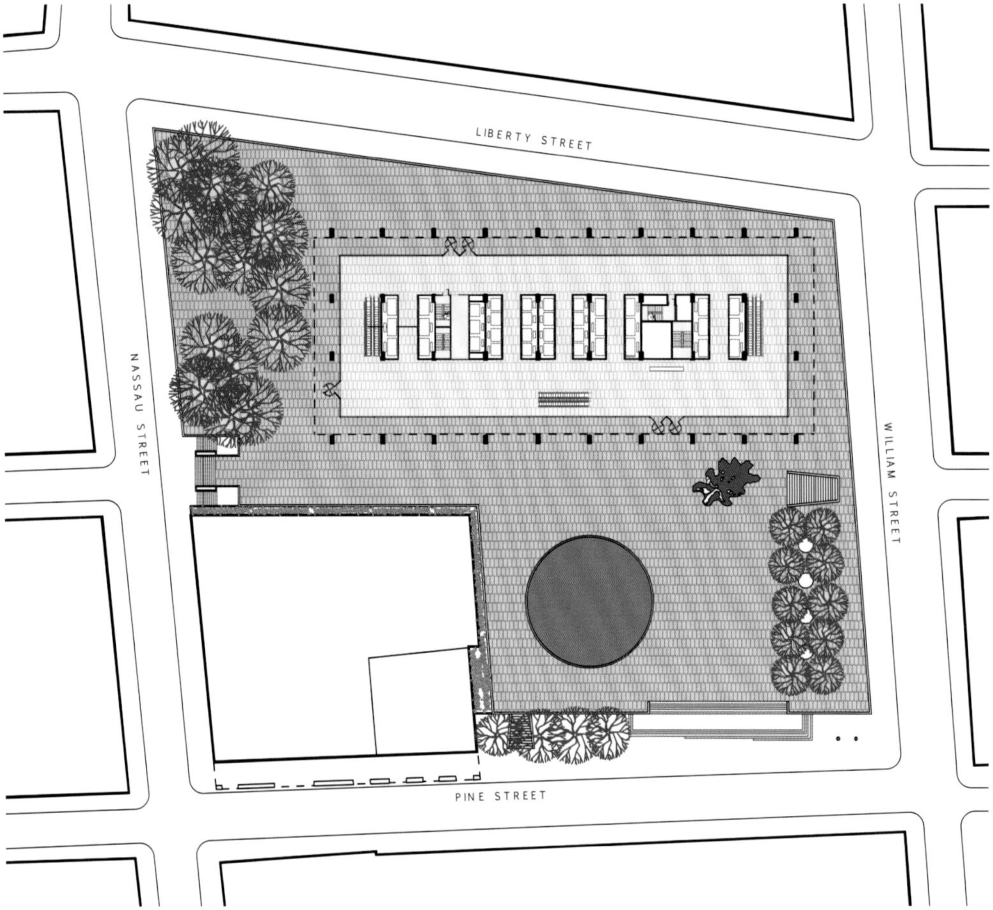

LIBERTY STREET
NASSAU STREET
WILLIAM STREET
PINE STREET

Ground Floor

6'
30 m

SCALE 1/1250

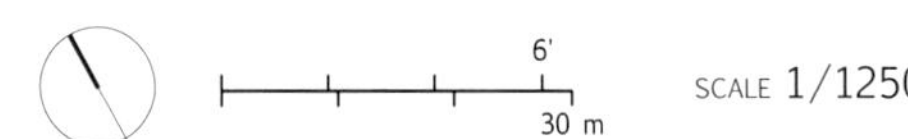

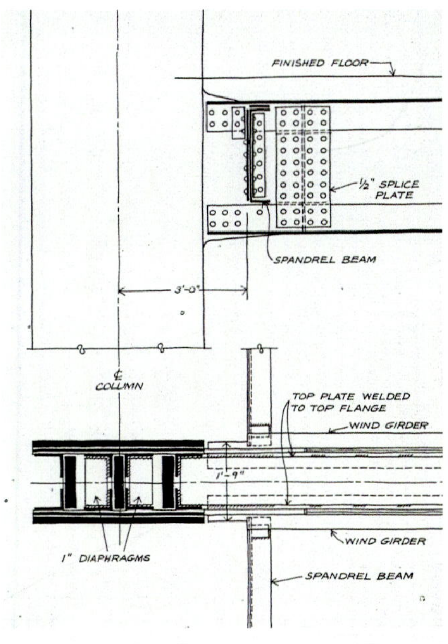

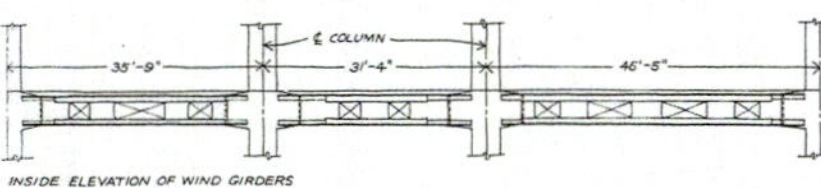

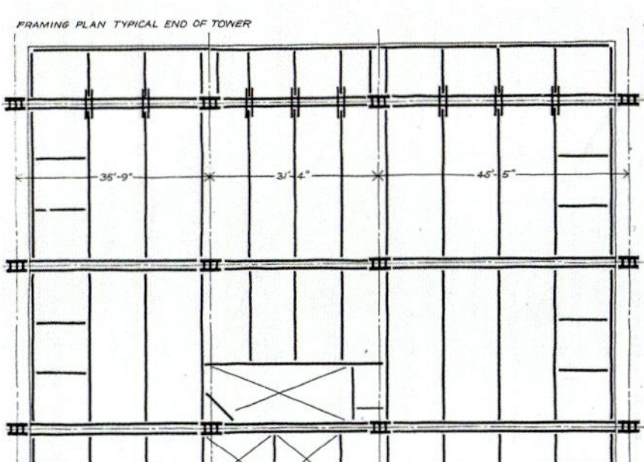

Structural details of the Chase Manhattan Bank. Connections between columns and beams and wind girders details.

On the right

View of the Chase from William Street, immediately in front of Federal Reserve.

Photo by author, 2010.

Innovative for the time of its construction, the design of the structure generated valuable attributes for the typical plans. On these floors, except for two columns placed near each of the two shorter façades, there are no structural elements in the space. The rows of columns are placed outside the glazed enclosures and within the circulation and service core, which allows a high level of flexibility for the occupation of the floor. The two large spaces between the larger façades and the central core are not the same width, one being 30' and the other 40' (9.14 and 12.19 meters, respectively).

From a real estate point of view, having two spaces for rent with different sizes (one for small and the other for medium and large offices) on the same floor can be advantageous when it comes to finding tenants.

Regarding the open floor plan, Bunshaft and his team developed mock-up studies simulating the two situations: one depicting spaces with columns and economical structural spans and a second with the solution of columns which were external to the building envelope. The result indicated that the first solution, described as conventional, had space for 6% fewer desks, but its

Pages 81 and 83 of *Architectural Record* magazine, November 1959. Advertising for the Bethlehem Steel Company structural elements using the Chase Manhattan as a showcase.

shorter span structure cost 5% less than the proposed scheme, with taller beams required for long spans.[46]

The chosen system, with higher beams and external columns, proved to be very efficient. According to reports, when the time came to occupy some of the spaces in the new building for the first time, new configurations arose that were not elucidated with the help of the mock-ups made to foresee alternatives for the placement of internal partitions, tables and equipment.

The interior design of the Chase was also carried out with extreme care, precision and resourcefulness. David Rockefeller, executive vice president and later president of the bank during the years when the building was conceived, designed and constructed, was a lover of modern art and architecture and earmarked USD 500,000 for art pieces and artifacts. Some of the most valuable were on the 17th floor, which housed the offices of top management, including that of “Mr. David” himself. That level had a private barbershop, meeting room with 60 chairs and a large table; and was directly connected by express elevators to the street level and the 60th floor, where the executive dining room was located.

Bunshaft had planned a spectacular sculpture for that floor, which would be placed at a specially chosen focal point in order to welcome bank executives and their guests as they left the elevator. But according to him, when the 60th floor structure was completed, he and the other team's architects realized that no sculpture was needed: the external view to the ornate

View of the Chase from Maiden Lane. Federal Reserve in the foreground.

Photo by author, 2010.

pyramidal tip of the 40 Wall Street Building (designed by architect H. Craig Severance, built in 1929 and considered a landmark of lower Manhattan) with the sunset backdrop of land and sea would more than recompence the absence of a statue.[47]

As part of this sophisticated interior design project, it is worth mentioning the design of all the furniture and accessories made especially for the Chase, as well as some of the technical details that allowed for its implementation and operation in workspaces.

The project proved to be an important testing ground for the manufacture of products related to architecture. Backed by the client, the SOM team set about defining all the elements down to the smallest details; specifying everything, from panel push buttons for elevators to faucets for sinks. And when a model of any of these could not be found on the market that would satisfactorily fit the project, exclusive models were designed for the occasion. The quality, quantity and diversity of products designed for the Chase eventually set new standards for high-end construction, and even influenced the American industry, which came to have a new benchmark for architectural components.

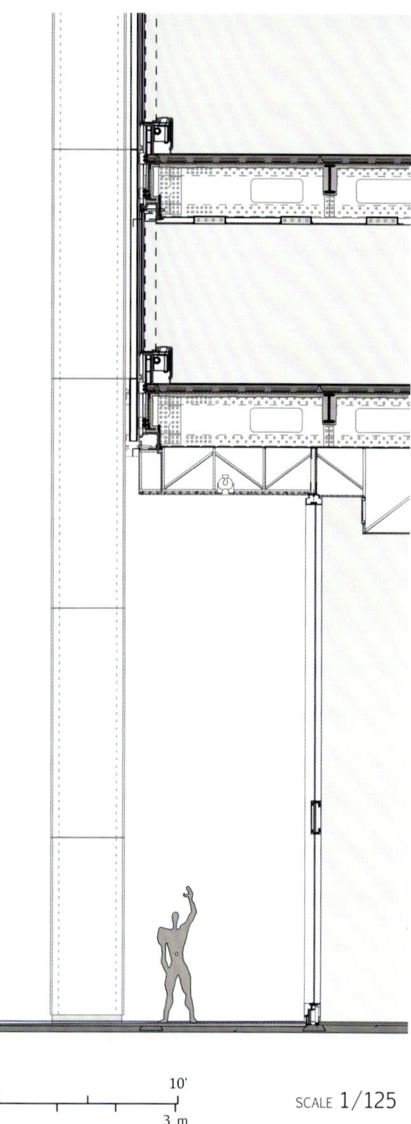

On the left:

View from the 60th floor's lobby where the executive dining room was located. The external view, which has the ornate pyramidal tip of the 40 Wall Street Building as focal point, can be seen as a spatial protagonist.

On the left:

Typical façade section.

Drawing by the author.

On the right:

Office of the president, David Rockefeller.

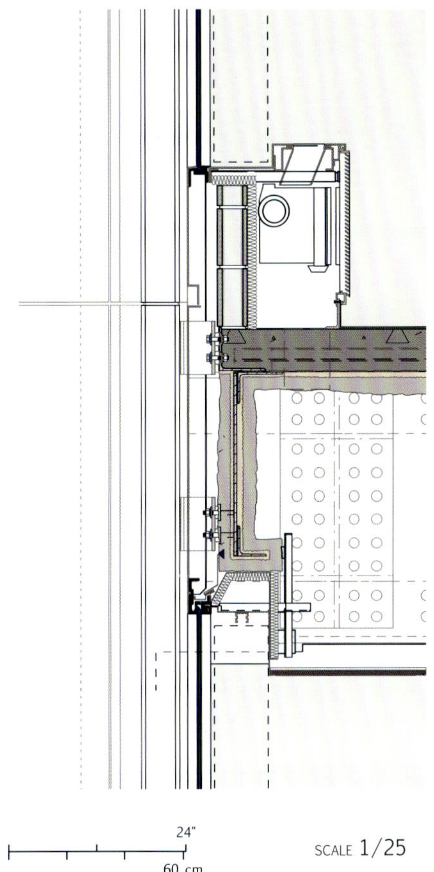

Detail showing the encounter of the floor slab of the typical floor with the curtain wall.

Drawing by the author.

External finishes of the building were also the subject of extensive studies by Bunshaft, his team and the clients. After initial discussions, a decision had to be made whether to build the curtain wall with anodized aluminum or stainless-steel profiles and sheets. In order to have a closer definition on aspects such as durability, maintenance, fine finishes, economy, etc., and also regarding the visual result that each of the two materials had, a prototype of a portion of the plant was built with all the components that would make up its façades. The dispute ended up being tied together in technical terms, with the architects and their clients deciding to build with aluminum due to preferences related to the appearance of the finish, costs and extended warranty time offered by the manufacturers.[48]

The cladding of the structure and also of the curtain walls were designed in order to accentuate certain visual attributes devised for the building. Confirming the argument that the complex blends into the dense area of Lower Manhattan, finishes and their glossy texture make the body of the building reflect the scarce light that filters down to the surrounding streets that form the "canyons of the Wall Street area" (a nickname given to the appearance of a mountain range that southern Manhattan acquired with the construction of so many tall buildings). This effect even helps to transform the plaza of the complex into a peaceful space in the midst of the dark neighboring skyscrapers. In addition to enhancing the immediate surroundings, the tower's cladding stands out visually amid so many tall buildings when viewed from neighboring boroughs such as Brooklyn or Staten Island.

Reynolds Metals Company, 1953-1955
Richmond, Virginia

On the left:

Detail of the south-west corner of the building, facing the bucolic area at the South.

The Reynolds Metals Company headquarters was built between 1953 and 1955 in Richmond, Virginia. One of the main goals of the project was to showcase the company and its ability to develop and produce aluminum building components for the booming US industry. At the time of its inauguration, the building had a capacity for 1,000 workers and the work cost $11.5 million, million at the time of construction. In addition to the investment in its own headquarters, Reynolds Metals already had a history of commitment to high quality, demonstrated through sponsorship of a series of books and annual awards related to good architecture.[49]

After the construction of the Connecticut General Insurance Company, Bunshaft and his team were again faced with an assignment for a large corporation that decided to locate in a peripheral area on the outskirts of a major urban center. In this case, a site with a rural character in the suburbs, five miles from downtown Richmond. The complex basically consists of a two-story, square-based prism suspended by pilotis, which sits on a podium-

On the right:

Site plan of the Reynolds Metals Company, Richmond, Virginia.

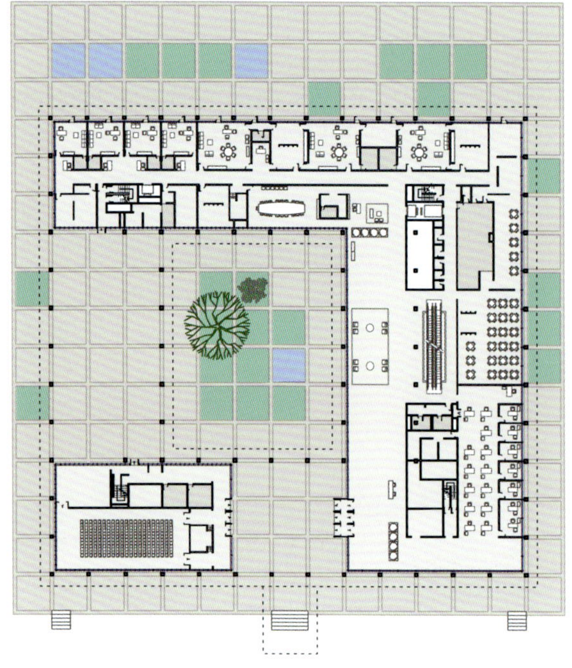

Ground Floor

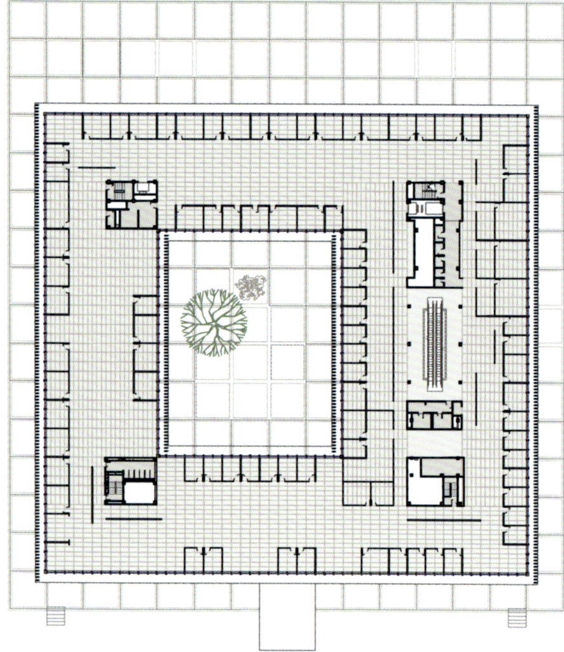

Typical Floor

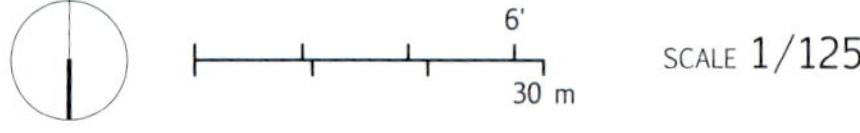

SCALE 1/1250

like base. The base accommodates the building to the site itself, which has slopes of almost one level high. The prism has a perforation in its center that projects onto a first-floor garden. The central courtyard, adorned with a fountain with five additional fountains with a background consisting of holly trees and a 12-meter-high southern magnolia tree, is a fundamental formal element, arranging interiors and bio-climatically qualifying the building.

The designed environment completes the composition, accentuating its classical formal attributes even more. In front of the north façade, where the main access is located, there is a 250-foot-long linear water mirror, flanked by two roads framed by rows of oak willows. These paths are used for the passage of cars and each gives access to a large parking area.

As was common in his projects, Bunshaft did not hold back on inducing visual cues to anyone moving through the complex by establishing points of interest. From the entrance through the main access deck, one immediately discovers the courtyard with its dominant magnolia tree. From there, different perspectives open up, depending on the direction taken.

The article "Reynolds Wraps Iself a Package in Aluminum", published in September 1958 in *Architectural Forum* magazine, tells the story:

> *To the left, a colonnade beneath the upper office floors opens up an eastward view and makes the side of the building toward the main road from Richmond more interesting to the passing motorist. [...] Turning to the right from the entrance portico, the visitor passes through a glass and aluminum entrance vestibule into the main reception lounge, which overlooks the court and colonnade view (photo right). Generously proportioned and sparsely furnished under a 14-foot ceiling, this lounge has ample space opposite the entrance for displays of Reynolds products and processes.*[50]

On the first floor, in addition to the large lobby, from which it is possible to ascend the typical floors or descend to the lower level via escalators, and the executive offices and meeting room, there is an auditorium and a space for the company's staff. To the south, the executive offices open onto an exclusive terrace that overlooks an extensive forest of native trees.

The main room on the lower level is a dining and living area for employees. It is located on the south façade and, like the executive offices, has an adjoining terrace that opens onto the forest. Besides that, the lower level houses a medical room, sourcing and supply facilities, boiler space, two six-ton air conditioning compressors and an automatic control center for the building's mechanical networks.

The materials and finishes that form the base give it a solid appearance. The first ground floor top surface, which forms a "lid," is made of red colonial brick panels, very common in the state of Virginia. Between these panels are strips of 2' wide precast concrete veneer aligned to the first-floor columns. The external walls are also clad with precast concrete veneer.

In contrast to this choice of materials, the façades of the first and typical floors are made of lightweight materials, almost all of which being covered with glass or aluminum. According to Reynolds, approximately 1.25 million pounds of aluminum produced by the company were used in the project, which was applied for façade elements, partitions, ceilings, push buttons, door handles, etc.

The typical floors basically house collective work areas. As previously reported, Bunshaft and his team sought to free the internal spaces of obstacles through the use of large structural spans. Thus, they were able to

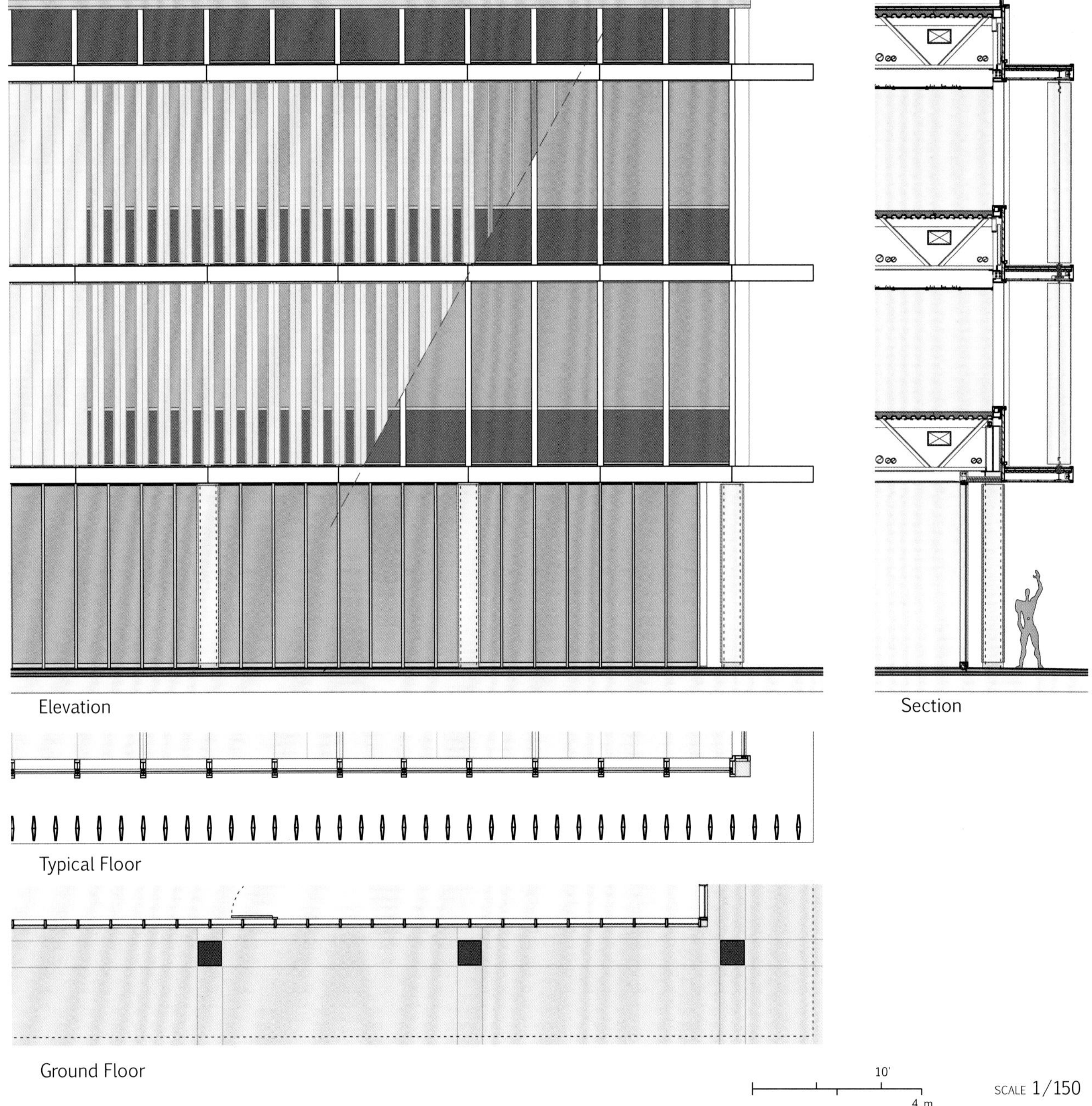
Elevation
Section
Typical Floor
Ground Floor
10'
4 m
SCALE 1/150

View of the north-east corner of Reynolds Metals Company. The presence of a system of louvers in the east façade can be noted.

construct clear spans 62' (18.9 m) long by means of trusses placed in two directions, generating 47,000 sq. ft. of surface uninterrupted by columns. The trusses reach 1.17 m (3' 10") in height and are supported by structural mullions placed at the internal boundaries, that is, next to the glazed panels that make up the façades. The steel mullions are spaced 5' 2" apart and clad with aluminum, an economical but non-fireproof solution, which was possible because the plot is a quasi-rural site with much less stringent regulations than those of large American cities. Spans smaller than 62' are generated in areas where vertical circulation and service cores pass through. The latter also function as vertical structures.

The ceilings, interior partitions and installations are arranged under the same modulation. Aluminum suspended ceilings integrate air conditioning diffusers into their design and help to shade the fluorescent light over the workstations. The honeycomb pattern of each panel consists of 3/8-inch-diameter hexagonal cells that block the unsightly view of fluorescent lights, ductwork and steel trusses to anyone looking up at an angle of 45 degrees or less. They are mounted on a modulated 2' 7" grid of "tee" profiles, which serve as a frame for partitions, offering great flexibility. Partitions are composed of aluminum mullions and painted baked enamel insulated sandwich panels.[51]

The façades have a sophisticated solar protection system consisting mainly of vertical louvers and eaves attached to the outer edges of the slabs. The latter serve as a walkway for inspection, maintenance and window washing.

> *In one of the largest installations of its kind, the 880 louvers, each 14 feet high and 22 inches wide, are power-operated on a predetermined program by a master clock which anticipates the daily movements of the sun, gradually opening the east-facing louvers and shutting the west-facing ones as the day progresses. Seasonal differences in sun position are automatically taken care of. An overcast of more than 3 minutes causes photoelectric cells to open the louvers to their widest setting, admitting maximum light; with the return of full sunlight the louvers resume their proper position in the program. By stopping sun heat outside the building, the louvers reduce air-conditioning needs sufficiently to offset their $270,000 cost over a period of years*[52].

The north facade, where the main access is located.

There is a 250-foot-long linear water mirror, flanked by two roads framed by rows of oak willows. The paths serve as passage for vehicles and each gives access to a large parking area.

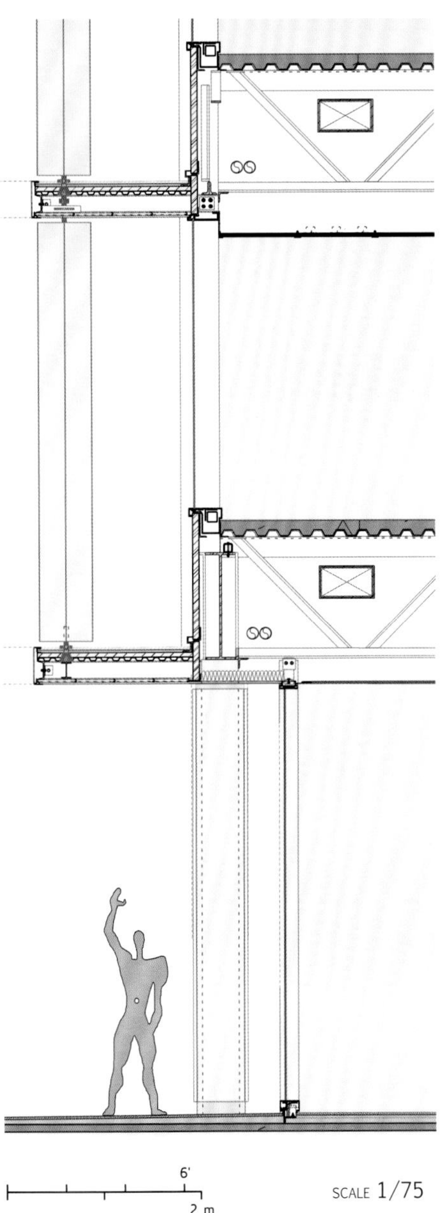

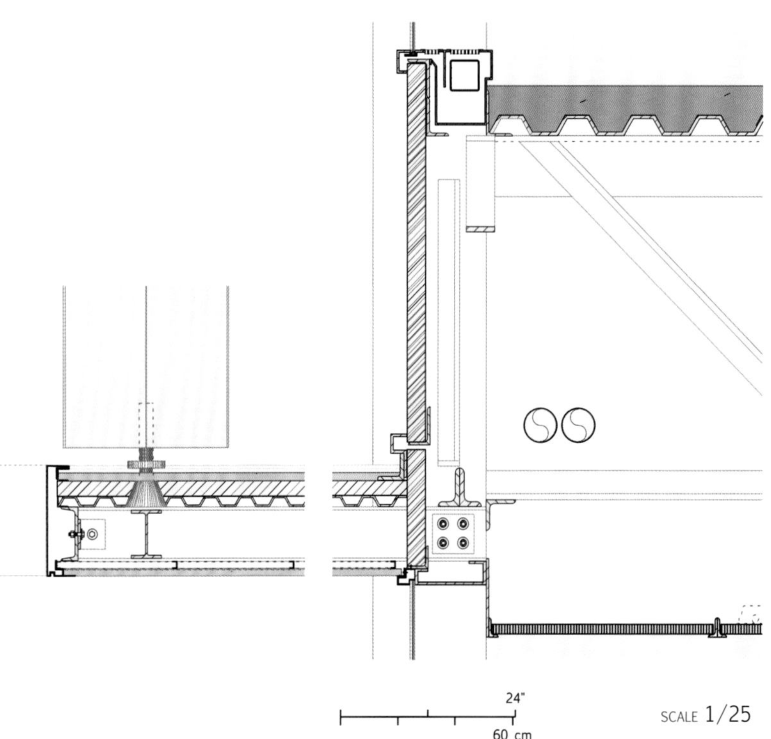

Typical façade section and floor slab and catwalk detail.

Photo and drawing by the author.

Beinecke Rare Books and Manuscripts Library, 1961-1963

New Haven, Connecticut

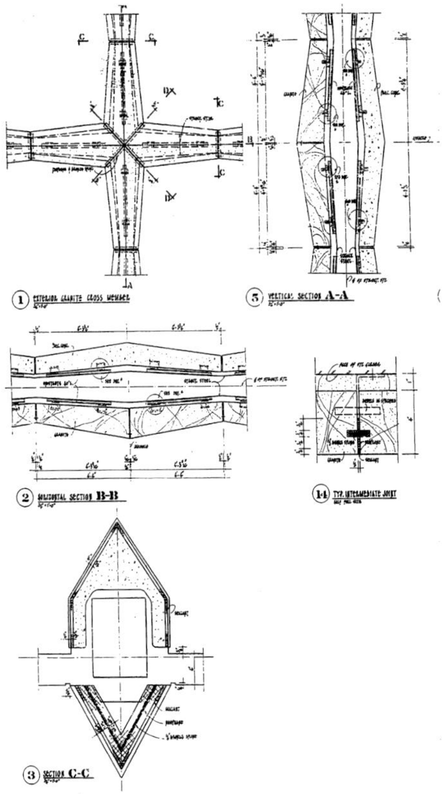

The Beinecke Library, inaugurated in 1963 at Yale University in New Haven, Connecticut, houses one of the most famous American collections of rare books and manuscripts, being one of the most sophisticated buildings on the campus where it is located. The complex consists of a plaza on which is placed a main volume, a prism of rectangular base elevated from the ground by four pyramidal columns set at its corners.

The 200' x 350' (60.96 x 106.68 m) access plaza is configured as a large platform, a base that delineates through the floor, walls and benches, covered with the same type of granite cladding as the external limits of the complex. Its prime formal attribute is to act as a backdrop for the main volume to look like a hidden jewel in the midst of the environment formed mostly by neo-Gothic buildings.

The interior of the prism is a monumental space with an atmosphere that induces contemplation. And in this case, the objects of contemplation are (in addition to the building itself) exquisitely displayed books and manuscripts of great historical value. Access to the complex is through a glazed hall on the first floor where there is a reception area from which one goes up to the exhibition level or down to the lower levels. In contrast to the neighboring buildings of eclectic and neo-Gothic style, the entrance hall transparency makes it attractive to the public, establishing visual integration between indoors and outdoors.

At the center of the exhibition hall is a tower of glass with shelves. It is a stainless-steel structure containing 180,000 volumes, out of the total of 820,000 stored in the library. The shelves are accessed by perimeter circulations as walkways from which the entire exhibition space can be appreciated. The whole structure measures 35' x 60' (10.67 x 18.29 m), and is 50' (15.24 m) above ground level; it wraps around the building's reinforced concrete circulation and service core. The latter measures 18' x 19' (5.48 x 5.79m) in plan. The enclosing curtain wall is made of polished translucent glass panels supported by extruded bronze profiles and neoprene gaskets, which in turn wrap around the tower's structural steel mullions. Inside, the relative humidity and temperature are controlled and measured at a constant 50% and 70ºF (21.1 ºC), respectively.

Detail of the steel crosses that compose the Vierendeel trusses of Beinecke Library building. Drawing from the executive project.

On the left:

The south façade of Beinecke Library.

Photo by author, 2010.

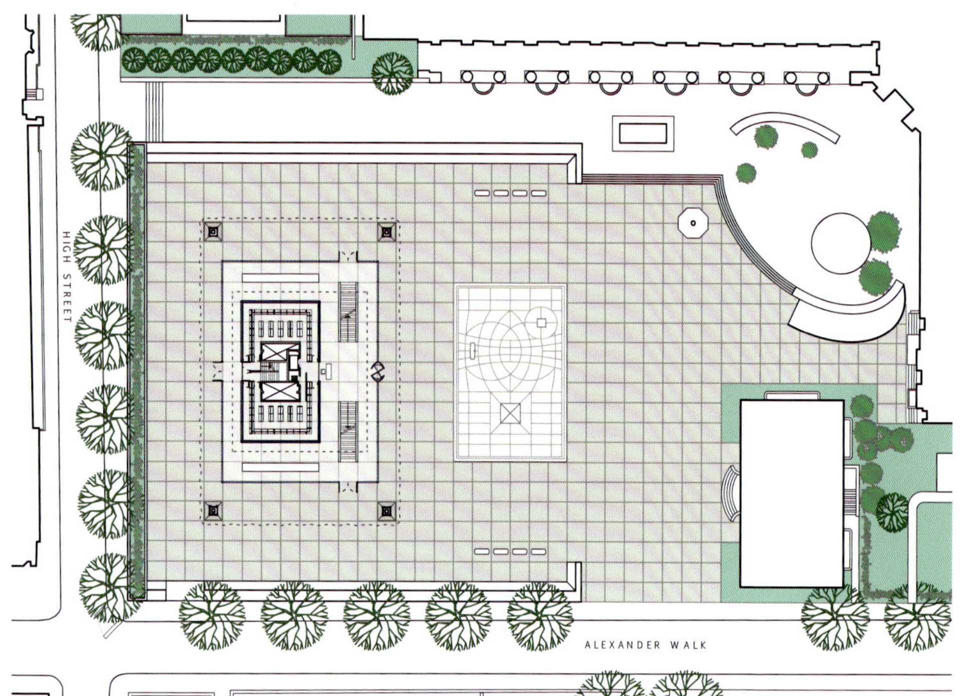

Ground Floor

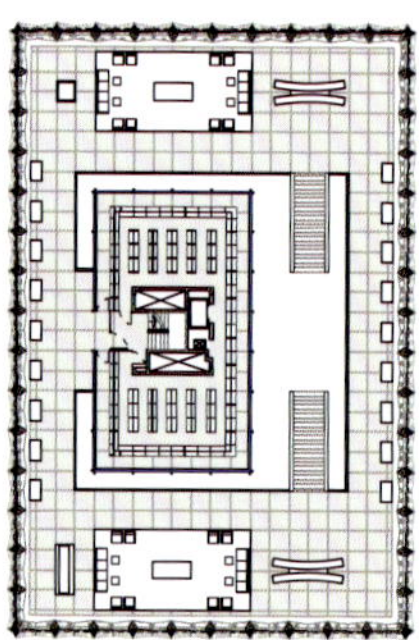

First Floor

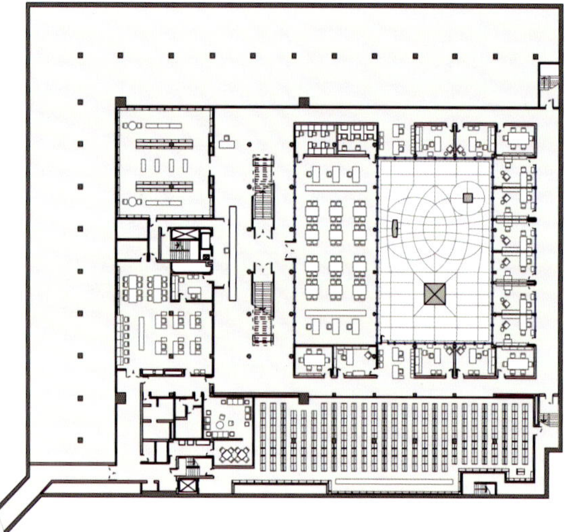

Basement

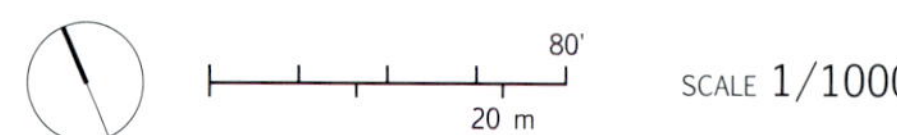

On the right:

The interior of the library, a monumental space with an atmosphere that induces contemplation.

Photo by author, 2010.

Elevation

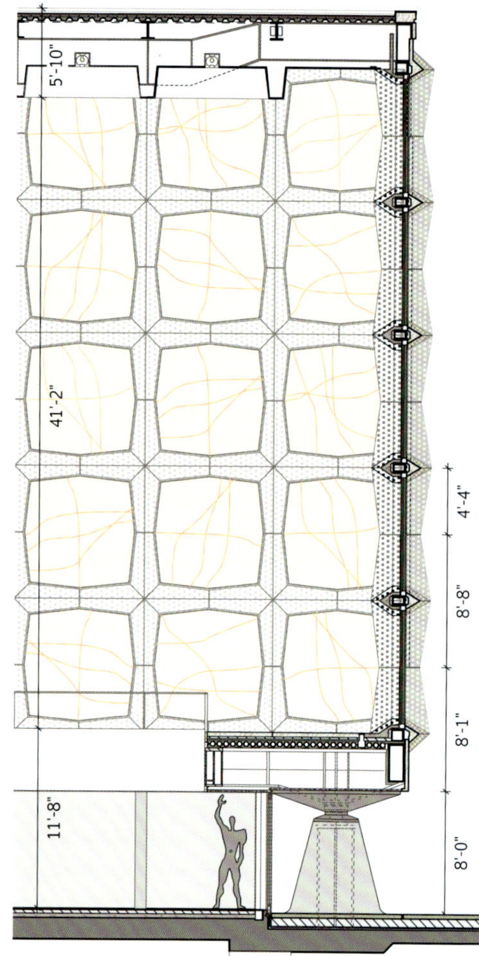

Section

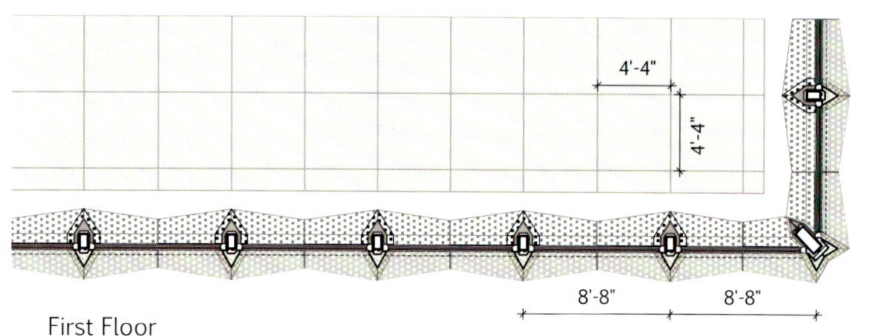

First Floor

SCALE 1/125

On both sides of the room are lounges with sofas and coffee tables. Next to the façades and composing the layout with these pieces of furniture, there are individual showcases.

All other library functions are carried out on two basement levels which are under the floor of the plaza. Researchers and scholars wishing to use the rare documents go directly to the first basement level – one floor below ground – where, after passing an identity check, they are allowed entry to the guarded reading room. This level also contains administrative facilities, curators' offices, which surround three sides of a sunken courtyard and a light well, staff function spaces, card files, additional stacking areas, toilets, etc. From the southwest corner of the floor, one can pass through a tunnel to the Sterling Memorial Library. The second basement floor, two levels below the plaza, is dedicated to book storage and to house mechanical equipment.

The sunken patio aforementioned measures 50' x 77' (15.42 x 23.47 m). Its large dimensions allow it to be appreciated from the plaza. In addition to adding spatial quality to underground areas, it was intended as an additional element in the formal composition of the whole library. Bunshaft and his team hired Isamu Noguchi to collaborate and made a proposal for him to turn it into a horizontal plane in which a piece of art should fit the entire area. Noguchi composed it with three elements in white marble: a pyramid (earth), a circle (sun), and a cube (chance) on a floor as a background formed by cladding of the same material.[53]

Detail of the south façade. In the foreground, the sunken patio with Isamu Noguchi's composition. *The Cube (Chance)* stands out.

Photo by author, 2010.

Structure

The exhibition space features an ingenious structural system. The façades are composed of large Vierendeel beams that transfer their loads to the four large 8'-high (2.5 m) ground-floor columns. All the beams are 50' (15.25 m) high. Those comprising the north and south façades are 88' (26.83 m) long, and those corresponding to the east and west façades are 131' (40.9 m) long.

The columns are made of steel and covered with large granite slabs, which have the function of giving the columns mass and a pyramidal shape. Below the columns, reinforced concrete piles penetrate approximately 50' (15.25 m) to meet the bedrock of the site.

Early in the project process, Bunshaft believed that the structure forming the façades should be built with precast concrete units, using the concept adopted for the John Hancock Company building in New Orleans. Discussions with engineer Paul Weidlinger eventually defined that the large Vierendeel trusses would be formed from the union of steel modules in cross format.

The crosses were shaped with their vertical and horizontal members in pyramidal format, tapering their tubular sections from the central crossing point to the tips. The upper and lower chords of the trusses are prismatic, that is, they have a continuous rectangular cross-section. The crosses measure 8' 8" high by 8' 8" (2.64 m) wide. The size was determined by the basic module of the building and the surrounding plaza, which in turn was established by the 4' 4" (1.32 m) spacing of the rows of book storage shelves.

After extensive design and calculation work, Weidlinger determined that a fully welded grid system should be adopted to form the Vierendeel beams, as it allowed a great deal of freedom in the selection of the structural components necessary to economically meet the architectural requirements.

The assembly, in turn, could contribute to the reduction of in-situ welding. It was proposed to assemble the Vierendeel beam in large sections: (1) corner unit with a row of four or five cross modules; (2) top and bottom end beams with first row of vertical members; (3) corner unit for top and bottom end beams with first row of vertical members.[54]

Some building fire regulations required the façade beams to be covered on both sides. Precast concrete cladding finished with a fine granite aggregate was specified for the interior surfaces; and Woodbury White granite – the same material that was used to pave the 70,000-square-foot (6,500 m2) plaza, as well as the enclosing walls that surround it – was specified for the exterior surfaces. Despite its name, the granite has a gray hue and was chosen to contrast with the panels filling the openings between the crosses, which should have had shades of bronze to white. Specimens of this stone, obtained from a quarry in northern Vermont from which it had not been extracted for many years at the time, were found to be extremely durable and to meet well the aesthetic requirements of color and texture established by the architects. The quarry was reopened for the sole purpose of providing the material needed for the work.[55] Before it was decided to cover the exterior with granite, Bunshaft had proposed to cover it with the same precast concrete cladding used on the interior.

The interior of the prism, the main space of the library. The central glass tower houses shelves of rare books and works of art.

Photo by author, 2010.

A lengthy investigation of about two years was carried out into the most important material for the library, the panels that fill the hollows in the façade trusses. Bunshaft and his team searched for marble quarries abroad, sent samples to the US and made full-size models, but none of the foreign alternatives proved to be suitable.[56] Finally, the Montclair-Danby marble was also discovered with the Vermont supplier, which, according to Bunshaft's testimony, was a last, desperate thing.[57]

The marble chosen complies with Bunshaft's initial wishes for white and bronze. The octagonal panels are 1-1/4" (3.175 cm) thick, translucent and faintly filter the light, protecting the valuable books from the sun's ultraviolet rays. From the outside, the marble gives the building a solemn character, helps to highlight the crosses of the structure and at the same time accentuates the visual purity of the built prism. From the inside, the natural shades of the material combined with its partial transparency intensify the solemn and welcoming atmosphere.

At Yale, Bunshaft once again refutes those who placed him, together with modern American architecture, within the category of monotonous, repetitive and merely functionalist buildings, which were supposedly represented almost exclusively by steel skyscrapers and their curtain walls. In the Beinecke Library, architectural form brings together recognition of the existing environment, the most precise technical and engineering skills, spatial considerations of monumental character, and a precise response to a varied programmatic problem.

Exploded axonometric of the complex, showing in black the huge viereendel trussers that form the main structure of the library prism.

Drawing by author, 2010.

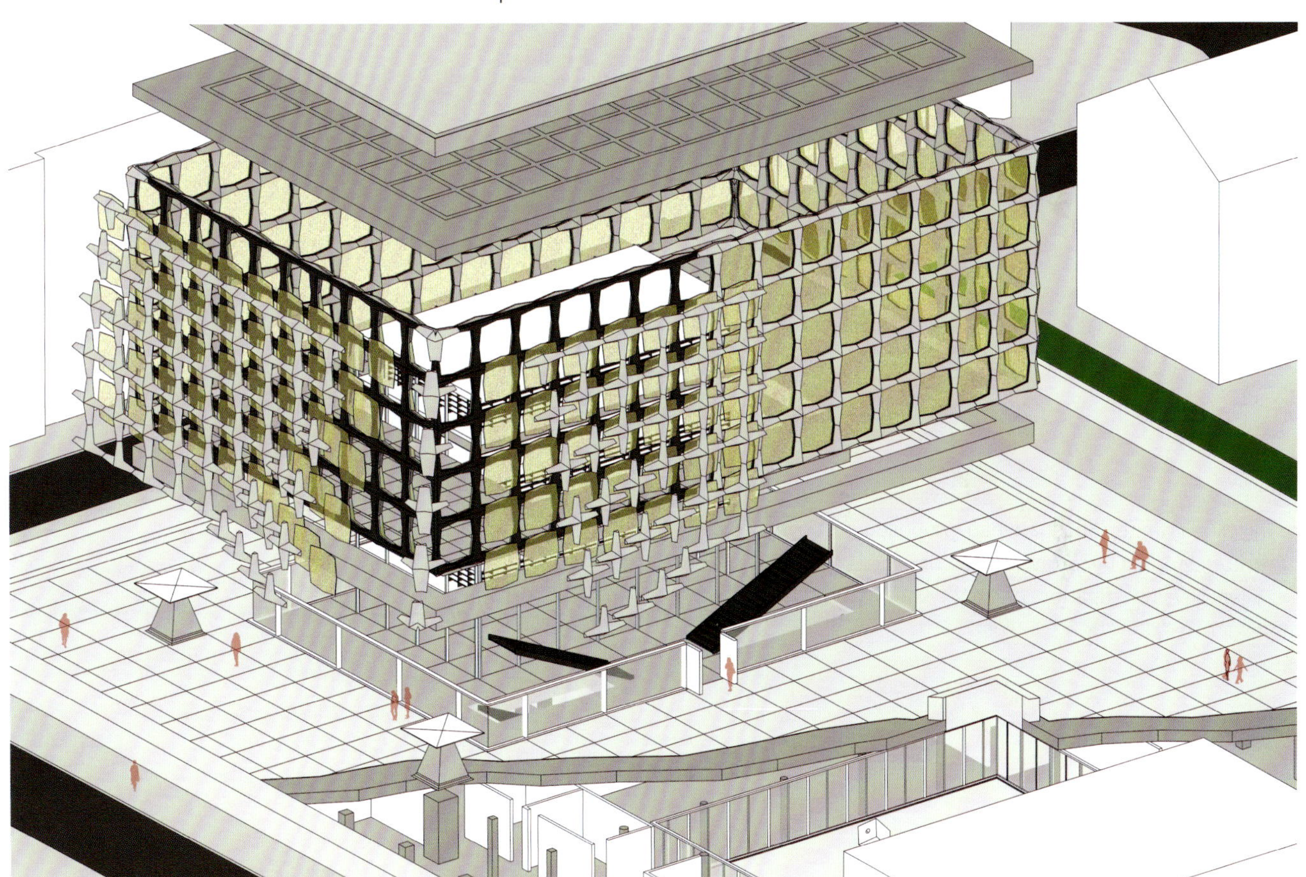

SCALE 1/75

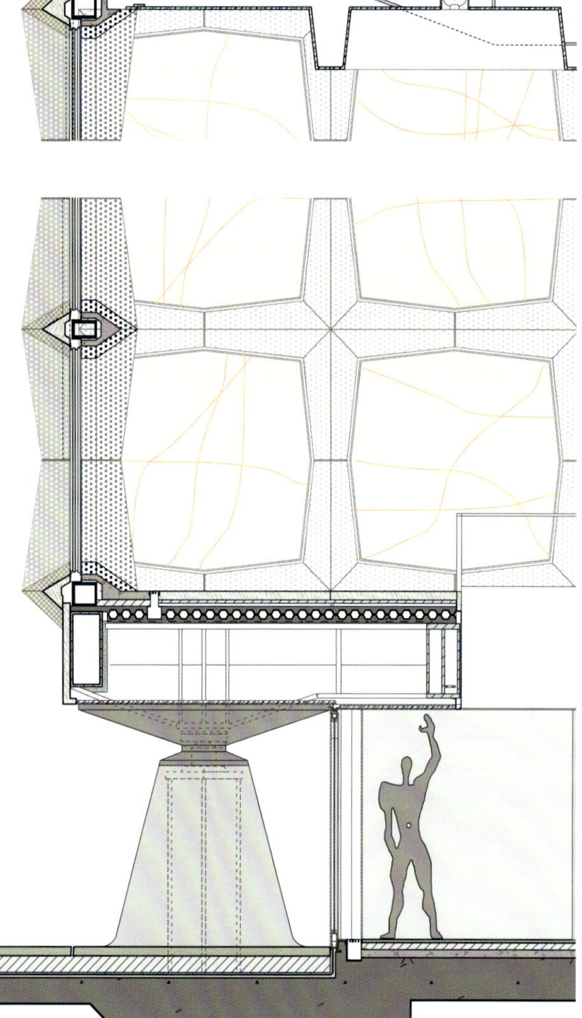

Section

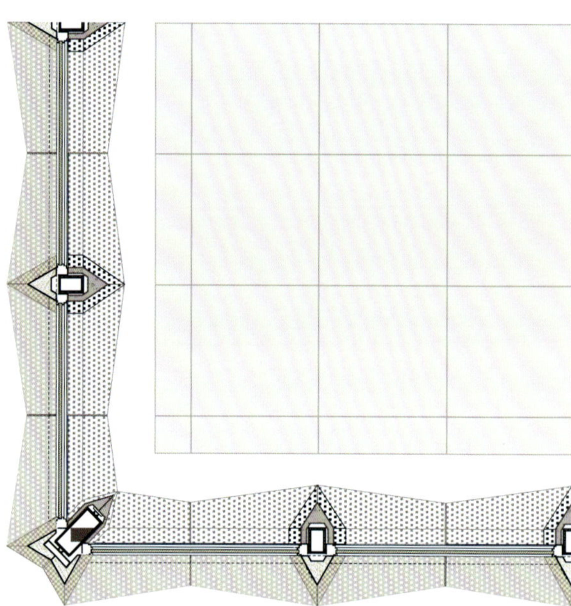

First Floor

On the right:

The Beinecke Library with Lillian Goldman Law Library in the background.

Photo by author, 2010.

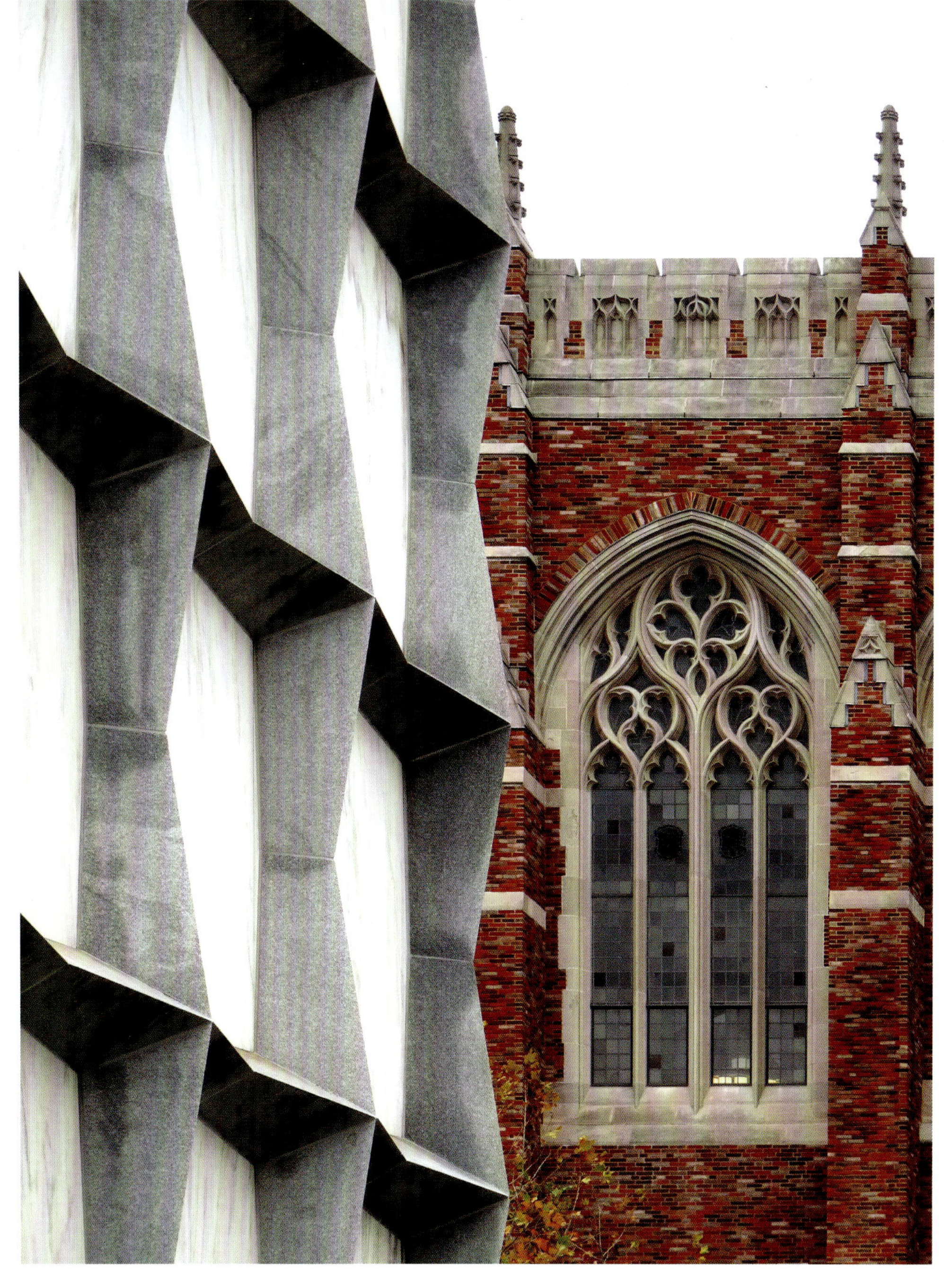

Made of Concrete

Lambert Bank, 1956-1965

Brussels, Begium

Framing diagrams *(below) compare a typical structural system with that proposed for the Brussels bank. In the former the exterior columns are husky and widely spaced, and the curtain wall is "stretched" directly over them. In the Banque Lambert the exterior columns will be smaller and closely spaced and the curtain wall will stand behind them.*

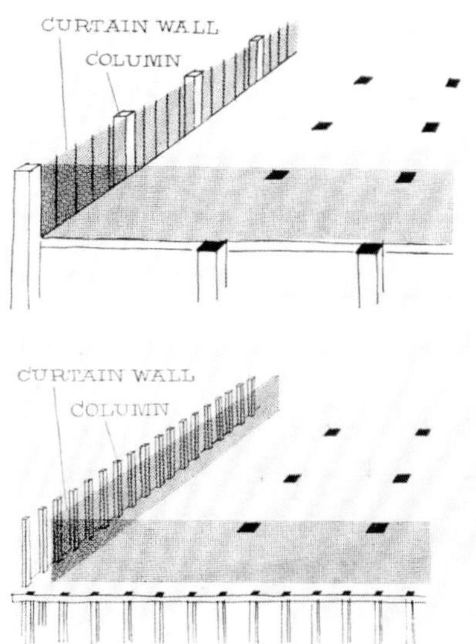

Diagram of the perimeter structure used in the Lambert Bank, Brussels. Published in *Architectural Forum* magazine, May of 1959.

On the left:

Photo of the model for the Lambert Bank (first version, 1959).

In mid-1956, Gordon Bunshaft was contacted as part of a search for architects to carry out a project in Brussels. The building for the Lambert Bank began to be designed by Bunshaft and his team in 1957, and in 1959 a fairly advanced version of the project was published in some media, but it did not fully correspond to what would be completed in 1965. The finished building consisted of a body of eight stories supported by columns on the ground floor.[58]

The ground floor extends over a platform that houses an underground parking garage and raises the entire complex above the level of the surrounding sidewalks, bridging the slope between the northwest and southeast portions of the site. The typical floor plan measures essentially 245' 5" x 103' (78.40 x 31.4 m). Matching with European practice, a basic module of 4'7" (1.4 m) was stipulated for the project. The module governs the internal spaces, coordinates partitions and roof installations, and coincides with the structural grid.

The complex included a bank office open to the public on the ground floor, administrative offices on typical floors and a huge apartment for Baroness Lambert and her family, occupying the seventh floor and the penthouse.[59]

The basic premise of having free floors to be able to occupy them as much as possible with work spaces was of course implicit and continued to serve as a formal stimulant. The configuration adopted placed the structure in the center and at the limits of the typical floors, and on the ground floor on evenly distributed columns. The central supports are concentrated in the service and vertical circulation core and also in four additional columns. The necessity for these columns to be placed outside the core is due to the rectangular geometry of the building, in which the two large façades are almost two and a half times longer than the smaller ones.

It is important to mention that Bunshaft's proposal to use an exposed precast concrete structure instead of a steel curtain-wall structure was justified, according to the architect himself, by the environment in which the complex would be inserted. The *Architectural Forum* article entitled "SOM

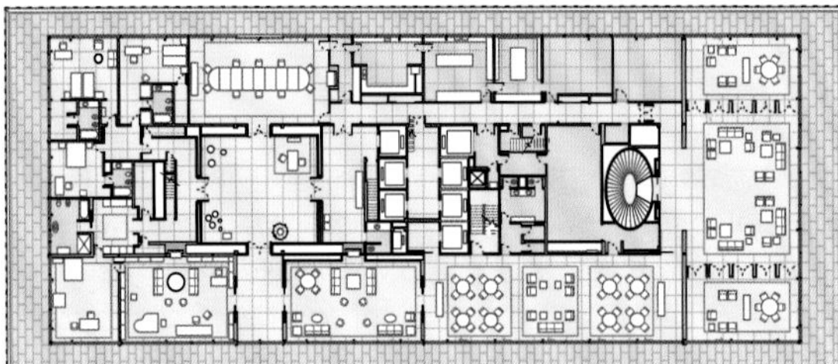

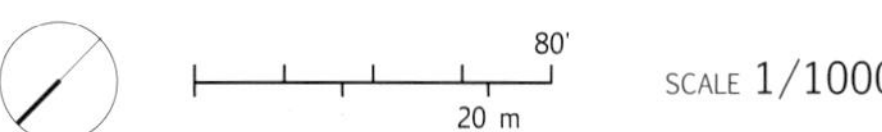

SCALE 1/1000

Penthouse

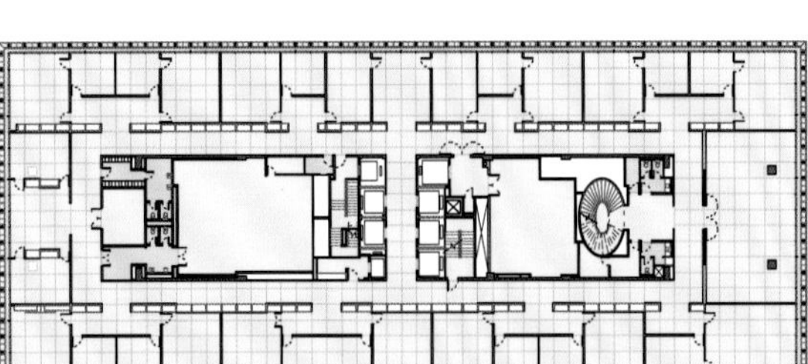

7th Floor

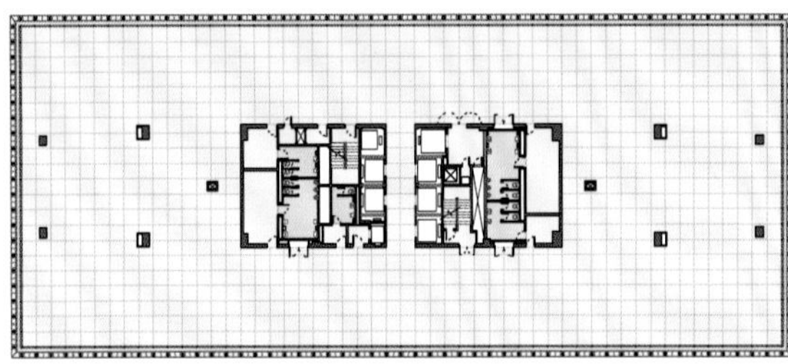

Typical Floor

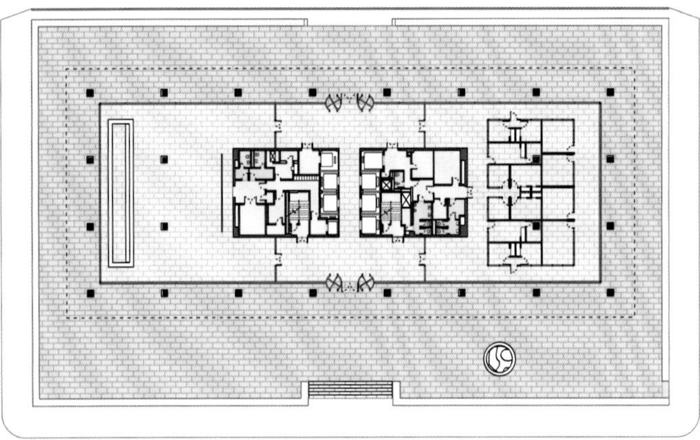

Ground Floor

Puts the Bones Outside the Skin", dated May 1959, presented some of the basic project guidelines taken by the architect:

> *Now SOM's Gordon Bunshaft (with Project Manager Frederick C. Gans, and Design Assistant Whitson M. Overcash Jr.) is about to build his first, big commercial office structure in Europe; and in doing so, he has decided to turn away from the sleek skin he helped make famous and, instead, to develop a rugged, three-dimensional façade of structural, precast concrete elements reminiscent of the limestone facings of older European buildings. [...] He feels strongly that some degree of continuity in urban design is mandatory where the existing townscape contains handsome buildings of the past, as it does in Brussels. Moreover, he believes that concrete is essentially 'the' material for Europe. [...] It was felt that the texture of a glass-and-metal curtain wall would be out of place in such a setting; instead, the architects developed a structural system of precast, 'Schock-beton' units that are expressed on all façades and echo the scale of neighboring buildings.*[60]

The building is located just in front of one of the entrances to the Royal Palace complex in Brussels, across the Marnix Avenue.

Although the structural system was not entirely new, the supporting structure was undoubtedly the most important and differentiating aspect of the building when it was completed. For the first time at SOM, a building was conceived with primary structural components of precast concrete. The façades of the Lambert Bank consist of a structural grid formed by precast concrete cross-shaped elements that go from half the height of one floor to half the height of the next. In other words, their height dimension is equivalent to one distance from floor to floor.

The building opened up a new range of formal possibilities, not only within the company, but also in the field of American architecture during those years. The solutions generated by the collaborative work with engineer Paul Weidlinger and his structural design office were of fundamental importance for the successful conception of the structure and, within the same cooperation, other solutions were derived for various SOM commissions.

Structure

The perimeter frame of the building body is composed of solid concrete cruciform units that combine the functions of edge beam and column. The cruciform units have a height equal to that of one story, i.e., 10' 10" (3.30 m), and measure 4' 7" (1.40 m) in length from end to end of their horizontal members. These members were designed with a volumetric subtraction in the form of a gutter on their internal faces of the horizontal members, leaving

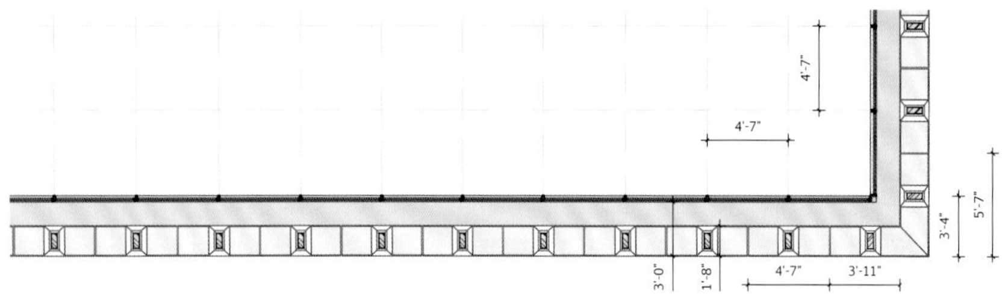

Typical Floor

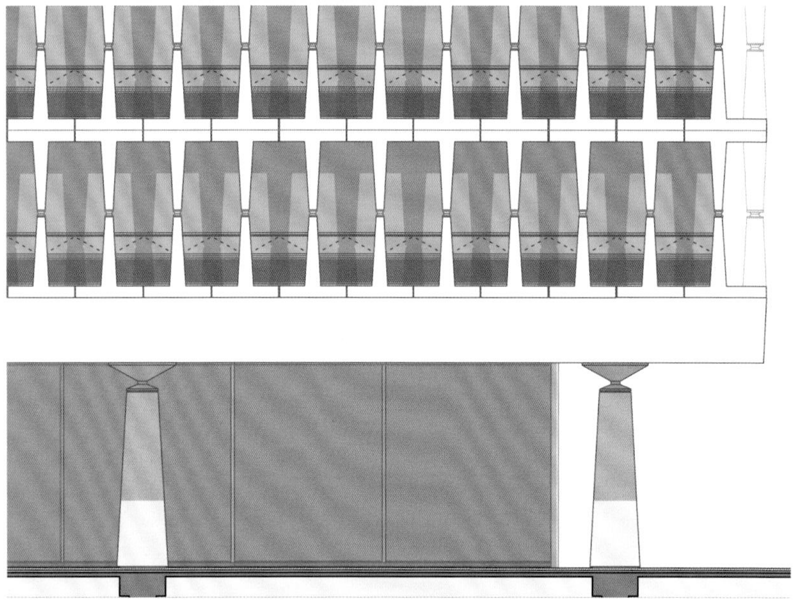

Elevation

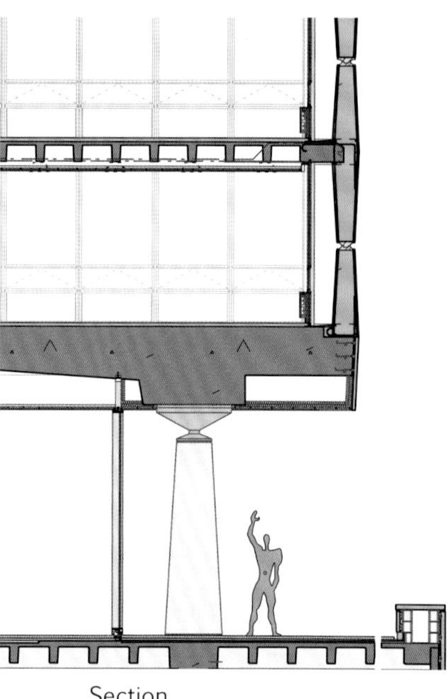

Section

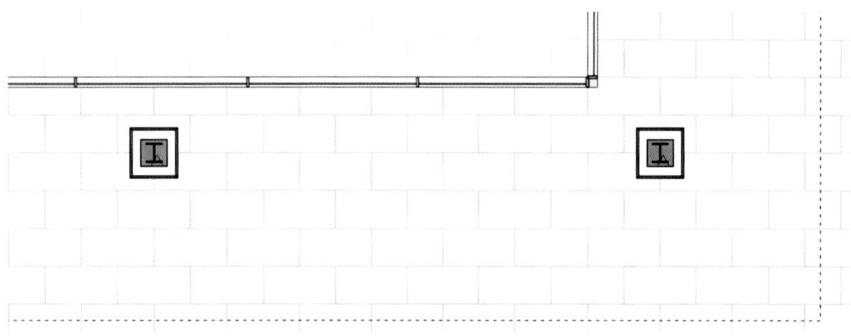

Ground Floor

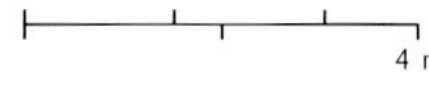

SCALE 1/150

On the right:

The repetition of precast concrete crosses creates a uniform grid for the façade of the Lambert Bank.

Photo by author, 2010.

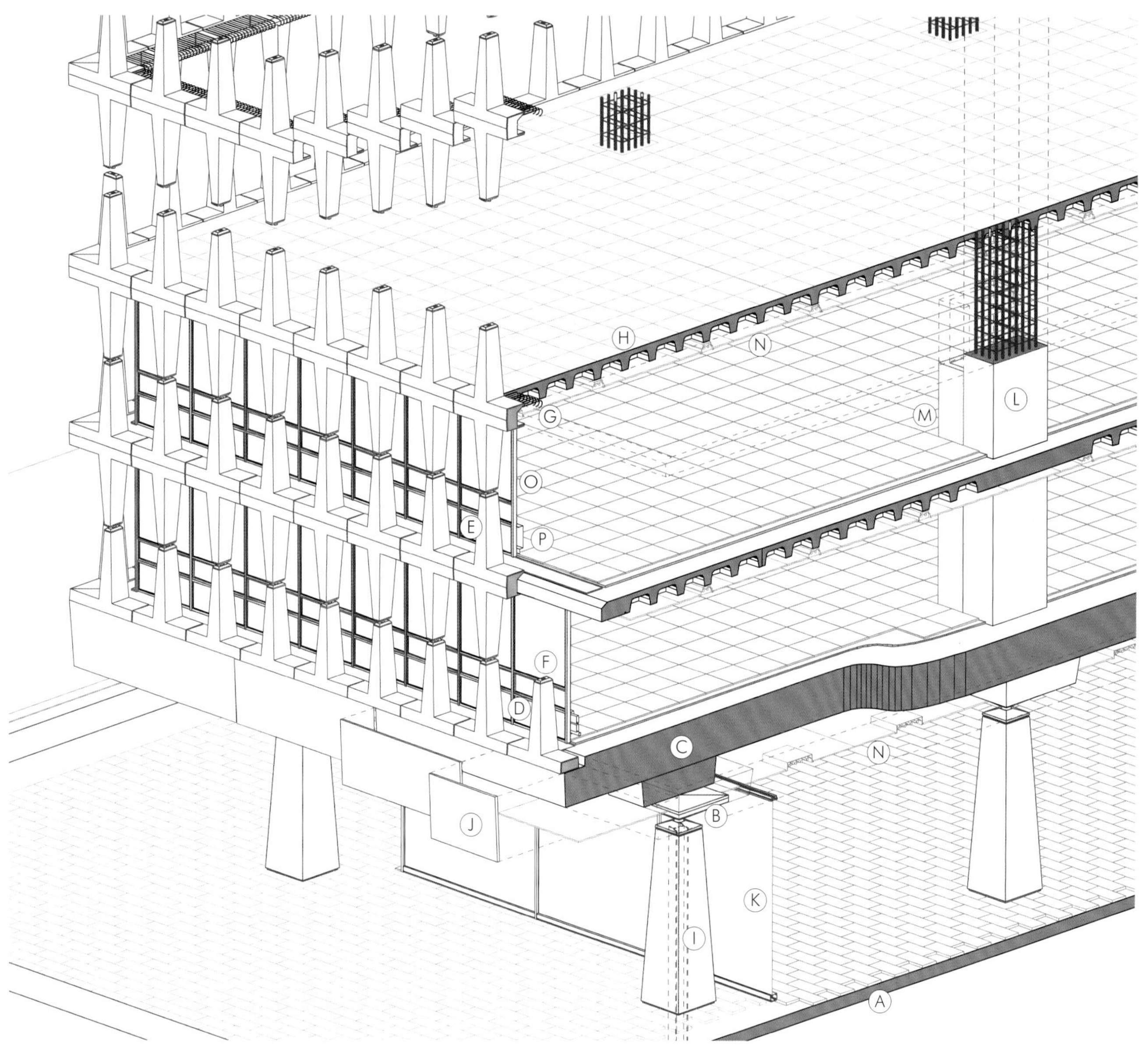

Axonometric drawing of the building for Lambert Bank, showing the structure and its installations.

Drawing by the author, 2012.

Ⓐ Cast-in-place reinforced concrete floor slabs

Ⓑ 'H' section steel columns covered with prefabricated façade panels finished with fine quartz aggregate

Ⓒ First-floor slab (beams and slab) in cast-in-place reinforced concrete

Ⓓ Special precast concrete structural units, cast to form the base of the façade structural frame

Ⓔ Precast concrete structural units finished with fine quartz aggregate

Ⓕ Steel connectors integrated into the precast structural units, with internal tongue and groove for interlocking with adjacent units

Ⓖ Protruding reinforcement rods of the precast units for connection with the reinforcement of the floor slab

Ⓗ Reinforced cast-in-place concrete waffle slab

Ⓘ Precast façade panels finished with fine quartz aggregate

Ⓙ Precast column cladding panels finished with fine quartz aggregate

Ⓚ Fixed glazed windows

Ⓛ Reinforced cast-in-place concrete columns

Ⓜ Shaft for vertical passage of installations

Ⓝ Acoustic ceiling

Ⓞ Glazed enclosures with lower hopper windows

Ⓟ Technical cabinet with passage of electric, plumbing and HVAC installations

a sort of linear void that is filled when the concrete of the slabs is poured. The prefabricated crosses also have rebars that protrude from these hollows and that are embedded and tied to the slabs during their casting on site, receiving the bending movements coming from them. The slabs are bidirectional and cast in situ. They reach a span of 33' 5½" (10.20 m) and play a fundamental role in the horizontal interlocking of the structure, helping to tie the perimeter supports to those inside the floors. The glazed windows are spaced about 2' (60 cm) from the perimeter, establishing an exterior walkway.

In addition to the basic cross type – the most recurrent throughout the building – the structure also includes four other types derived from it: top cap and attic parapet units; corner units for top cap and attic parapet (these first two types make up the top row of structural screens); corner cross units; bottom units and bottom corner units (the latter two types are located on the first-floor cast-in-place concrete structure).

The crosses act as columns and also as edge beams, resisting forces of different natures. The horizontal forces acting on the perimeter structure

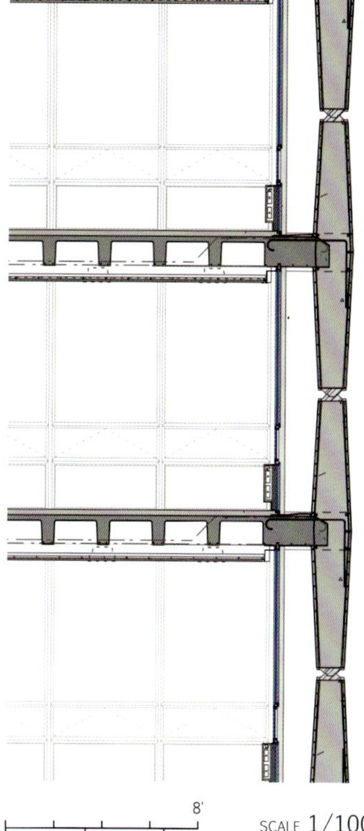

On the right:

Photo of a workspace during renovation works, and enlarged section of a typical floor of the Lambert Bank.

Photo and drawing by the author, 2012.

produce moments of bending that vary in height from zero at the midpoint between slabs to a maximum at the level of the slabs. Structural engineer Paul Weidlinger felt that the units he designed in collaboration with SOM should clearly express this stress flow, so the columns were shaped wider at the encounter with the edge beam and narrower at the connections with units adjacent in height. The "thinning" of the columns helps to reduce the abruptness of the internal stress change caused by bending moment variations.

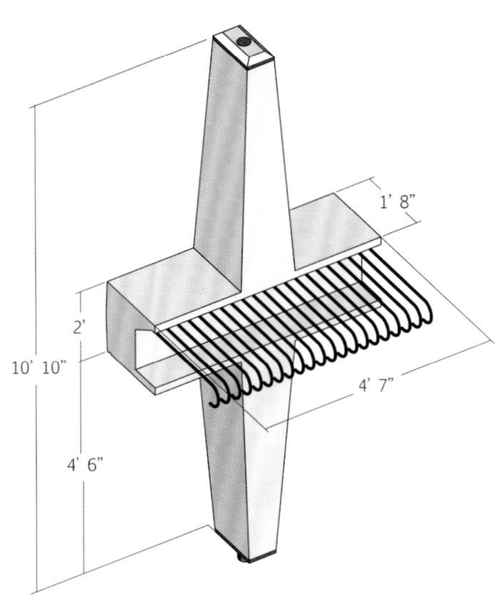

The typical prefabricated units for the Lambert Bank.

Drawing by the author, 2010.

All precast parts for the Lambert Bank were cast in Rotterdam by a company called Schokbeton,[61] which at the time was a pioneer in the use of an innovative casting method, and began to be manufactured in the USA in 1959.

The joints between crossings were solved with stainless steel connections already integrated into the precast concrete parts. Prior to casting in the factory, spherical bearing joints were welded to the reinforcement of the units at each of their two vertical ends, allowing a perfect fit on site.

All those design criterion solve three problems with a single gesture: constructively, by way of saving material when fabricating parts with the exact volume to an adjusted and excellent structural performance; from a commercial point of view, by giving exclusivity to each building and leaving a unique solution; and formally, lightening the visual weight of the structure, allowing for its multiplication along the length and height of the façades, making it elegant and projecting a delicate three-dimensional tissue.

Differences in the plumb and span between the perimeter screens of the typical floors and the ground floor columns made it necessary to use a transfer load mechanism in the second-floor slab. Edge beams (which are effectively transfer beams), secondary beams and bidirectional ribbed slabs form a large cast-in-place concrete tray, which redirects the upper loads to the central core and the ground floor columns. The presence of the vertical supports is reduced on the ground as they are more widely spaced and set back from the perimeter of the typical stories.

As a formal repercussion, the main body appears externally elevated from the floor plan, enhancing its visual independence from the plaza platform. The perception of volumetric purity already established by the uniform treatment of the façades is much further perceived.

On the left:

The Lambert Bank viewed from Marnix Avenue.

John Hancock Mutual Life Insurance Company

1960-1962. New Orleans, Louisiana

With Nolan, Norman & Nolan

Between 1960 and 1962, one of several John Hancock headquarters commissioned to SOM was built in New Orleans. It was the insurance company's second project to be built outside of Boston. Of all Bunshaft's career projects, the one in New Orleans was the first building with precast concrete structure to open.

SOM's New York office was the first to introduce precast concrete in its projects, giving rise to most of the material's later applications. In those years, many of the corporate clients demanded an avant-garde image for their new headquarters, and at that time this condition was directly linked to the use of an innovative material such as precast concrete. From the beginning, Bunshaft and his team focused on the exploitation of the material in matters of structural systems, always having as precedents those experiences with steel structures that proved to be successful.

Erected on the site of an early 20th century public library, the complex is located in front of Lee Circle, which was inaugurated in 1807 and articulates the junction between St. Charles Avenue and Calliope Street[62].

The New Orleans building for the John Hancock Company consists of a six-story body elevated on a base that occupies almost the entire site and protrudes in height above street level. The typical floors measure 92'5" x 142'5" (28.16 x 45.23 m) and the basic building module governing the entire building is 4'8" (1.42 m). The base houses service and parking spaces, and on its roof there is the first floor with the main access to the building and a surrounding plaza with an external area of 26,102.48 sq. ft (2,425 m2). From the sidewalks, the public reaches the plaza via a staircase that has as its focal point a granite sculpture-fountain by Isamu Noguchi. According to the artist himself, the work suggests *A River of Plenty* and has been named *The Mississippi* by locals.[63]

When Gordon Bunshaft and his team were commissioned, they were working on the plans for the Lambert Bank and, coincidentally or not, ended up using a structural approach very similar to that used in the Brussels building. Both works are structured vertically with structural precast members placed at the outer boundary of the floors. This type of system, classified here as perimeter load-bearing framing, stands out from the vertical struc-

On the left:

The John Hancock building viewed from Lee Circle.

Photo by author, 2010.

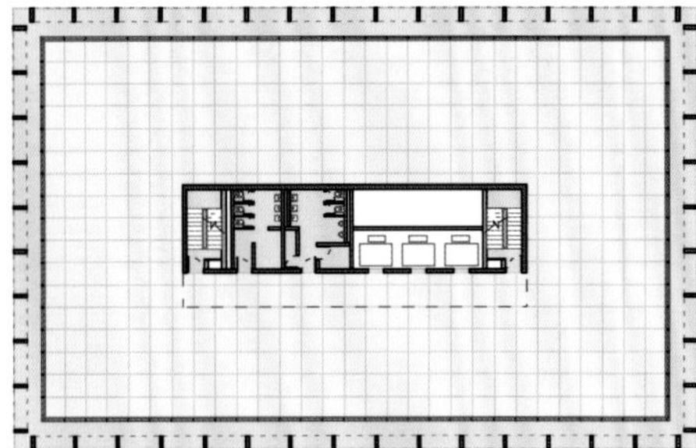

Typical Floor

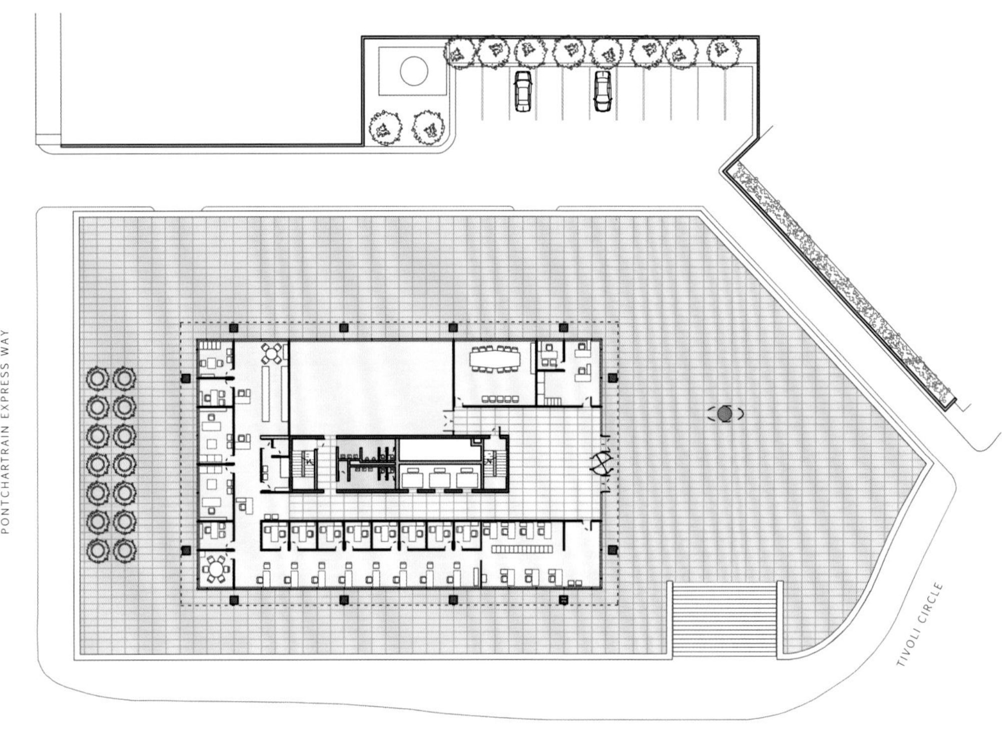

Ground Floor

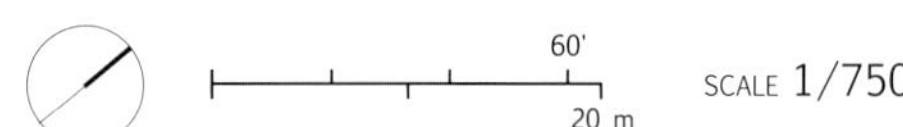

turing of the building, in which prefabricated concrete elements formally and technically guide the composition.

Prefabricated parts and load transfer elements

The perimeter structure consists of prefabricated vertical supports measuring 8" (20.30 cm) wide, 3' (91.5 cm) deep and 11' 12" (365 cm) high, spaced 9'4" (284 cm) apart. The latter dimension represents half of the construction modulation. In addition, part of the system are horizontal panels, 5" (12.7 cm) high, 36" (91.44 cm) deep and of 8' 11" width (271 m), which bolt to the vertical supports at a height of 84" (213 m) from the floor on each typical plan. The vertical supports, or external columns, are reinforced by rods capped with a 1" (2.54 cm) thick steel plate, which extend 10'1" (44 cm) beyond the concrete tops of the units. Another steel plate is also welded at the bottom of the column to the internal reinforcement rods.

The transition between the typical floor and the first-floor structures depends, as in the case of Lambert Bank, on a transfer structure. In the John Hancock building, the second-floor slab, which makes the transition aforementioned, is formed by double "tee" section edge beams made of welded steel plates, and the overhang with respect to the first-floor columns is about 16" (40 cm). It should be noted that the spans between the ground-floor columns is 37'4" (11.38 m) on the long façades and 56' (17.07 m) on the short ones, and that the corners are cantilevered by 16'4" (4.98 m) on each side, formally intensifying the independence between the base and the body of the building.

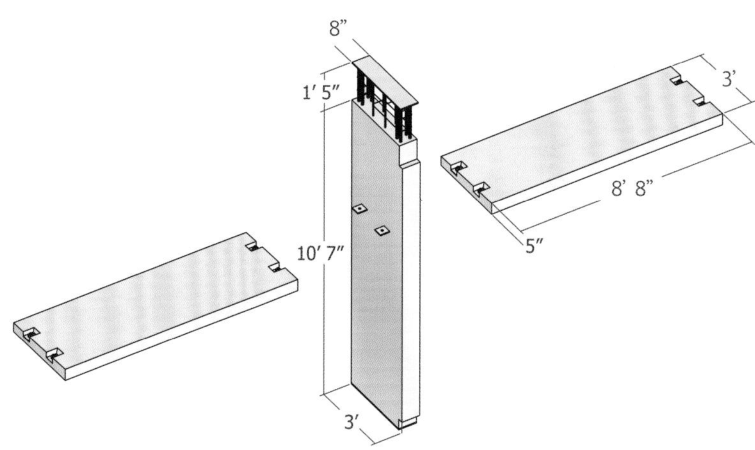

On the right:

Vertical and horizontal prefabricated units form the perimeter structure of the John Hancock building.

Drawing by author, 2010.

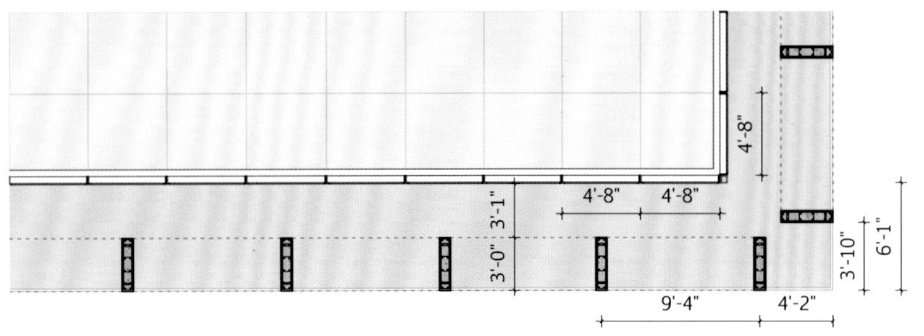

Typical Floor

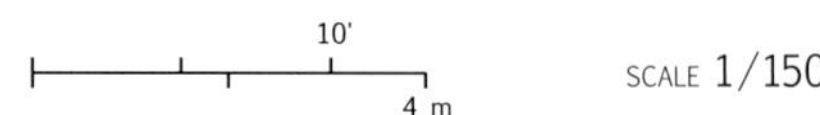

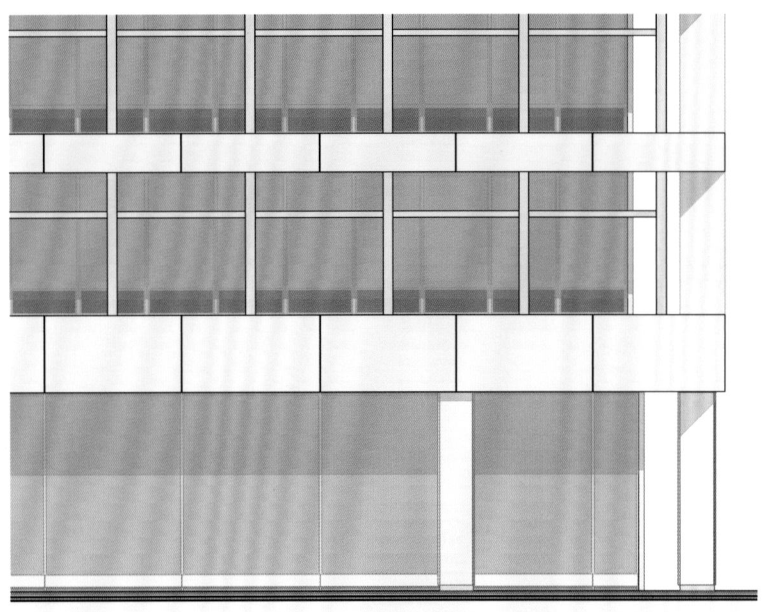

Elevation

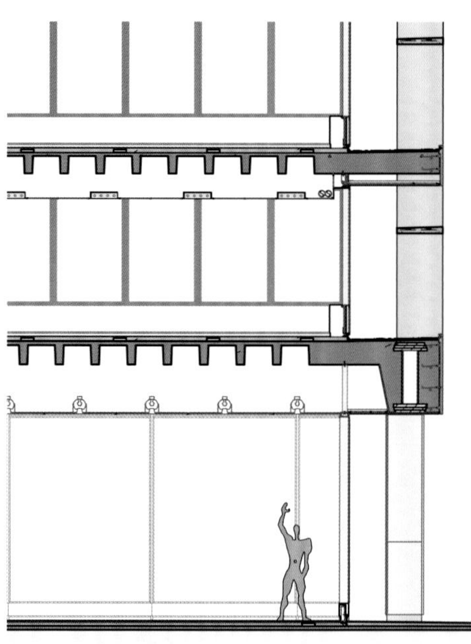

Section

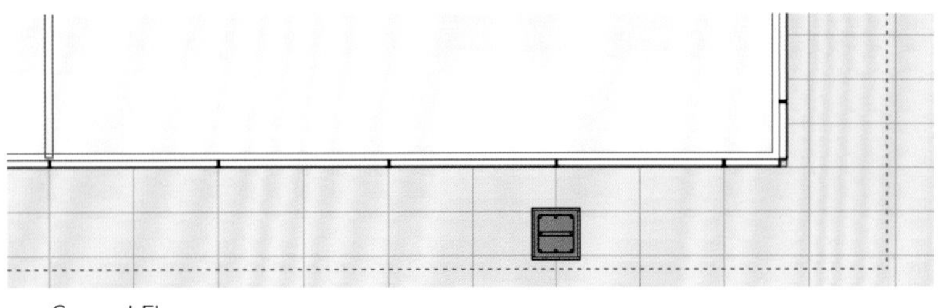

Ground Floor

On the right:

From the access, partial view to the building, showing in the foreground the fountain-sculpture *A River of Plenty*, also known as *The Mississipi*, by Isamu Noguchi.

Drawing by author, 2010.

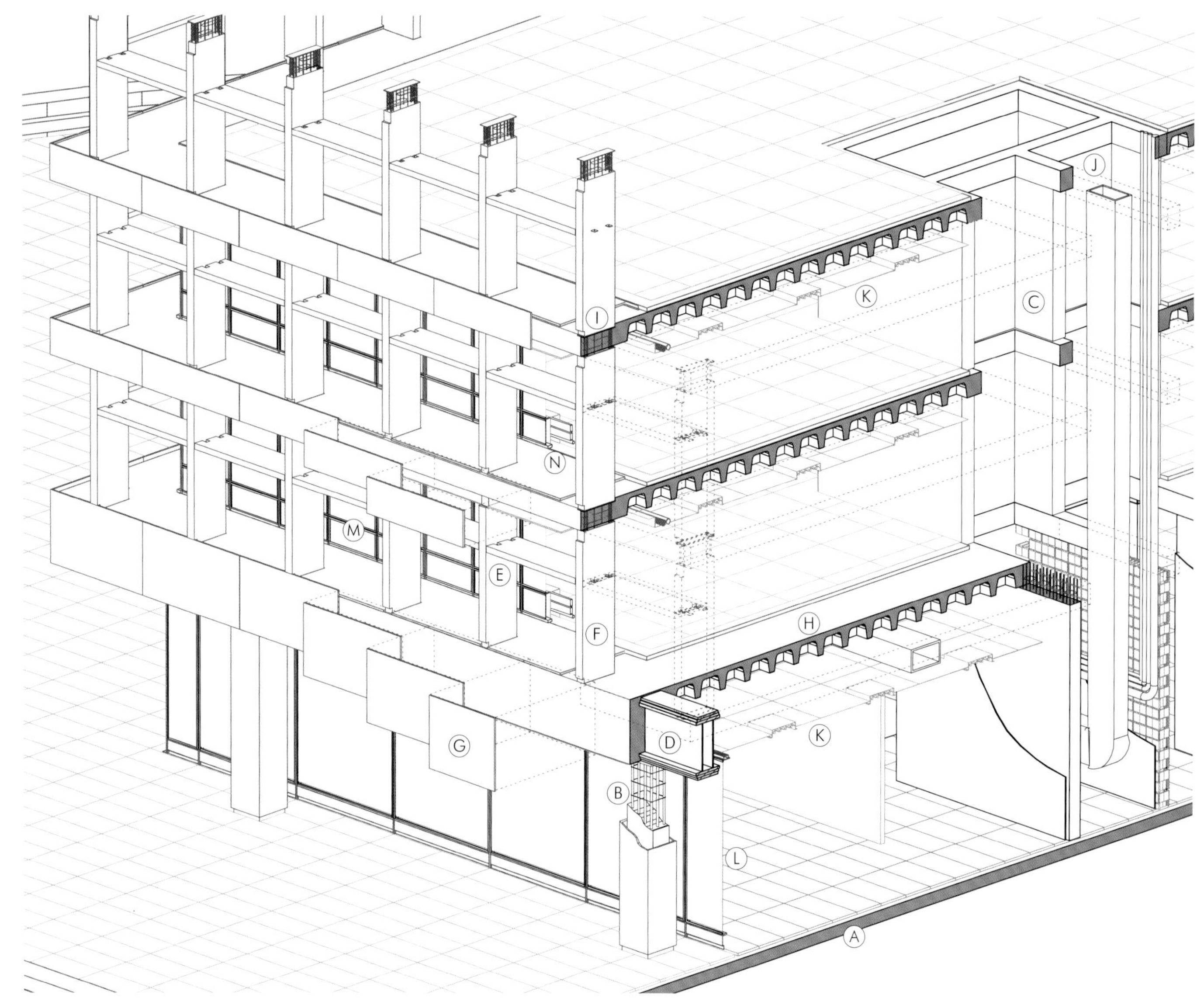

Axonometric drawing of the building for New Orleans' John Hancock, showing the structure and its installations.

Drawing by the author, 2012.

(A) Reinforced cast-in-place concrete floor slabs

(B) Reinforced cast-in-place concrete columns clad with precast panels

(C) Central core of the building

(D) Steel transfer beams for shoring of superior level loads

(E) Perimetral precast concrete columns

(F) Precast concrete slab that functions both as a sunshade and as a structural interlocking element of the perimeter structure

(G) Prefabricated concrete cladding panel for the edge of transfer beams

(H) Reinforced cast-in-place concrete waffle slab

(I) Connection between subsequent external precast columns by welding of their vertical ends

(J) Shaft for vertical passage of installations

(K) Acoustic ceiling

(L) Fixed glazed windows

(M) Glazed enclosures with lower hopper windows

(N) Technical cabinet with passage of electric, plumbing and HVAC installations

Bi-directional slabs

Far from being an obsession, or the result of the search for novelty in itself, the use of pieces brought from the factory sought to benefit the projects economically and formally. Depending on the characteristics of the commission, the use of these elements could solve just one part of the structural system, requiring the adoption of other materials and techniques. For Bunshaft and his team, in-situ casting of concrete elements was almost indispensable for structures using precast systems.

This type of structural combination was detected in more cases in North America at that time. With reference to buildings with perimeter supporting frames, cast-in-place slabs play a key role in the appropriate use of precast concrete elements.

In an article published in *Progressive Architecture* magazine from October 1960, Edward Friedman, a collaborating architect in the office of I.M. Pei, justified its use:

> *Shortly after World War II, the steel shortage, coupled with the appearance of the flat slab, gave impetus to reinforced concrete construction. Cities where zoning regulations limited building heights, gratefully received the shallower floor-to-floor height of flat-slab construction. An entire floor could be gained, an advantage impossible with the greater floor depth of structural-steel construction. The advantage of flat-slab design was further augmented by 'scatter columns' which could be shaped and placed at will according to plan dictates. Taller and more powerful cranes and improved ready-mix concrete service were additional encouragements.*[64]

Another aspect that confirms the benefits of the combination of cast-in-place slabs and precast perimeter supporting frames is the fact that the four façades of the buildings are protected from direct sunlight. The shading provided by the façade structure allowed for a reduction of loads in the calculation of the air conditioning systems, which directly led to a reduction in the cross-section of the air conditioning ducts and, consequently, in the total slab height between the top face of the false ceilings and the finished floor level above. The two-way slabs used in the New Orleans building span up to 33' 9 1/2" (10.3 m).

Regarding the façade, these slabs enable adequate formal articulations, allowing for a very satisfactory integration with the frame established by the prefabricated vertical supports. In the case of the John Hancock building, the relatively reduced frame edges make them visually integrated into the whole, like a uniform fabric, in which the lines must be sufficiently slender and elegant to maintain the continuous appearance both vertically and horizontally.

Photo of a workspace of a typical floor of the John Hancock building, lately used for art exhibitions.

Photo by the author, 2010.

Internally, the spaces generated are isotropic: floor and ceiling induce an even perception of space, i.e., equivalent in both directions of the plan and toward the four façades.

Formal elementality

It is also important to mention the visual qualities brought by the modular façade proportion and dimensions, as well as those coming from certain composition strategies present in the projects, such as the load transfer mechanisms or the elevated ground-floor platforms. The importance of the perimeter structure for the construction of a clear volumetry in the works can be easily recognized. Yet, beyond being a purely aesthetic quality related to what is clear and geometrically identifiable, the perimeter frames and their uniform treatment of the four elevations add formal elementality to the buildings. It is pertinent to quote Carles Martí Aris in order to explain the fundamental formal conditions stemming from the supporting structure found in both the Lambert Bank and the John Hancock building in New Orleans:

> *The simple is of a piece: it lacks ingredients and, therefore, composition. The elemental, on the other hand, arises from the composition of some elements following certain rules (...) "Elementality" and "complexity" form a complementary conceptual pair that has a capital importance for the artistic procedure. The work of art is always a complex construction in which the elements that form it are recognizable (...) There is no complication in them [the complex and elemental works], but there is, on the other hand, a remarkable complexity and recognizability throughout the whole process.*[65]

It is clear in these two works by Bunshaft, that structural rules or parameters govern, influenced by a strong visual sense, the placement of units of all types in the system. The prefabricated units that make up the supporting structure are recognized both internally and externally, reflecting directly and indirectly through a precise metric the previously stipulated formal and visual order.

Section and matching photograph showing the façade system for the Jonh Hancock building of New Orleans.

Photo and Drawing by the author, 2012.

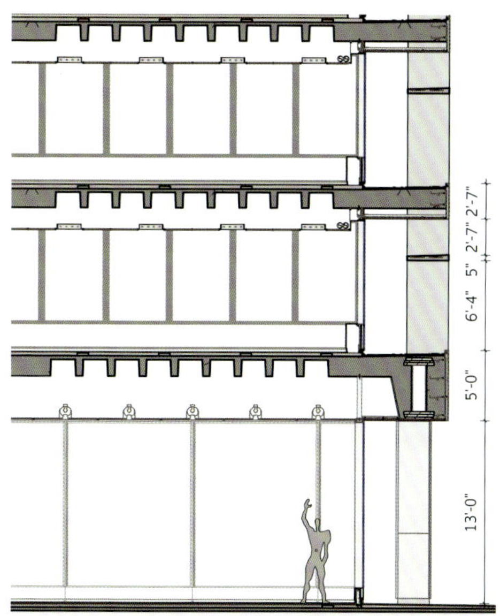

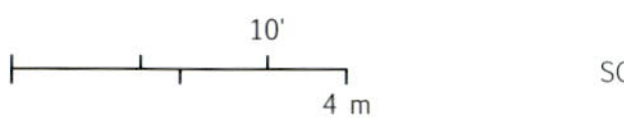

SCALE 1/175

Watson Powell Jr

American Republic Life Insurance Company
1960-1965. Des Moines, Iowa

In the early 1960s, Watson Powell Jr., president of the American Republic Insurance Company and a lover of art and modern architecture, approached SOM to inquire about the possibility of the firm's New York office taking on the project for the company. At first there was no interest on the part of the architects in carrying out the commission due to the small scale of the building and the investment that the project would entail, something that had already happened in the same period when Watson had tried to contact other prominent architectural firms in the US. The executive ended up hitting it off with Gordon Bunshaft and finally convinced him to take part in the project for his company's headquarters. Bunshaft agreed to a deal on the condition that he would be given free reign over the project decisions he would make. The architect and his team began to study the needs of the client, whose basic demand was for open working spaces without obstacles or interruptions such as walls, columns or poles.[66]

Regarding the materials and techniques that should be employed, the client already had some initial ideas. Watson was hesitant about constructing a concrete building, having seen all the cracks in the recently opened terminal that Saarinen designed for Dulles Airport in Washington, DC. Watson and Bunshaft were entertained on that topic, which resulted in them visiting the Portland Cement Association (PCA) in Chicago together. For two days they studied the risks and, finally, Watson was convinced that his future building could be made of concrete and that it would stand the test of time.

In 1965, the building was at last completed on a site located on the outskirts of downtown Des Moines, Iowa. The complex was initially intended to accommodate some 650 company workers at what would become its headquarters, and consists basically of a prism raised on eight large columns, under which a two-story podium is placed. The prism corresponds to the typical floors[67] and the podium houses within its walls an access plaza, the building's reception area, six offices for public service and a space for group work with computers. On the roof of the podium, which is the second floor of the complex, there is a collective dining room and a large open common room with an adjoining terrace.

On the left:

The American Republic Life Insurance building viewed from 6th Avenue in Des Moines, Iowa.

Photo by author, 2010.

PARK ST

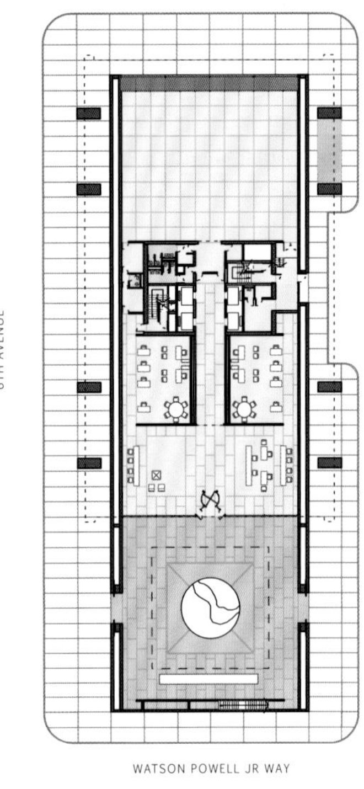

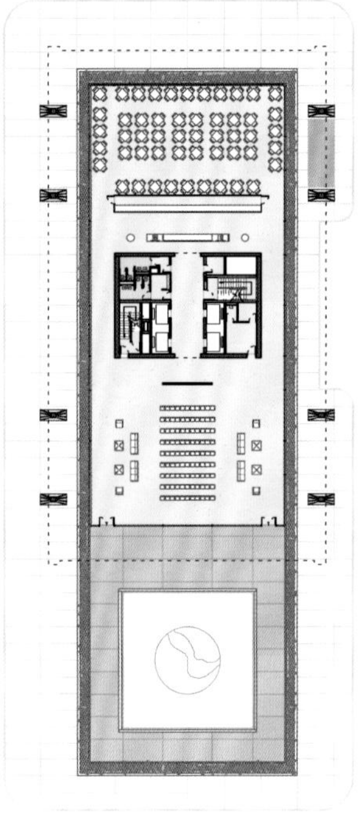

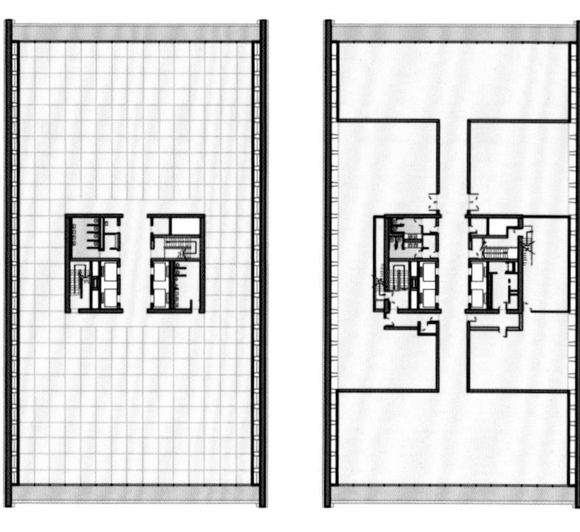

Ground Floor

First Floor

Typical Floor

7th Floor

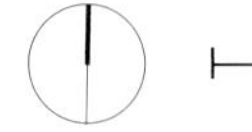

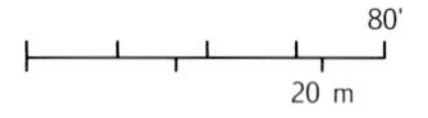

SCALE 1/1000

One-way slabs on load-bearing walls

The eight-story main volume is basically made up of two large lateral load-bearing walls between which are supported slabs made of precast concrete slabs. At the second-floor level, each of these cast-in-place concrete side walls is supported by four large columns, which raises the block above the podium-like base of the building. In the center of the floor there is a vertical circulation and service core with cast-in-place concrete walls that helps to stiffen the building horizontally.

This structural configuration relied heavily on an elaborate and ingenious union of cast-in-place and prefabricated reinforced concrete elements. In addition, the main members were designed and engineered to allow for efficient integration with the building's required subsystems.

The two supporting walls are 90' 7 1/4" (27.62 m) high by 180' (54.86 m) long and vary in thickness from 4' (122 cm) at the base to 21" (53 cm) at the top. The tapering of the sections, from the upper extremities to the bases, reflects the reduction of the stress applied to the walls.

The floors are composed of precast and prestressed concrete slabs. The ends of these elements (consisting only of the web of the profile) fit into cavities formed in the load-bearing side walls. These cavities were lined with neoprene pads to adequately support the precast tees.

On the interior of each floor, concrete block partitions running parallel to the load-bearing walls were erected on the floor slabs. The resulting linear space serves as a passageway for mechanical and electrical installations and runs vertically between the second and eighth floors. In addition to freeing the working floors from columns or vertical supports, the adoption of supporting blind walls was justified on the grounds that they would control excessive light and reduce the energy required to air-condition the rooms (in fact, the air conditioning loads required to cool the building's internal parts were reduced by 20%, in comparison with a building with the same size and four glazed façades).

On the right:

View of the north (rear) façade from 6th Avenue.

Photo by author, 2010.

The "tee" slabs

The precast slabs that form the floors perform some key functions for the operation of the entire system. These precast-prestressed "tee" section units weigh approximately 36 tons each.

All were cast at an industrial plant located in Lincoln, Nebraska, approximately 210 miles (340 km) from the site and transported to Des Moines in pairs, in 12 rail cars rented to work exclusively during the construction and assembly period. Once in the destination city, two trucks were positioned with their "backs" to each other with the trailer axle in the middle so that they could be maneuvered back and forth more easily through the streets. Transport and delivery time was critical as there was no storage space at the job site and the slabs were placed on the structure as they arrived. The basic and predominant "tee" slab type in the building is 99' 4" (30.27 m) long, 4' 6" (1.37 m) high and 3' 11 1/2" (1.21 m) wide.

On the right:

Section and matching photograph showing one of the structural *in-situ* walls and the series of precast concrete slabs.

Photo and drawing by the author, 2010.

From the executive project, a detail of the "hinge," structural element between the body and the columns at the base of the building.

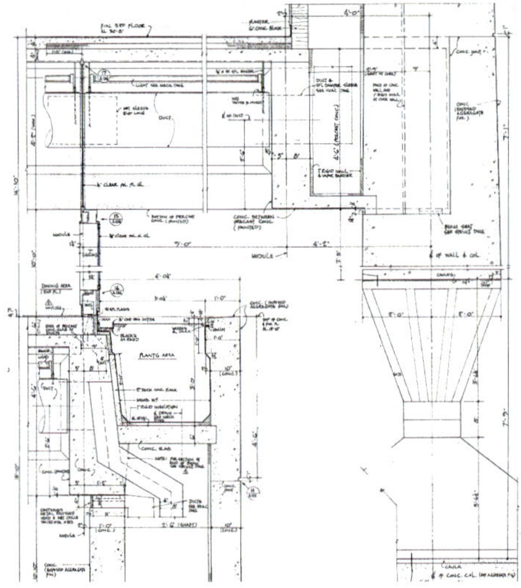

On the left:

Partial view of the north facade, from Park St.

Photo by author, 2010.

SCALE 1/100

4'-10"
14'-4"
9'-6"
4'-10"
14'-11"
10'-0"
4'-4"
15'-8"
11'-4"

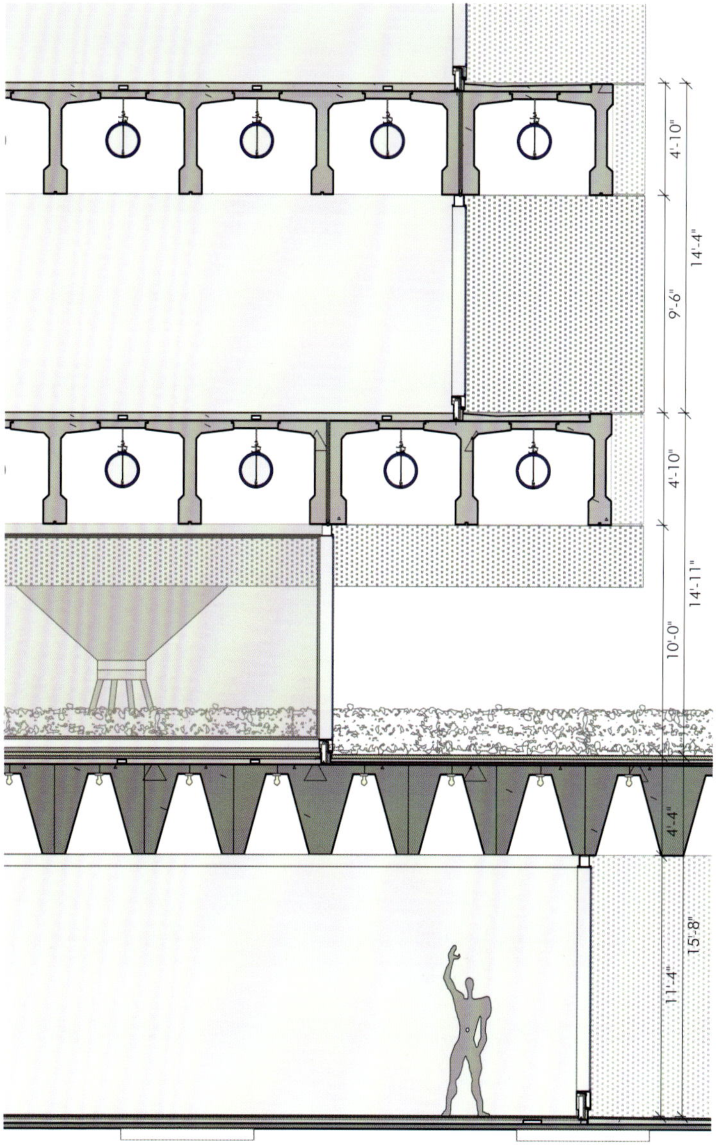

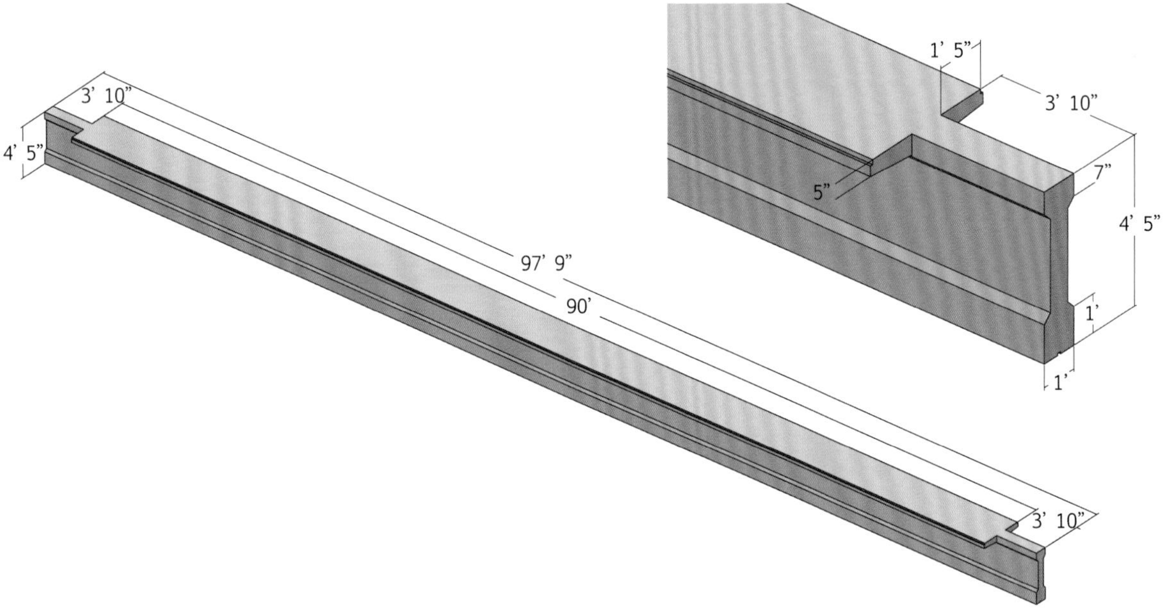

1' 5"
3' 10"
7"
5"
4' 5"
1'
1'

3' 10"
4' 5"
97' 9"
90'
3' 10"

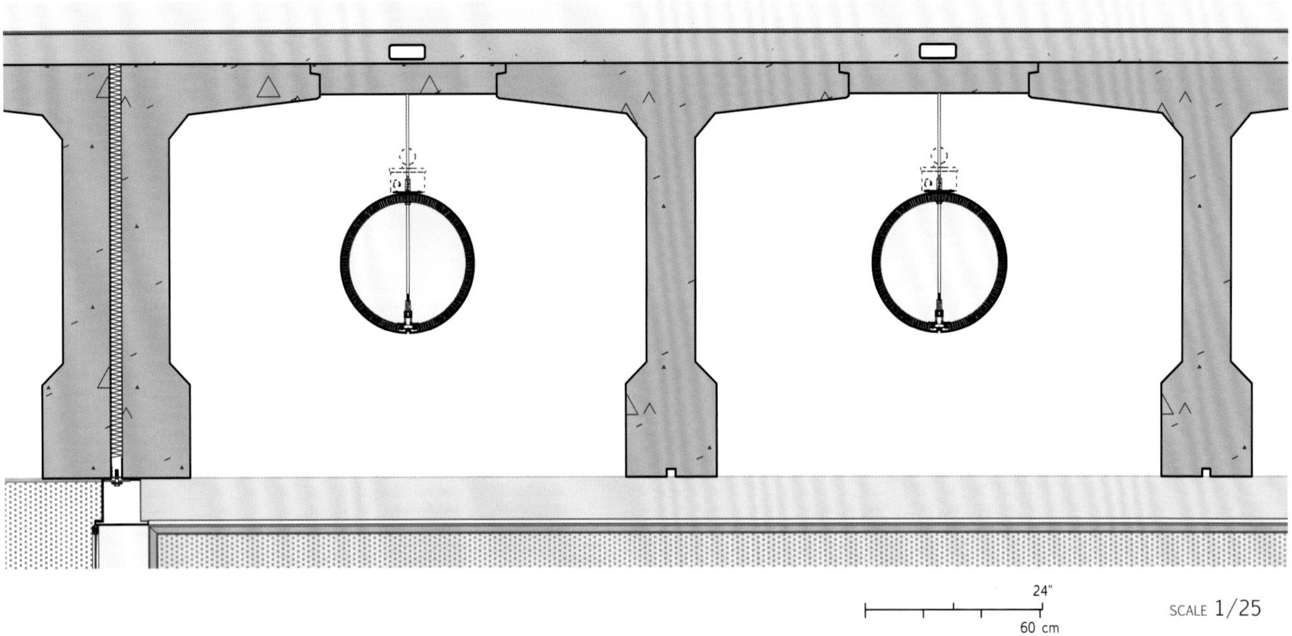

24"
60 cm
SCALE 1/25

On the left (top):

The typical precast concrete "Tee" slab that form the floors in American Republic Life Insurance Company.

Drawing by the author, 2010.

On the left (bottom):

Section detail of the slabs. Circular ducts for HVAC system and fluorescent tubes were installed along the vaults, formed by the flange and the webs of the floor slabs.

Drawing by the author, 2010.

In two situations of the complex, the lengths of the prefabricated tees are different. The northern part of the second-floor slab, between the central core and the building boundary, was built with prefabricated "tee" slabs equal to those of the typical floors, but 72' (22 m) long. In the typical floors, between the structural cores and the load-bearing side walls, the slabs have slightly shorter spans, being 21' (6.4 m) long.[68]

Directly related to the use of prestressed "tees", the technical ceilings of the American Republic Insurance Company were developed by Gordon Bunshaft and a team of consultants from outside SOM, including structural engineer Paul Weidlinger and mechanical engineers Syska & Hennessy.

Circular ducts for the heating and air-conditioning systems were installed along the vaults formed by the flange and the webs of the floor slabs. Fluorescent tubes were attached over these ducts to shed light on the vaults, which also function as perfect reflectors, creating ideal lighting for office work. With respect to acoustic comfort, the performance obtained by the combination of the carpet floor coverings with the exposed undersides of the floor slabs was considered satisfactory when the building was finished.[69]

The perception of spaciousness in height in the workspaces was also increased by the use of the precast slabs, as the upper limit of the ceilings is provided by the upper flanges of the slabs. In this way, the height of the floor slabs is also integrated into the overall height, which would not be the case if there were false ceilings or elements with the same function under the horizontal structures.

It should be clarified that, although the American Republic building used somewhat sophisticated "tee" slabs compared to those used in engineering works, the concepts and guidelines for the calculation, design and molding of these elements were practically the same as those applied to the manufacturing of similar units found in bridges and large infrastructure.

Form: structural efficiency and integrated systems

The structural system of the American Republic building reveals a considerable number of structural element types and, consequently, results in the prefabricated "tee" slabs having less visual prominence. The vertical structure of the building's body, consisting of the side walls, the steel connectors and the eight columns, volumetrically defines the prism that stands out from the base as a whole. The slabs and the large free spans they bridge add lightness to the prism, which, despite the robustness and great mass of the two concrete screens, does not appear heavy or grotesque.

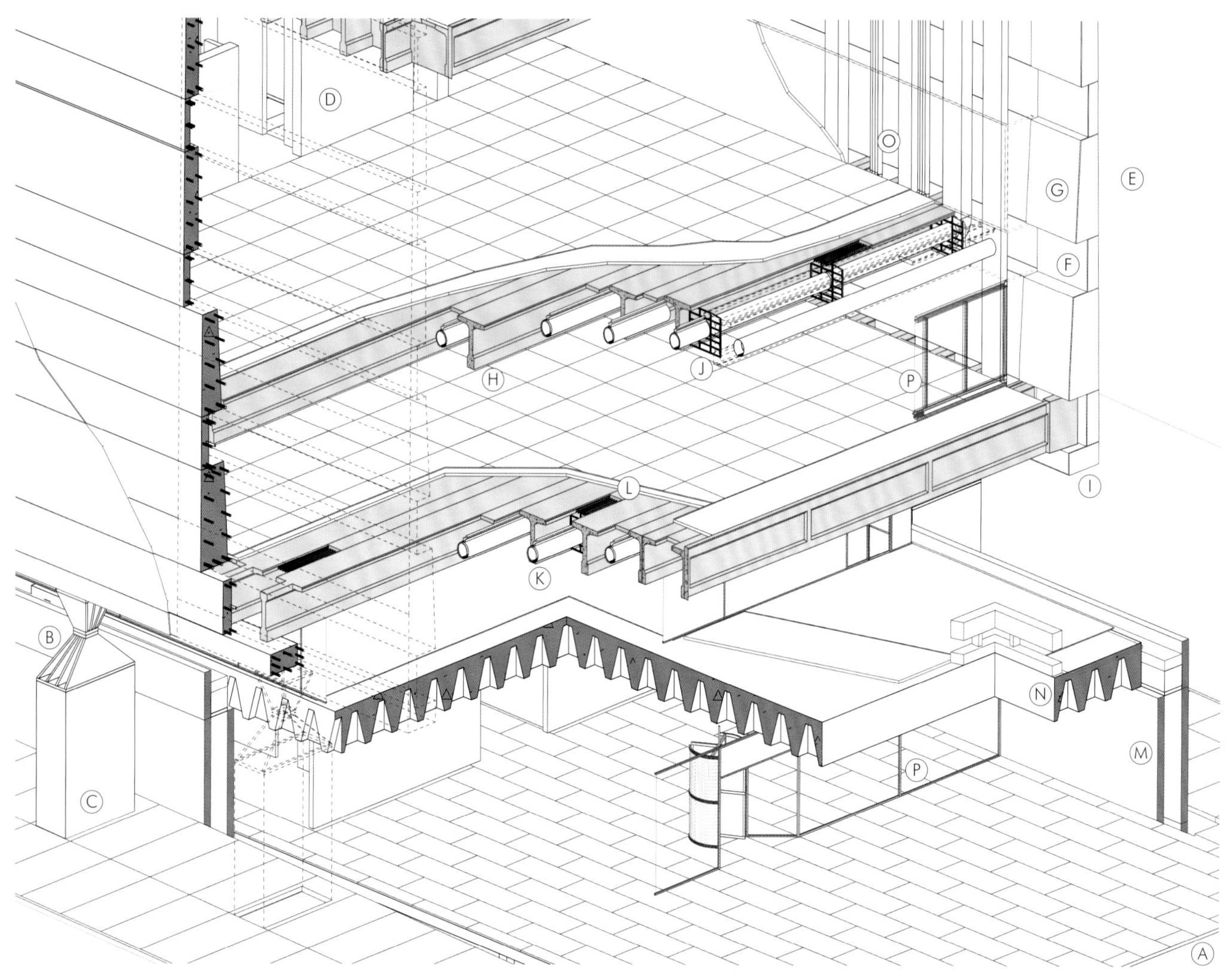

Axonometric drawing of the American Republic building, showing the structure and its installations.

Drawing by the author, 2012.

(A) Reinforced cast-in-place concrete slab

(B) Double pyramid-shaped steel connector finished in black vinyl paint

(C) Reinforced cast-in-place concrete columns

(D) Structural, circulation and services core

(E) Reinforced cast-in-place concrete structural lateral walls

(F) Structural wall layer at the level of the standard floor slabs

(G) Structural wall layer at the level of the clear heights between slabs of typical floors

(H) Precast and prestressed "tee" section concrete floor slabs unit

(I) Solid base of the structural wall that connects to the eight first-floor columns

(J) Panels acting as diaphragms for horizontal stabilization of the "tee" slabs of the floor slabs

(K) Tubular ducts of the integrated HVAC and lighting systems

(L) Floor slab compression layer

(M) Double exterior walls at the base of the complex

(N) Cast-in-place concrete bi-directional ribbed slab

(O) Lateral shaft with passage of electric, plumbing and HVAC installations

(P) Fixed glazed windows

This condition is made extreme by the presence of the black vinyl coated steel hinges connecting the first-floor columns with the cast-in-place concrete walls.

The "tee" slabs appear on the exterior in their full height, and the glazed windows of the typical floors seen from the outside correspond to the full clear height. From the offices, the spatial limits that are visually perceived are, to the east and west, the continuous planes of white-painted walls that cover the lateral structural walls; and, to the north and south, the glazed windows. No vertical structural elements, such as columns or supporting walls, are visible within these spaces.

After understanding how the building for the American Republic Insurance Company works structurally, perhaps the most obvious (or the first) feature that comes to mind is that the load-bearing elements virtually define its built form. In addition to the usual and obligatory demand for structural efficiency, the load-bearing elements are given great aesthetic and visual importance. The precise work of integration between the load-bearing structure and the installation systems, which is revealed in a categorical way in precast prestressed concrete slabs, is a fundamental condition for the structural system to play such a leading role.

Interior of the seventh floor of the American Republic building.

Photo by the author, 2010.

American Can Company
1967-1970. Greenwich, Connecticut

On the left:

The American Can Company building, in Greenwich, Connecticut.

Photo by author, 2010.

Following the construction of a series of low-rise corporate buildings in which precast concrete structures had been employed with complete skill, Bunshaft and SOM were commissioned to design a new headquarters for the American Can Company on the outskirts of New York City. The site on which the building was constructed is located in the small town of Greenwich, Connecticut, about an hour's drive from downtown Manhattan.

The total site area is approximately 70.8 hectares (175 acres). The surrounding nature is rich, with many trees and native species. The land (16.2 hectares, 40 acres) is preserved in its natural sanctuary state with many native birds and other animals. A large mansion that formerly dominated the property was maintained and converted into a guest house for the company.

There are large slopes throughout the area. An artificial lake was built in a depression in the terrain, next to the portion of the site chosen by the architect and his clients for the complex. All these elements were part of the overall conception of Bunshaft and his team, including the landscaping and the relationship of the building with its surroundings.

The complex occupies an area equal to 2,810,220 sq ft (24,255 m2) and can be described as two blocks – one with a rectangular base and the other with a square base – (the rectangular one having three floors and approximately four times larger than the square one, which has one floor) placed on a base with five levels of parking and infrastructure. The structure of the two blocks is formed by columns, beams and double "tee" slabs in precast concrete, practically defining its volumetry. The base also functions as containment for the waters of the artificial lake.

The base has its four lower levels occupied by 1,700 parking spaces (1,600 regular and 100 for the presidency block), with a total of 219,460 m2. The fifth level is occupied by a well-equipped restaurant/cafeteria in the northeast area – from which there is access to a large balcony overlooking the lake – by classrooms for staff training, multipurpose rooms and medical services in the central area; and by other auxiliary functions in the southwest area.

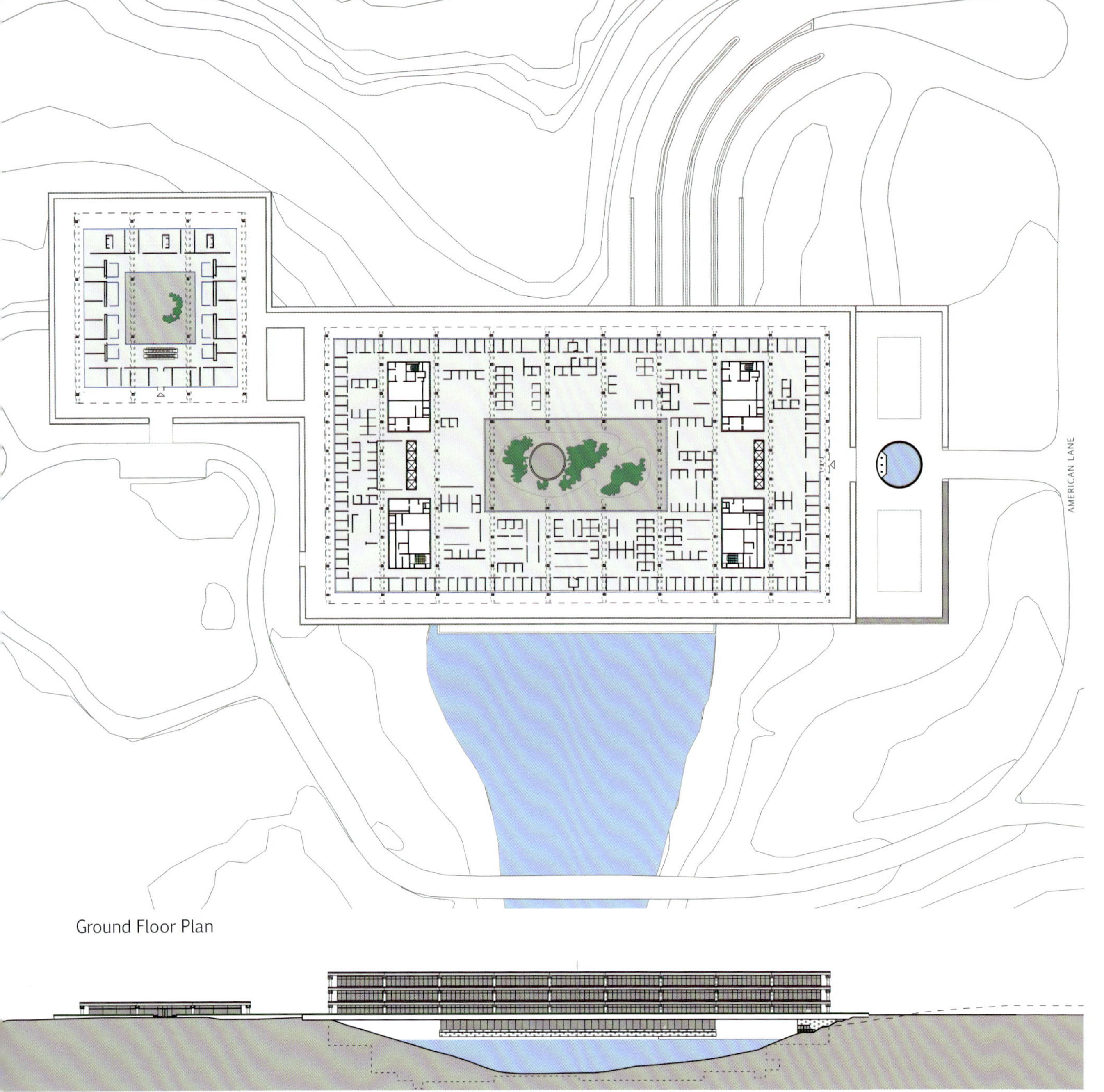

Ground Floor Plan

Southeast Elevation

The American Can Company building viewed from the south, across the lake.

Photo by author, 2010.

The roof of the base constitutes a large terrace that makes the transition from the outside of the complex to the two blocks and provides beautiful views over the entire site.

The large block, which occupies the front area of the complex and houses offices for collective work, measures 544' x 288' (166 x 88 m) in plan and has a central courtyard with 180' x 95' (54.9 x 29 m). The small block, designated for the directors' offices, has an external projection in plan of 183' x 196' (56 x 60 m) and also has a central courtyard measuring 75' x 75' (22.86 x 22.86 m). The entire built-up area is designed to accommodate 2,200 employees.

One-way floor slabs on beams

In both the large block and the small block, the supporting structure is basically composed by a standard module repetition consisting of cast-in-place reinforced concrete portal frames – i.e., columns and beams – on which the floor slabs are born; the structural spans correspond directly to the dimensions of the precast slabs that make up the floor slabs. In plan, these elements are 60' (18.3 m) large and 3' (0.91 m) wide.

In the large block, the beams have a "U" section that is 3' (0.91 m) high by 4'9" (1.44 m) wide; they span 30' (9.1 m). In the other direction the span corresponds to the total span of the floor slabs, consequently measuring 60' (18.3 m).

The director's block has some interesting structural differences in relation to the large block. The most obvious one concerns the basic structural modules. While in the collective work block the module measures 30' x 60' (9.1 x 18.3 m), in the directors annex these dimensions are equal to 30' x 30' (18.3 x 18.3 m). These differences are due to the different loads on the slabs in each block. The smaller block has only one floor, which means that the weight supported by the beams is much lower compared to that supported by the beams of the larger block. Apart from that, the beams of the small block are massive and have post-tensioned cables inside them, which increases their strength. The beams of the large block could have been cast in the same way, but that would have raised the construction costs too much, considering the scale of the building and the fact that the structural module is distributed extensively in plan and also in height.

The difference between the types of beams and structural spans built in one block and the other denotes certain formal intentions. The adoption of the same intercolumniation for all elevations adds elegance to the managerial block and subtly highlights its greater refinement within the ensemble. In addition, the square plan also suggests that the four façades be treated

200'
60 m
SCALE 1/2000

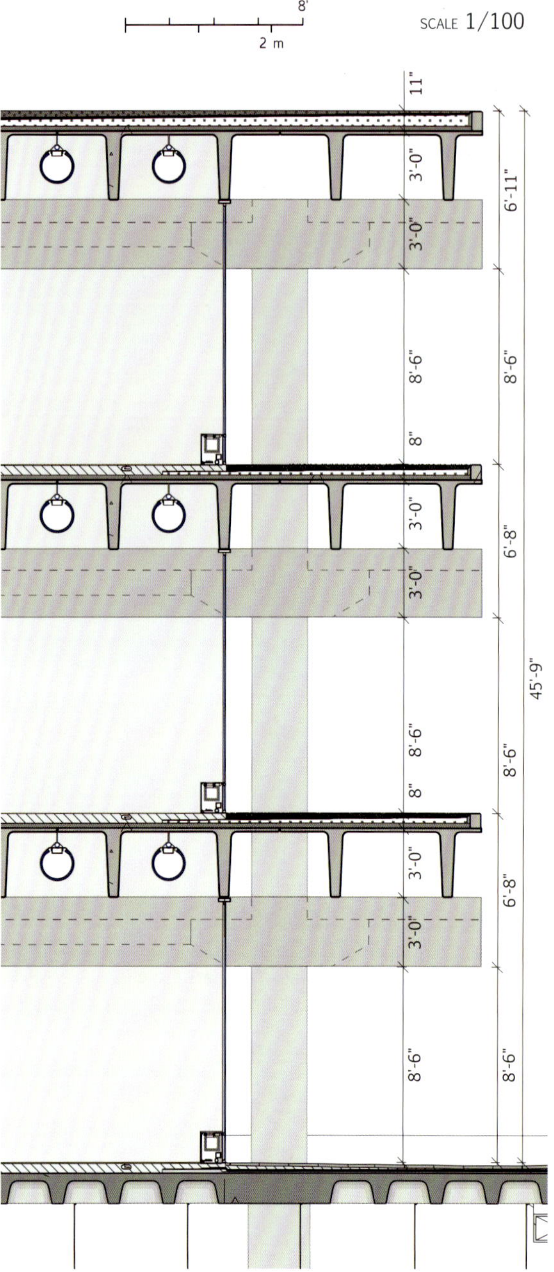
8'
2 m
SCALE 1/100
11"
3'-0"
3'-0"
6'-11"
8'-6"
8'-6"
8"
3'-0"
3'-0"
6'-8"
45'-9"
8'-6"
8'-6"
8"
3'-0"
3'-0"
6'-8"
8'-6"
8'-6"

Detail of the structure of the American Can Company's directors' block.

Photo by author, 2010.

On the right:

Partial view of the southeast façade of the American Can Company building.

Photo by author, 2010.

On the left:

Photo and southwest façade section of the American Can Company's collective work building.

Photo and drawing by author, 2010.

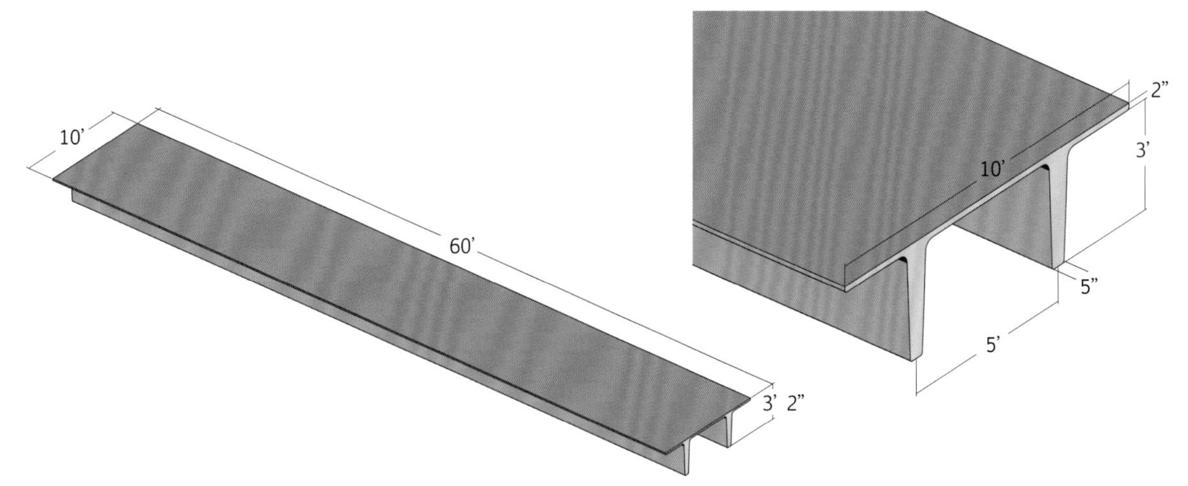

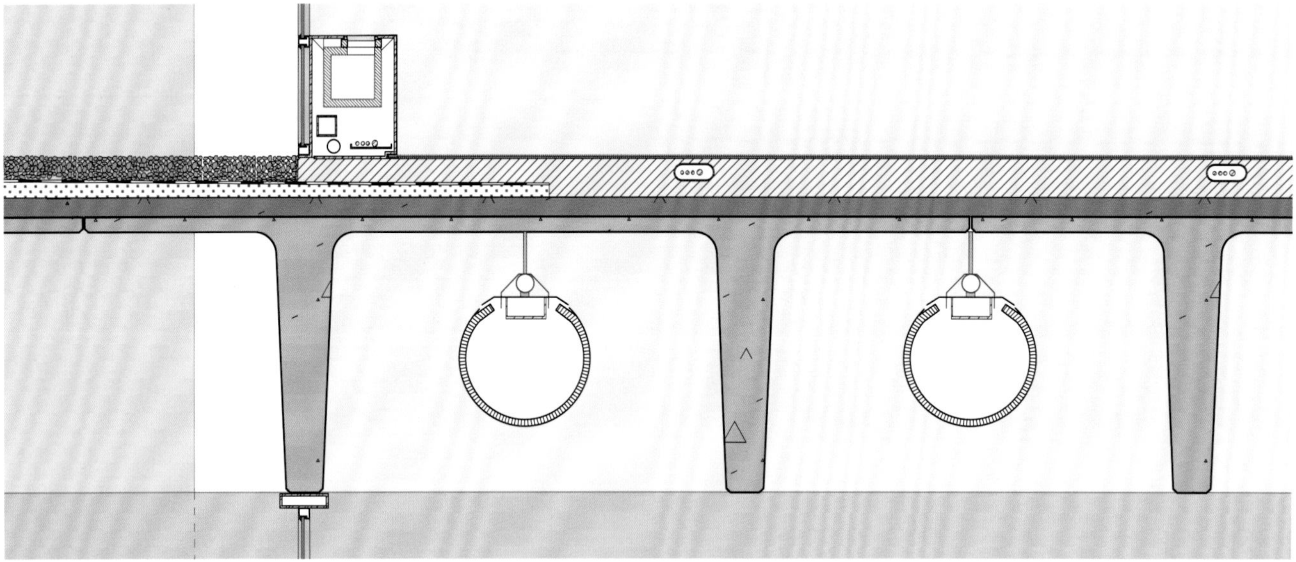

24"
60 cm

SCALE 1/25

Partial view of the northeast façade of the American Can Company building.

Photo by author, 2010.

equivalently, and this certainly influenced the decision to maintain the same structural span in both plan directions. A final but no less important aspect is recognized in the terminations of its beams. The anchor stops of the post-tensioning ribs are made of stainless steel and were left exposed as plugs, exhibiting the technique and at the same time showing the constructive precision employed.

The double "tees"

The double "tee" slab model used in the American Can Company's structure can be considered a standard within the North American industry in the years in which the building was constructed. The units were produced in the factories of Blakeslee Prestress Inc. in Branford, Connecticut, approximately 62 miles (100 km) from the construction site.

As mentioned above, the predominant type that makes up the floor slabs is 60' x 3' (18.3 x 0.91 m) in plan. Each rib is 34" (86 cm) high and 5" (12.8 cm) wide; the upper flange is 2" (5.4 cm) thick. The overall section dimensions are 10' x 3' (3.05 x 0.91 m).

But there are three other types derived from this basic model. In the northwest and southeast façades (the largest in the large block) of both blocks of the complex, the beams overhang 9' (2.74 m) from the axis of the columns, so that the slabs in these perimeter sections have the flanges cut off, their general section measurements being equal to 9' x 3' (2.74 x 0.91 m).

On the southwest and northeast façades, the floor slab terminations also consist of double "tees" with special dimensions. In these façades (in both blocks) the beams define the boundaries. In all the structural frames of the complex, the ends of the slabs are always placed on the longitudinal axis of the beams. This means that the slabs of the peripheral structural frames do not reach the perimeter of the façades. In order for the slabs to be flush with the outer faces of the beams, it was necessary to place "pieces" of slab 2' 4 1/2" (72 cm) long (half the 4' 9" – 144 cm – of the beam width), giving a satisfactory finish to the slabs.

The corner units, on the other hand, absorb both dimensional variations related to the perimeters aforementioned, measuring 9' x 3' x 28" (2.74 x 0.91 x 0.72 m).

It is worth pointing out that in a work of this size, the pieces are cast especially for the order. This is unavoidable due to the large number of units required and some project specificities, such as those mentioned above.

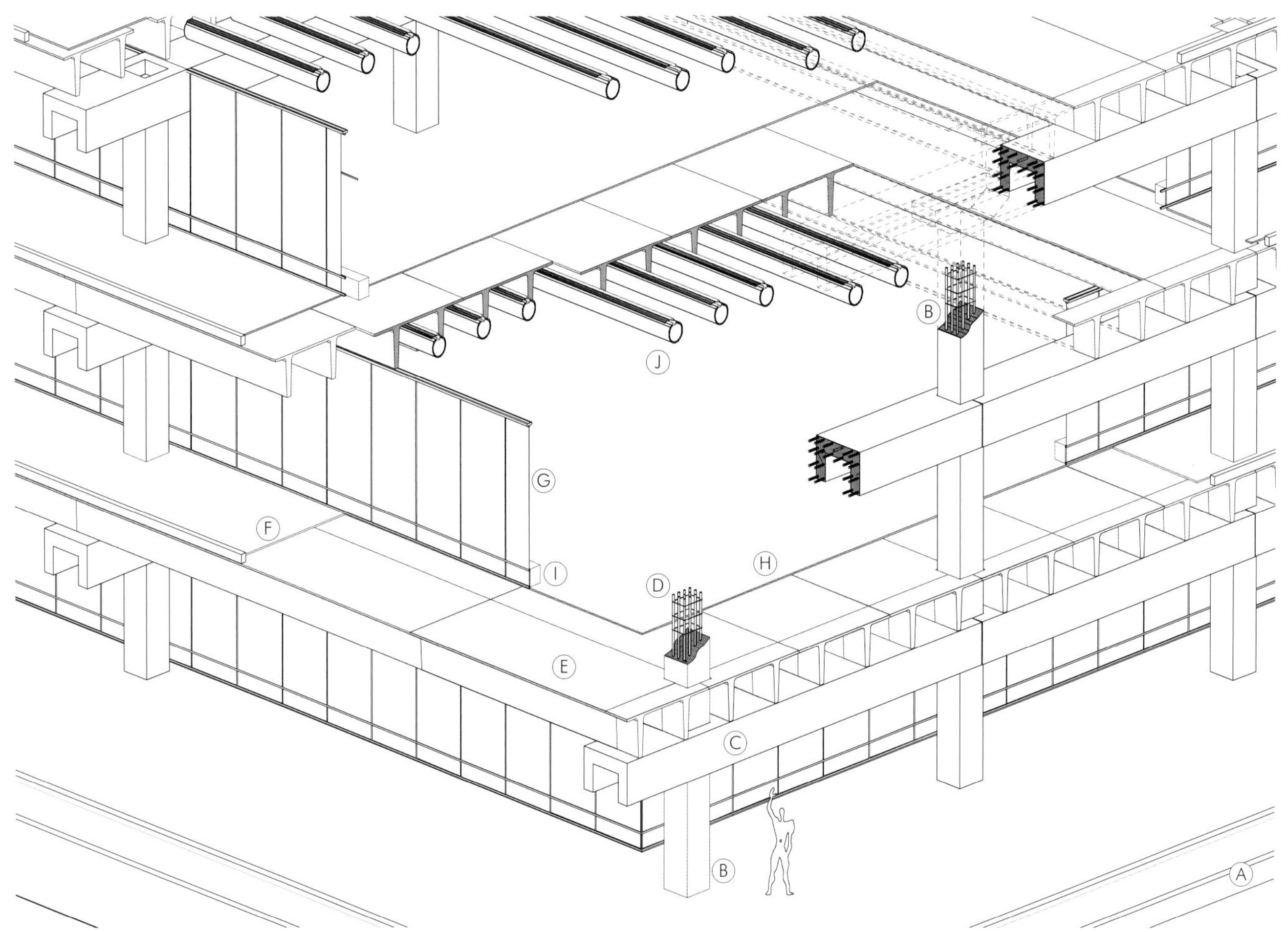

This is not at all an uneconomical aspect for the construction as the number of regular precast elements is much higher than that of special ones. Moreover, during those years, the basic section of the double "tee" slabs used could be found in the main catalogs of North American precast concrete companies, and they are still manufactured to this day. This means that no special molds or finishes had to be designed and produced for the American Can Company's slabs to be manufactured.

Axonometric drawing of the American Can Company building, showing the structure and its installations.

Drawing by the author, 2012.

An equivalent configuration to that created for the American Republic Life Insurance Company was devised by Bunshaft and his team to further exploit

(A) Reinforced cast-in-place concrete floor slabs

(B) Reinforced cast-in-place concrete columns

(C) Cast-in-place reinforced concrete beams

(D) Steel column reinforcements

(E) 'Double tee' precast concrete floor slabs

(F) Floor slab compression layer

(G) Fixed glazed enclosures

(H) Finished interior floor

(I) Technical cabinet with passage of electric, plumbing and HVAC installations

(J) Tubular ducts of the integrated HVAC and lighting systems

the double-tee slabs of the American Can. As in the Des Moines building, circular-section ducts carrying the heating and air conditioning systems were hung along the vault-like spaces formed by the space between the webs of the floor slabs. Fluorescent tubes were also installed above the ducts to provide indirect lighting in the work spaces.

The ductwork and electrical installations are somewhat different from those found in the American Republic building. Horizontal air conditioning and ventilation ducts that supply the ceilings run above the girders in the interior parts. Panels that fill the gaps formed between the webs and flanges of the double-tee slabs and the top faces of the beams (similar to the diaphragms used in the American Republic) conceal the installations and also help to horizontally lock the floor slabs. These elements were arranged in pairs, positioned about 8' to 12' (20 to 30 cm) from both lateral faces of the beams, forming a hidden but easily accessible channel.

All the façades of the American Can building are composed in the same way. The columns, beams and floor slabs give unity to the built volume through their repetition, both horizontally and vertically, on all four elevations. Visually, the floor slabs are perceived from all sides, and the double "tees" that form them are fully exposed along the entire length of the façades. It is possible to visualize them integrally – on all their faces – due to the fact that they are simply supported on the porticos cast in situ, suggesting the difference between the materials and a total exposure of the structural logic. The standard structural module, consisting of column and beam portal frames, in fact enhance the value of the precast concrete floor slabs in two ways. On the one hand, the simplicity of the portal frames contrasts with the formal originality of the double "tees" and their fully exposed profiles. On the other hand, the diaphanousness of this vertical structure means that the only elements that continuously frame the contour – and consequently the built form – at all vertical levels are the floor slabs.

The idea of making the logic of the system visually apparent was pursued comprehensively by Bunshaft. The precast concrete slabs were painted white and the cast-in-place elements were treated with rough finishes, highlighting the differences in casting and the nature of the fabrication of the structural parts. The cast-in-place reinforced concrete portal frames were covered with a warm, light gray granite aggregate, exposed by sandblasting. The precise finishing of the exposed structural elements is sufficiently refined to give the building a luxurious and sophisticated appearance and leave all the formal protagonism for the built structural system.

The Architect's House

1961-1963. Long Island, New York

In the early 1960s, Gordon and Nina Bunshaft lived in the Manhattan House, a building designed by the architect himself and his team at SOM between 1947 and 1950. The Manhattan House apartment, renovated by Bunshaft in the mid-1960s, prefigures certain design strategies and personal preferences that years later would be reflected in the house he designed and built between 1961 and 1963 for himself and his wife in Long Island, New York.

The 2,594 sq ft. (241 m2) rectangular house is structured by means of two large lateral walls and 19 concrete roof slabs. Both the shape and the dimensions of the latter guided the conception of the house and the arrangement of the other integral elements.

Until its completion, no other building by Bunshaft or SOM had been erected with prefabricated horizontal structures. The use of industrial concrete elements in his own house, where the architect applied all his design skills to subsequently house his prized and valuable collection of modern art and furniture, evidences a personal commitment to the material; a fact ratified throughout the sixties and early seventies in the headquarters for the American Republic Insurance Company and the American Can Company.

Gordon and Nina Bunshaft's apartment at the Manhattan House

In 1950, the Manhattan House apartment building, designed by Gordon Bunshaft in association with architects Mayer & Whittlesey, was completed. The building was the tallest and longest reinforced concrete-framed building in New York; the cast-in-place flat slabs provided column-free spaces for the 22' x 25' (6 x 7.6 m) living rooms, which were unusually large at the time. That same year Gordon and Nina moved into one of the apartments in the building. Some of the architect's personal photos indicate that in 1954 the couple moved to another apartment in the building, number C-903, located on the ninth floor.[70]

In 1956 the architect carried out a major renovation of his apartment. The project included the relocation of some installations, the lighting system, certain pieces of furniture and some finishings. The modifications took place

On the left:

View of the south façade of Gordon and Nina Bunshaft's house.

Gordon and Nina in the office of his Manhattan House apartment in 1968.

mainly in the first bedroom (converted into a study), the kitchen and the dining room adjoining the living room. The renovation foreshadowed some of the important project aspects conceived in the East Hampton house, completed almost eight years later.

Analyzing the plans produced for the renovation and the photos of the finished apartment, it is possible to recognize the prominence the Bunshafts gave to the display of their art collection in the home, primarily in the living spaces.[71]

Bunshaft took special care with the lighting. Two focal points of interest were bathed in light with specially designed lamps. The doorless half of the wall dividing the living-dining room from the bedrooms, positioned in front of the windows of the space, was bathed in indirect light spilled by a white linear luminaire with fluorescent lamps placed inside a channeled reflector. The five-module fixture was recessed between a beam and the wall. The lower part was completed with one of the two sideboards designed by the architect for the space, made with a stainless-steel structure, wooden panels with black high-gloss Formica and a white marble top. For the dining table, Bunshaft designed a linear lamp with a rectangular section in white painted aluminum and 3' 4" long (1 m).

Floor plan of the renovation project for Gordon and Nina Bunshaft's apartment in the Manhattan House building.

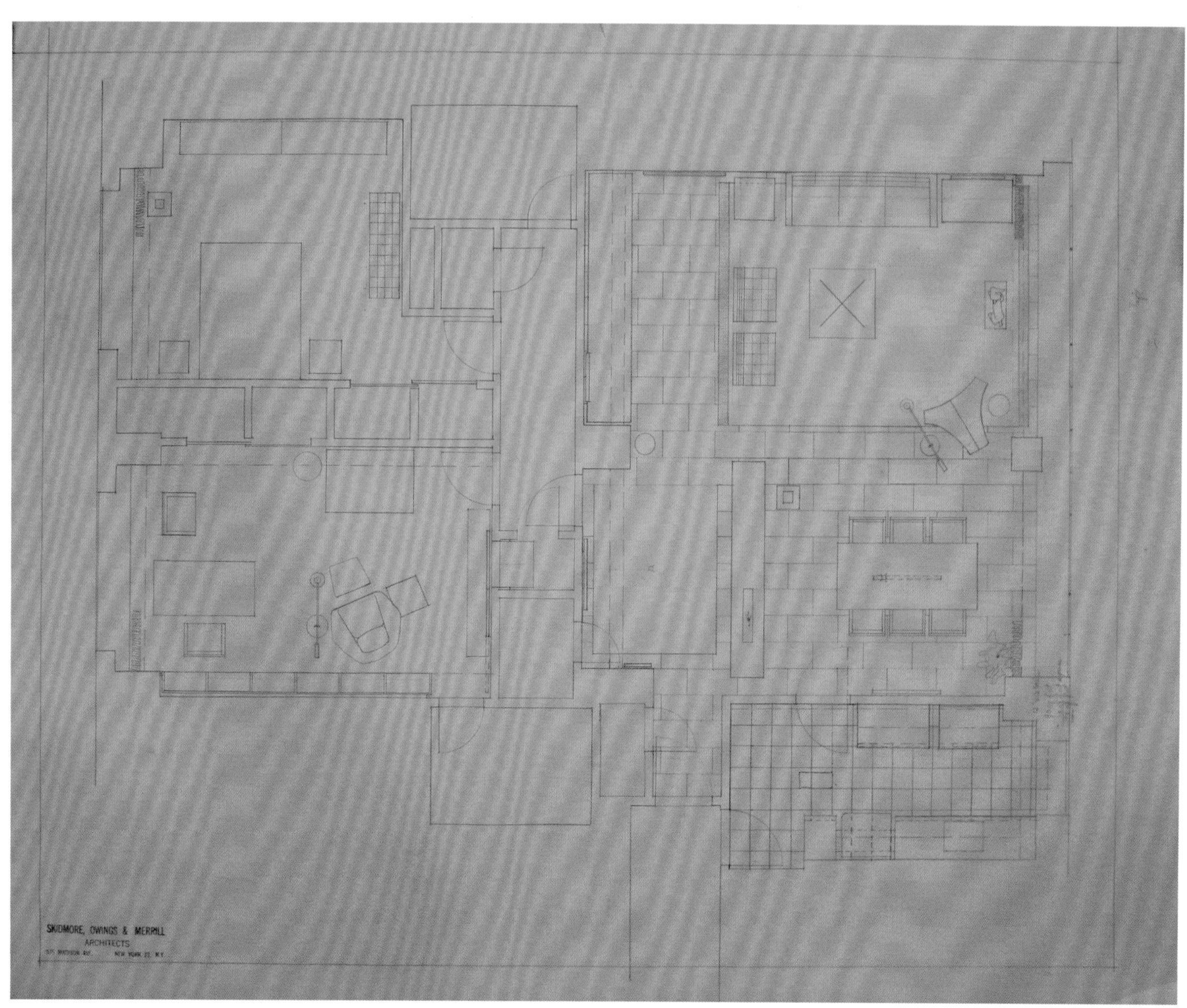

On the left:

View of Manhattan House apartment, southwest façade, from East 65th Street.

Photo by author, 2010.

Gordon and Nina's bedroom in their Manhattan House apartment.

On the right:

The living room in Gordon and Nina's Manhattan House apartment.

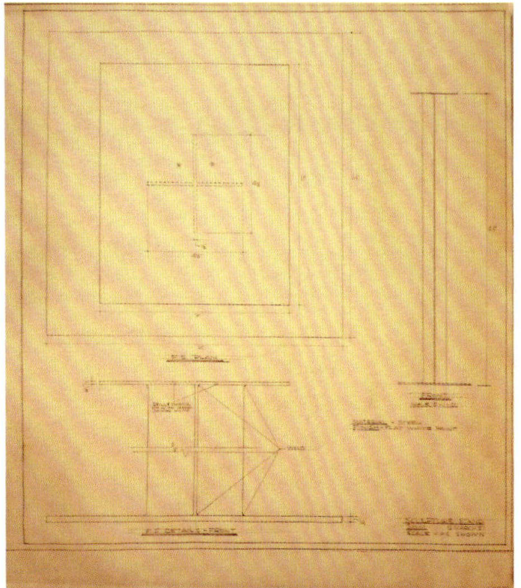

Detail of a sculpture stand designed by Gordon Bunshaft for his Manhattan House apartment.

The furniture organized the spaces and, together with the lighting, helped to define the placement of paintings, tapestry and sculptures. Another sideboard, with similar textures to the one just described, defined a circulatory axis between the dining room table and the back wall at a distance of 5' (1.5 m). Being of medium height, approximately 2' 4 1/2" (72 cm), it allowed the sensation of spatial amplitude to be maintained, serving as a support for sculptures.

For works of this type, Bunshaft designed a kind of pedestal in white painted steel, of which more than one unit was made for the studio, the living room and his bedroom in the apartment. These elements, together with all the other furniture, clearly demonstrate the architect's attention to design and his fascination with furniture design, which was present since he was a young architect.

All these built elements were part of some spatial arrangement strategies that were then repeated in the house built in East Hampton. More than verifying the coincidences that occurred in both projects, the recognition of the formal attributes of the Manhattan apartment gives clues to the conception of the house, for which the supporting structure and the prefabricated roof elements are fundamental.

Location plan of Nina and Gordon Bunshaft's house in East Hampton, New York (drawing attributed to a Bunshaft collaborator).

The roof of the buildings are represented in light beige. At the bottom, the studio; to the right, the garage.

The House of Mr. and Mrs. Bunshaft

The site where the house was built is located in a residential development in the small coastal town of East Hampton, Long Island, approximately 93 mi (150 km) from New York. The house occupies the center of the site; obviously this positioning was due to a direct relationship with the visual and solar orientation. The building can be described as a prism with a rectangular base measuring 95' x 26'4" (29 x 8.12 m), in which the two longest walls support the roof, which is formed by double "tee" slabs in precast concrete.

The area is quiet and economically valued, being occupied by mansions and large summer houses. The plot is approximately two acres (8,000 m^2) and trapezoidal in shape. The surrounding nature is rich, with many trees and native vegetation. The Georgica Pond, on the southern boundary of the site, enhances the site even more. From the center of the area, it is possible to have an almost 180 degree view of the water. The ground level in this portion had to be raised approximately 6' (1.8 m) prior to the construction of the house due to the advancing waters at certain times of the year.

The site and the executive drawings

In the 1960s, the Bunshaft residence became quite well known in various publications. In all of them the only building shown was the house. But the property included other spaces and built elements of interest. In addition to the house, the project contemplated the construction of a garage and also the design of most of the surrounding vegetation, access pavements and road for car traffic.

Through the executive plans made by Bunshaft it is possible to discover different interventions on the site throughout the sixties and seventies. The first drawings for the house are dated June 1, 1962. The first version consists of a set of 10 plans, in which all the building components are specified in detail.[72]

The landscaping project provided for the ground levels to be respected and those areas that would need to be filled in. Likewise, it indicated the areas where the previous vegetation and trees were to be maintained and where new trees and shrubs were to be planted.

Framing the front entrance to the house, Bunshaft designed a line of vegetation as a barrier 3' (90 cm) deep and 5' (1.5 m) high. It was composed of two rows of shrubs randomly placed. Using the same resource, an enclosure was also configured to visually protect the western portion of the adjoining lot, creating a sort of natural courtyard adjacent to Nina's studio

Gordon Bunshaft's architect stamp.

View of the Bunshaft studio from the south.

and guest room. The eastern part had no shutters on the windows, probably because the lot in that part ends at Georgica Pond. That last aspect must have been, with the solar orientation, fundamental to the choice of that end for the location of the couple's room.

In addition to the changes shown on the site plan, there is a plan for the garage extension dated January 19, 1970. The drawings indicate that Bunshaft added a carport to the existing one and also a storage room. The structure had load-bearing walls of concrete blocks clad with plywood. The last modifications made between January and May 1976 involved the construction of a studio on the eastern portion of the site. For the work,

Bunshaft produced a set of 10 plans. The studio had a nearly square floor plan measuring 28' x 26' (8.5 x 7.9 m) and a timber frame structure; plywood clad the building internally and externally. The floor and roof slabs were made of wood beams and joists.

It is interesting to note from the executive plans that, although the house itself and the other buildings in the complex were made of top-quality materials, such as travertine marble cladding brought from Italy, the drawings are austere and the construction techniques used were simple and conventional.

Bunshaft studio interior.

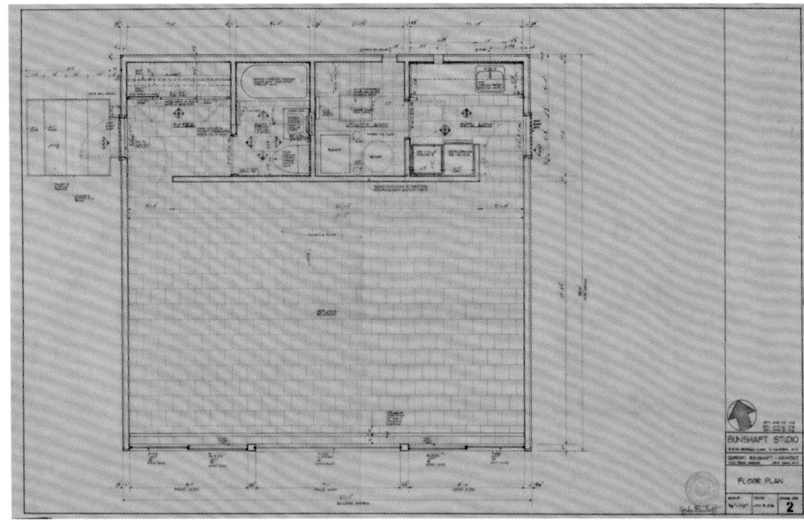

Bunshaft studio plant.

Double "tee" slabs on walls and beams

The structure of the house can be summarized as follows: two parallel 14" (35.5 cm) thick and 95' (29 m) long walls made of concrete block masonry standing 23" 12' (7.3 m) apart on which rest a roof formed by two pre-cast concrete beams and 19 precast concrete double "tee" slabs.

The configuration generated some interesting design possibilities. The center of the floor could be totally freed up because the vertical supports were the lateral peripheral walls. The absence of internal vertical supports was made possible by the adoption of double "tee" slabs for the roof. Bunshaft arranged the two intimate spaces at the ends and the main space of the house – the living room – in the center of the plan. In between these three spaces were service cores, with bathrooms, kitchen, storerooms and heating machine room. The master bedroom was on the east side. Guest room and an adjoining room used as Nina's painting studio was facing west.

It is an obvious, though still remarkable fact, that the project was conceived without any pressure or conditioning from industrialists, clients or other colleagues. After building some impressive works in steel, the architect had the opportunity of erecting his own Bunshaft house and, in the end, chose to do it by exploiting precast concrete elements.

Some of Bunshaft's works completed after the house, notably the American Republic Insurance Company and the American Can Company, confirm the architect's confidence in prefabricated elements, and demonstrate his skill in the use of the material and the structural systems that allow them to be put in place.

The constructive module

The structure also played a decisive role in the physical and visual integration of the interior and the exterior. The beams were placed along the entire length of the building, making it possible to remove the sections of the exterior wall that were of interest. In that way, both the bedrooms and the living room opened up to the surrounding open space – the lawn, trees and Georgica Pond.

Bunshaft also used the floor slabs as a basis for stipulating a basic constructive module for the work, and its dimensions were to be multiplied throughout the entire building. This decision defined the arrangement of the other elements and influenced technically and aesthetically, that is, concretely and abstractly, the final result. To better understand these ideas, it is necessary to precisely define the measurements of this key element. Each slab had overall dimensions of 26' 4" x 4' 12" (8.02 x 1.52 m) in plan. In

View from the front gate to the Bunshaft house lot in East Hampton.

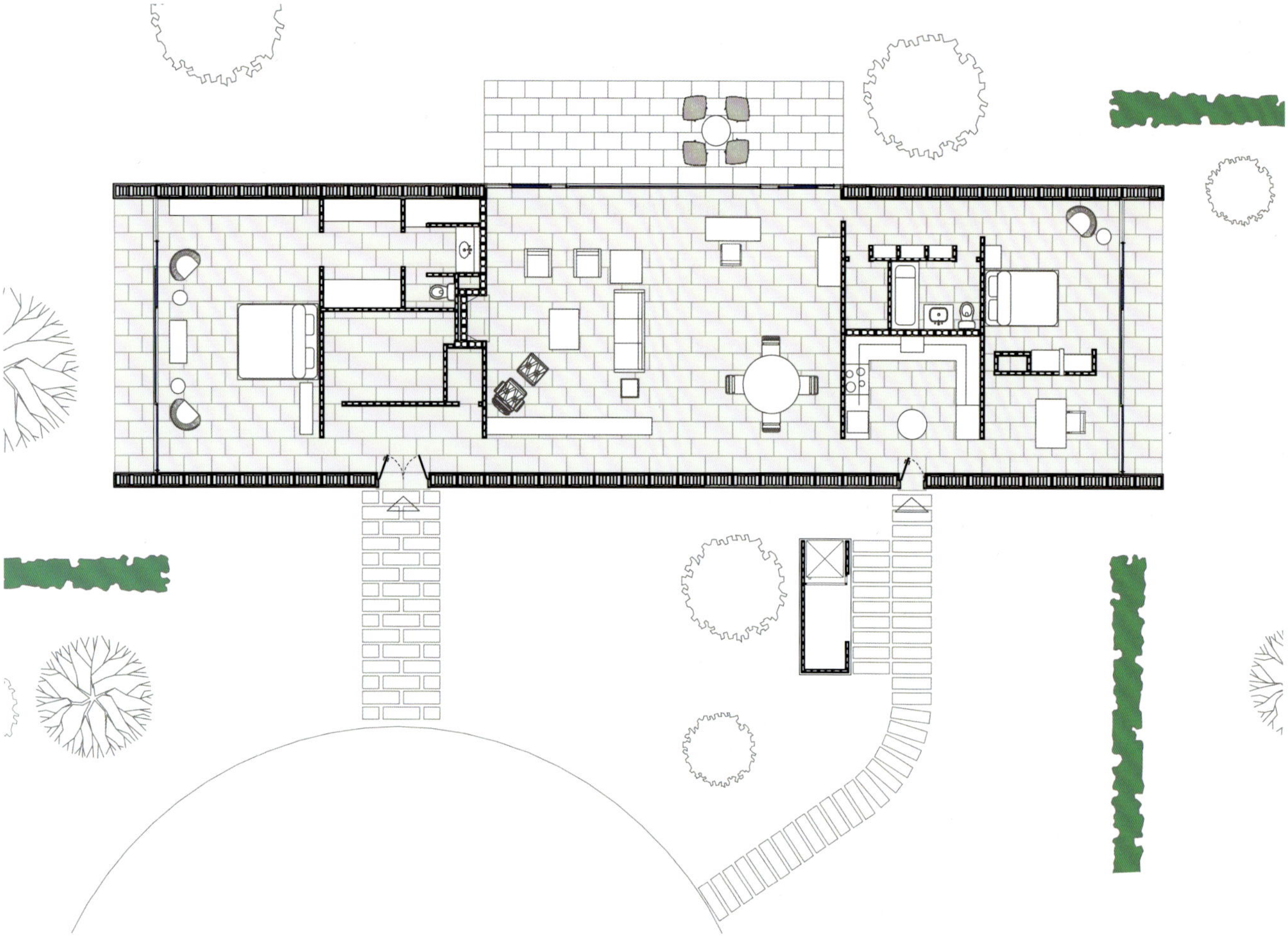

Ground Floor

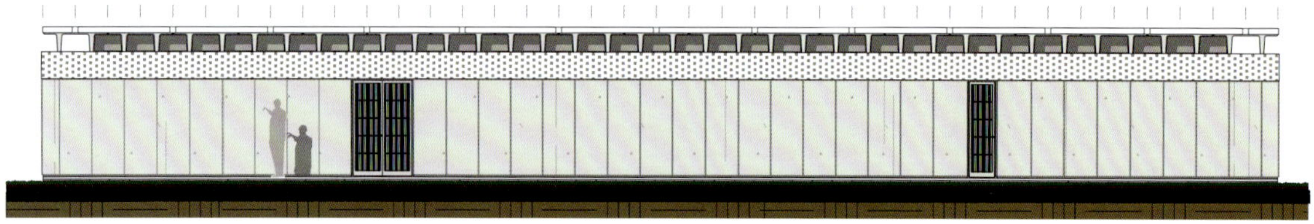

North Elevation

SCALE 1/200

section, the dimensions were 26' 4" (152 cm) wide by 1' 5" (42.5 cm) high. The distance between the webs was 2' 6" (76.2 cm) and the thickness of the upper flange was 2" (5 cm).

The basic construction module appears to be rectangular in shape. In the long dimension of the plan, it corresponds to the distance between the slab cores, which is 18" (76.2 cm), and runs from side to side of the building. On the short side, it is somewhat different. The side walls correspond to two free-standing strips, each measuring 14" (35.6 cm). Between them, other guidelines are established in which the modular lines are spaced 18" (45.7 cm) apart. This intramural modulation is reflected in the floor tiles. The standard size of these elements is 30" x 18" (76.2 x 45.7 cm), at a ratio of 1 to 2/3.

The systematic repetition of the basic module generates guidelines or regulatory grids, which permits clear visual relationships. One of the most direct dimensional and proportional correspondences is noted between the quartering of the travertine floor tiles and the webs of the double "tee" slabs. The measurements of the stones placed at the joint-breaker are exactly the dimensions of the basic module. The other elements placed inside the residence also follow this rule. The internal partitions were placed just below the webs, and the vertical mullions of the glazed doors coincide with these master elements. The travertine veneer panels that cover the external walls follow the same rule. Each of these elements is 30" (76.2 cm) wide; the joints between them coincide with the webs of the roof slabs.

Despite the rigor of the established system of constructive and visual order there were some variations generated by some functional demands internal to the project. The previously established rules that could impair the proper functioning of the building and its components were not taken to an extreme.

The external walls and their openings, both on the north and south façades, have measurements that correspond to the stipulated dimensional module and were all clad with the same travertine marble cladding. Even so, the elevations do not have symmetrical openings or regular repetitions; their arrangement on the façades clearly obey the distribution of the interior spaces and their demands.

From the outside, the visual unity and balance perceived in the building was due to the upper structural elements – the beams and roof slabs.

The south facade of the Bunshaft house. *Tall Figure III*, by Alberto Giacometti, and, in the background, *Seated Figure with a Slender Neck*, by Henry Moore.

Georgica Pond, seen from the living room of the house.

The east façade of the Bunshaft house and the sculpture *Animal Form* by Henry Moore (Roman travertine, 1969-70) in the foregroud.

Free-standing internal areas

It is important to note that in the interior, the criteria for the treatment of the wall surfaces were different from those applied to the façades. Internally, the finishes were adopted according to functional and aesthetic criteria established expressly for interior spaces. The roof beams are a good example of this idea.

The design and molding of these prefabricated and prestressed elements also contemplate these aspects. At the ends of the two beams, where they are fully exposed to the exterior, their widths are 14" (35.5 cm). The same situation occurs in the central portion of the beam on the south façade, which is over the glazed window and sliding door of the living room. In all the other parts of both beams, that is, in the sections that are on opaque panels of the side walls, their widths are 12" (30.5 cm). The external faces of the beams are completely regular.

Their external faces were only painted white. Their inner faces (the sections where the width of the beams was 30.5 cm) were covered next to the side walls with plaster cladding applied to the entire height from the floor to the lower face of the double "tee" slabs. The 5 cm subtractions made on the interior faces of the beams allowed the plaster cladding to fit perfectly into them, being flush with the 35.5 cm of the wider beam sections. These details are explained by the fact that the Bunshafts were collectors of works of art and the house was designed to have large free wall surfaces for the placement of tapestries and paintings.

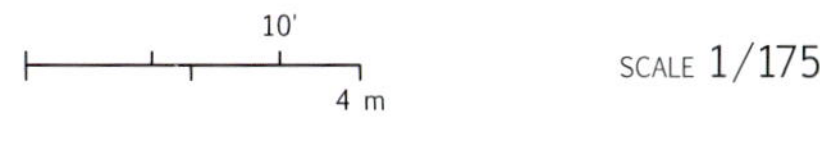

SCALE 1/175

East Elevation

South Elevation

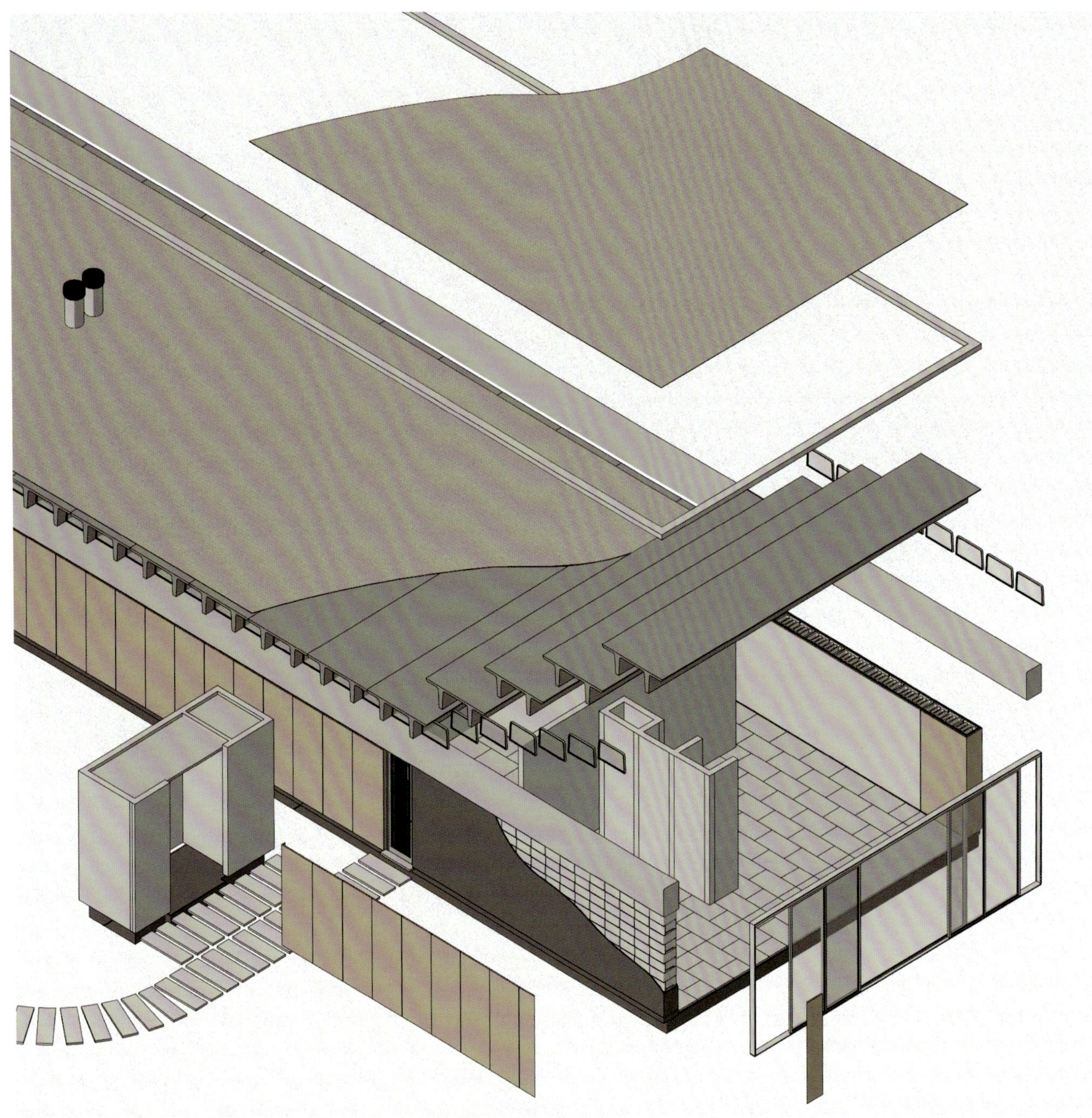

From time to time, the works in his Manhattan apartment were exchanged with those in the East Hampton residence. The white walls and travertine marble floor tiles endowed the space with a sobriety that enhanced the exposed works of art, helping to ensure that works with different nuances did not weigh down or visually conflict with each other in the room.

Another aspect that increased the degree of abstraction in the appreciation of the built space was the absence of doors in almost all the rooms. Except for works of art and pieces of furniture, the immobile spatial limits perceived by the eye are the roof slabs, the partition walls and the travertine floor cladding. In short, the constructive elements of the house played the role of configuring exempt background planes.

Regarding the roof, it is still possible to perceive that the uniform repetition of the slab cores, which were reiterated along the largest dimension of the floor plan, positively reduced the sensation of spatial depth and unified the adjacent rooms of the house from above. The space between their cores and the beams that supported them were covered with glass, creating appealing upper windows. The lighting effect achieved with these openings was very interesting. If on the one hand it allowed the daylight to bathe the rooms of the house, on the other hand it allowed the interior light to be diffused at night, framing the interior edges of the roof slab.

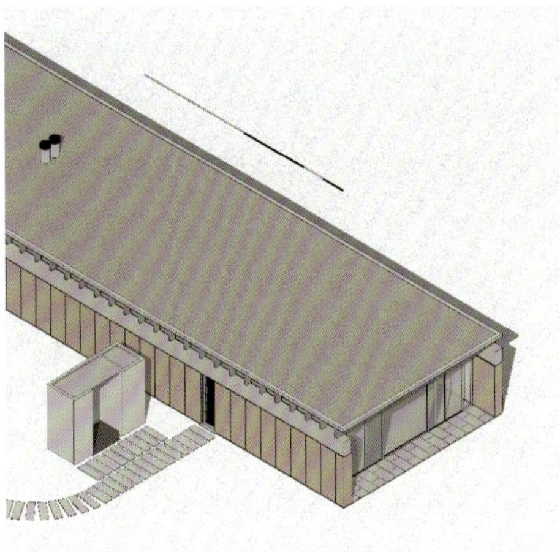

Complete axonometric drawing of the Bunshaft house.

Drawing by the author, 2008.

On the right:

The west façade, where the master bedroom was located.

On the left:

Exploded axonometric drawing of the Bunshaft house.

Drawing by the author, 2008.

Hidden installations

The achievement of the spatial qualities mentioned above was linked to some technical and constructive resources, and to the coordination between the different systems operating simultaneously in the building. Bunshaft's decision to preserve the internal and external surfaces from any and all visual influences other than the fundamental formal elements forced him to devise unconventional solutions to resolve the accommodation of the installations; the air conditioning and electrical ducts had to be specially positioned.

In order for all the systems to work together, it was necessary to pass the ducts and conduits under the floor of the house. This condition was also due to the architect's decision to keep the floor slabs free of visual interference. The electrical conduits passed through conduits embedded in the floor, placed between the floor tiles and the concrete slab. With respect to the ceilings, the conduits that carried the cables to the light fixtures passed over the roof, passing into spaces through holes previously made in the double "tees".

Along the central sections of the four façades of the house there were linear grilles to insufflate conditioned air. There was a radiant floor system, acclimatizing the house in the harsh winter days with snow in the region. The travertine tiling was perfectly suited for this use. The small room adjacent to the main entrance and the bathroom of the suite was intended to house the heating system machines. A small building measuring 4' 8" x 11' 7" (1.4 x 3.5 m) in plan and 6' 2" (1.9 m) in height, separated by 1.4 m (4' 7") from the north façade, housed the air conditioning generator and a storage cubicle.

10'

4 m

SCALE 1/175

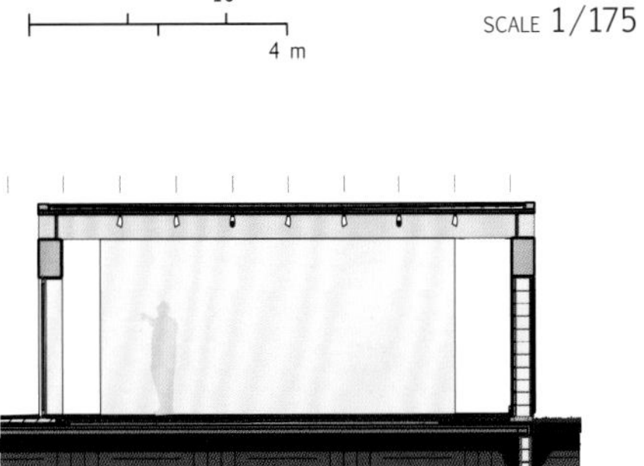

East-West Section

North-South Section

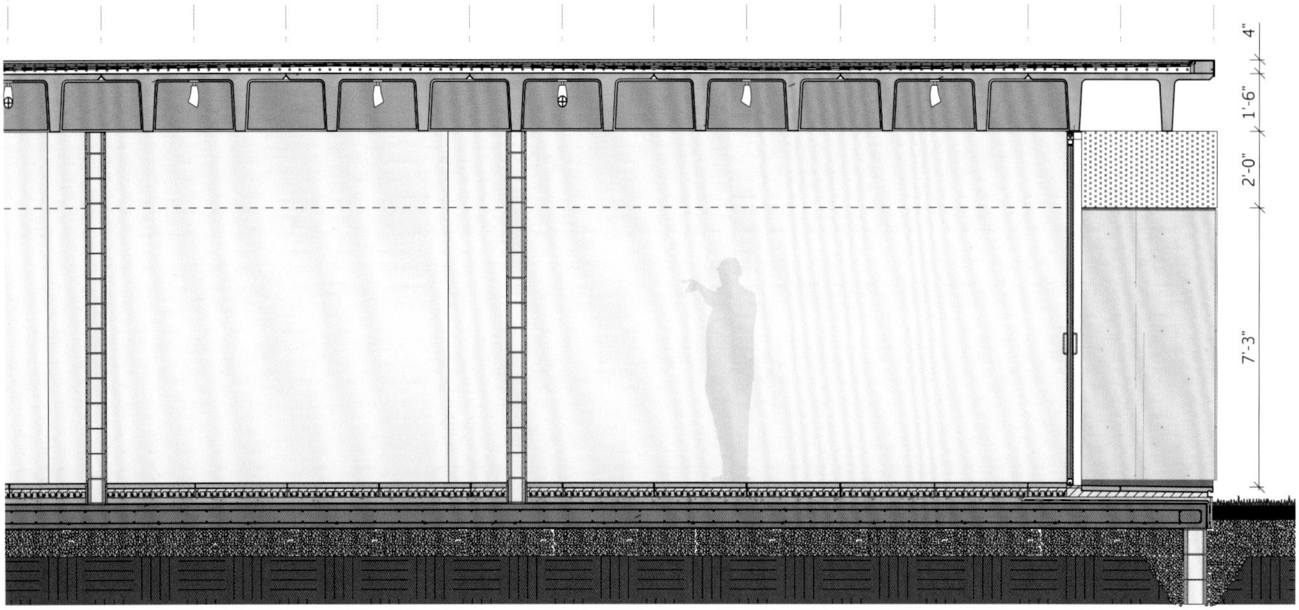

4"
1'-6"
2'-0"
7'-3"

North-South Section

East-West Section

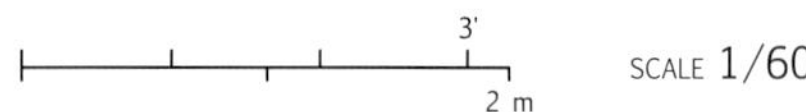

SCALE 1/60

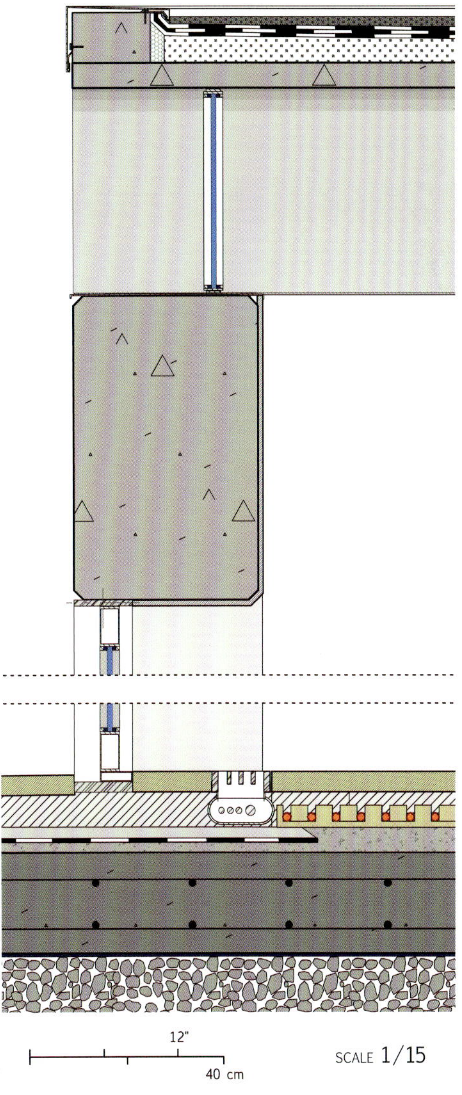

Detail of the west façade.

Drawing by the author, 2008.

On the right:

Travertine wall of the south façade. In the background *Moonbird*, by Joan Miró (2/5 bronze copy, 1966-1967).

North Façade

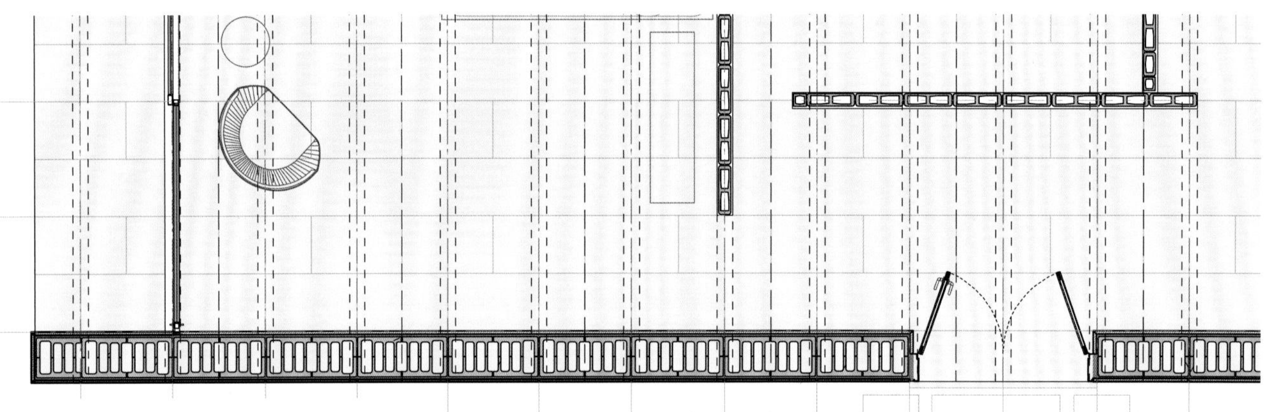

Detailed Plant

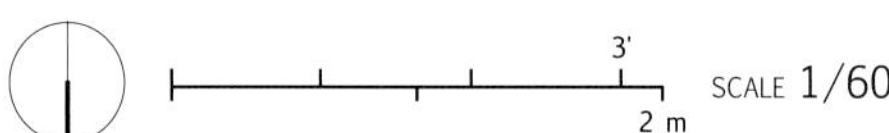

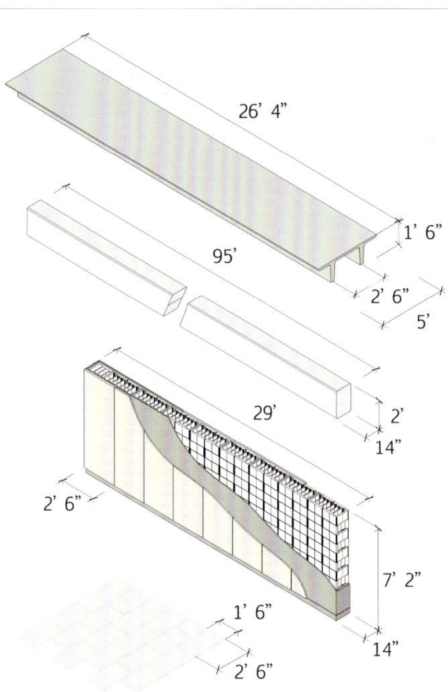

Structural components of the Bunshaft house.

Drawing by the author, 2008.

On the right:

The main entrance of the Bunshaft house.

The dining and living room: the main space of the house. The painting on the back wall is an acrylic on canvas by Helen Frankenthaler, titled *President of the Council* (1971). Silhouetted in front of it are, on the left, a bronze *Reclining Figure* by Henry Moore (1961) and on the right an Egyptian-Roman votive statue in black granite (1-11th century CE). And next to the glazed window, stands a work by Jean Dubuffet, *Amoucellement au Pain* (epoxy resin painted vinyl, 1968).

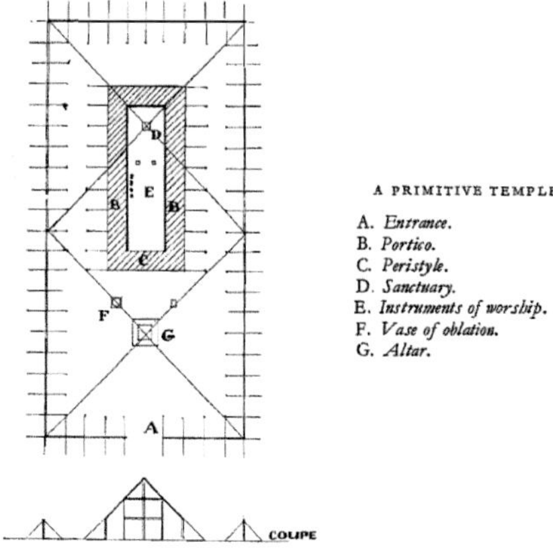

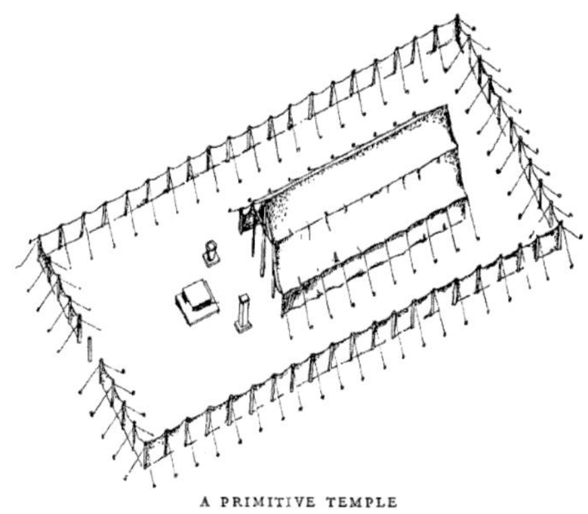

The primitive temple, by Le Corbusier.

Regulating Lines

In *Towards an Architecture*, in the chapter entitled "Regulating Lines", Le Corbusier explains some fundamental concepts of order using the description of a primitive tent placement in the jungle as a first example. In the midst of a supposed irregularity of nature, the members of a primitive tribe open a hole in the jungle and build their hut, whose plan has clear forms and is governed by simple mathematics. Referring to the primitive man, builder of the tent, and the way he acts:

> *In order to construct well and distribute his efforts to advantage, to obtain solidity and utility in the work, he has taken measures, he has adopted a unit of measurement, he has regulated his work, he has brought in order. For, all around him, the forest is in disorder with its creepers, its briars and the tree-trunks which impede him and paralyze his efforts.*
>
> *He has imposed order by means of measurement. In order to get his measurement, he has taken his pace, his foot, his elbow or his finger. [...] A unit gives measure and unity; a regulating line is a basis of construction and satisfaction.*[73]

The metaphor described above highlights the importance of the establishment of precise rules and their fundamental role when applied to construction, being the main strategy for the mastery of a place or situation.

The reference seems quite pertinent in relation to the East Hampton house. The executive plan number five produced for the construction of the house may serve as an example for that idea to be clarified. Entitled "roof slab plan with lighting layout," the plan consists of a roof plan with top views and elevations of the two beams drawn with a continuous black line; in thick blue dotted lines are drawn the projections of the interior partitions and side walls of the house.[74]

What can be observed is the correspondence between the internal spatial divisions and the webs of the prefabricated floor slabs. As previously stated, the design of the surrounding spaces was also guided by the continuity of the alignments corresponding to the floor slabs; these master lines correspond to the tensors that would support the primitive cabin sketched by Le Corbusier.

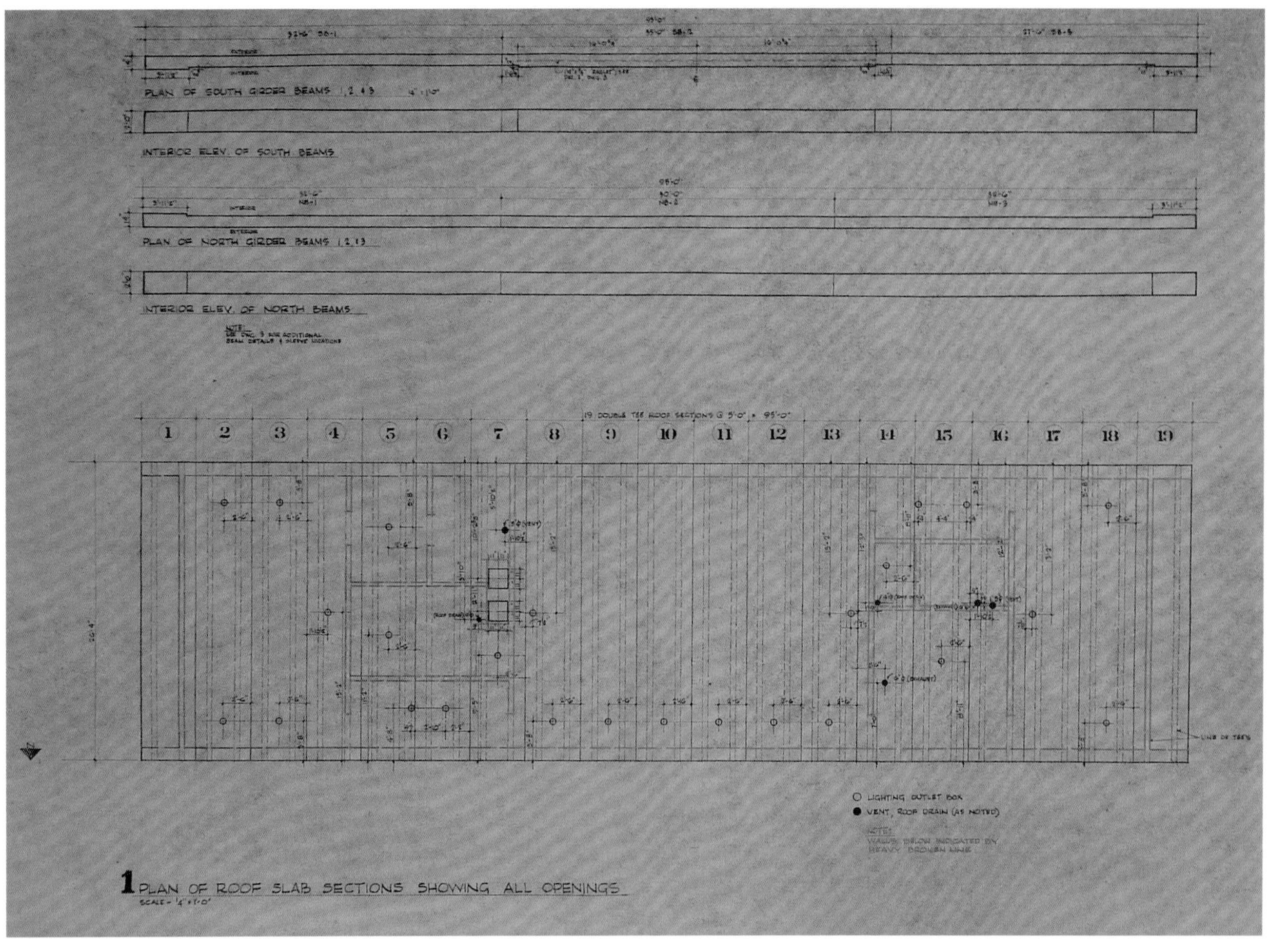

The executive plan of number 5, made for the construction of the Bunshaft house.

Gordon and Nina enjoying the living room of their East Hampton home.

The guidelines are not only adapted to the construction, but also to the establishment of previously studied perspectives that allow us to appreciate the whole elements under the same formal order: landscaping elements, the Georgica Pond, the works of art inside and outside the house and obviously the supporting structure. The “rules,” as in a game, must be clear enough so that individuals can recognize them through their own eyes and reflection. Only in this way does architecture fulfill its role as a work of art.

Epilogue: Form and Tectonicity

The American Can Company.

Photo by author, 2010.

The Work of the Architect

Gordon Bunshaft's career demonstrates that his professional profile hung on two basic functions: designing buildings and managing the fundamental decisions of a team dedicated to solving large architectural commissions. His temperament and objectivity in directing efforts toward specific goals earned him a place of prominence in the firm and with his professional environment. His prestige in New York society, and throughout the US, was not the result of his sales ability or good relations with important figures in New York society, but rather of his skills as a designer, which, together with his great leadership ability, opened up a wide range of work possibilities. In addition, the triad of SOM's work practice – modern architecture, American organizational methods, and the mastery and development of available industrialized construction techniques and materials – fully supported him.

Outside of the firm, Bunshaft sought out a few more allies to make his architectural ideas viable. After the Connecticut General Insurance Company headquarters project, the architect recognized the desirability of early coordination between architects and engineers. Undoubtedly, the most fruitful and long-lasting collaboration was with engineer Paul Weidlinger. Regarding this relationship, which grew closer after the completion of the project for Connecticut General, Bunshaft stated:

> *We knew we could do all sorts of things with concrete, [...] but we needed education. As soon as we got some rough ideas, the senior designer and Paul [Weidlinger] and I – mostly Paul and I – would get together. Sometimes Paul would say, 'You can't do this,' but he never made design suggestions.*[75]

Throughout the 1960s, Weidlinger contributed to Bunshaft and the New York's office skillful use of precast concrete. The engineer's work was important in ensuring that these buildings had a good assembly of the different construction elements and a perfect match between the formal structure conceived and the construction process adopted.

This condition is objectively explained in the May 1962 *Architectural Record* article entitled "Precast Apartment Structure Saves Cost, Shows Its Design" – which featured an apartment building designed by architect Tasso Katselas and engineer R. M. Gensert, the latter being the author of the ar-

ticle: “How to join precast elements efficiently is a difficult problem for the engineer. How to join them in a way that makes sense spatially and visually is a difficult problem for the architect.”[76]

Regarding Bunshaft’s projects, his recognition of the importance of technique for architecture, combined with the great team of advisors he had inside and outside SOM, ensured the resolution of the two just mentioned problems.

The large second-floor space at the American Republic Insurance Company. The spatiality achieved reflects the architect’s efforts to reconcile technique and form.

Photo by author, 2010.

The Building Parts

Among the six structural types composed of precast concrete elements identified by A. E. J. Morris, Gordon Bunshaft used two in his works. In fact, the English architect and scholar credits Bunshaft and his team with the development of one of them: external structural screens for building façades. The other, which Morris called columns and beams and roof "tees", also ended up being technically and formally exploited by Bunshaft, proving rather more fruitful than might be suggested in the early engineering employment of this type. The external structural screens, in this study called perimeter supporting frames, were embodied in the buildings for the John Hancock Company, New Orleans, and for the Lambert Bank in Brussels. In these two buildings, the vertical components of the structure were prefabricated, while the floor slabs – the horizontal components – were cast-in-place.

In the buildings for the American Can Company and the American Republic Company, the logic is reversed: the floor slabs - horizontal components - were assembled with precast concrete slabs and the vertical supports were cast in situ. Either way, it is possible to affirm that for Bunshaft projects, the casting-in-place of the concrete elements was essential for the works using precast systems. In this case, the architect masters the technique, puts it at his service and exposes the applied structural logic.

> *The architecture is serving the needs of the people who use the building. And [it does] something else, which is to take the materials and explore and exploit them to their fullest expression. A bold idea that, coupled with precision, care and thoughtfulness, makes a good building.*[77]

The use of pieces brought from the factory sought to benefit the projects economically and formally. Depending on the characteristics of the commission, the use of these elements was given in one way or another. The fact that their use was partial within the totality of the structural systems did not mean that they had no formal or constructive relevance in the whole.

By not totally prefabricating the structure, the architect transforms industrial prefabricated units and cast-in-place elements into complementary structural entities. In certain buildings, the set of prefabricated parts resolves the vertical structuring, while the cast-in-place elements account for the horizontal structuring. For other buildings, the logic is the reverse. In addition to the evident coordination, a coherent functional definition is perceived between one and the other type of elements.

Technique and Location

In the works studied, the use of precast concrete elements entailed certain design criteria related to the site where the buildings were constructed. Even the choice of the type of piece, which could be of different dimensions, anchoring characteristics, etc., were defined according to these conditions.

From a technical point of view, the weight and large dimensions of the precast units demanded transportation and assembly requirements, and it was necessary to adapt their design to the sites so that the construction work could be carried out correctly.

The American Can building and the Lambert Bank exemplify these ideas. The former has more than 700 large precast floor slabs 60' (18.3 m) long, which are distributed in the center of the 70.8 hectares (175 acres) site located on the outskirts of Greenwich. The second is integrated into the old town of Brussels and consists of 10' 10" (3.30 m) high and 4' 4" (1.33 m) long precast units. In both cases the assembly and design of the pieces matches the location of the ensembles.

From a formal point of view, the construction with prefabricated units implies the construction of buildings with certain visual characteristics specific to the material. The vertical structures placed on the perimeter form buildings with homogeneous façades; the horizontal structures are visible from the outside in their full height, which is sometimes equivalent to one third of the free height of its interior space. The podiums or bases adapt the built complex to its urban limits, and the main volume is placed in the best position under functional, formal and bioclimatic criteria.

In both cases, the considerable thickness of the parts that make up the prefabricated units adds considerable visual weight to the assemblies, making them better suited to clear sites, where they can be viewed from a distance from the outside. On relatively small plots, the architect creates these conditions by setting the built volume back from the perimeter, thus establishing a certain distance from the surrounding roads. The podium or base adapts the building complex to its urban limits; and on them, the main volume is placed in the best position according to functional, formal and bioclimatic criteria.

On the left:

The Manhattan House.

Photo by author, 2010.

Externally, the situation is reversed. In buildings with perimeter supporting frames, the expression of the precast elements is visually extreme from the outside. The structural units are spaced at a distance equal to that of the construction module, and the established perimeter frame directly reflects in three dimensions the arrangement stipulated for the entire building. In the works composed of "tees" or double "tee" units, the floor slabs appear to the outside in their full height and length but do not define the built volume integrally, with it being the glazed windows that expose the living spaces perceived from the outside.

The delicate façade texture of the Beinecke Library, which is nothing more than the vertical supporting structure of the building.

Photo by author, 2010.

Expression of the Constructive Logic

Tectonic considerations can be identified in different architectural attributes of Bunshaft's work with industrialized structures.

Generally, one can identify in his work an elementary project strategy linked to the use of the dimensions and proportions coming from the supporting structure. The architect arranges the totality of his projects through the use of strict modulations. In the case of the works studied, this criterion takes on even greater importance. For office buildings, workspace arrangement modules are fundamental, and the architect's skill lies in reconciling the dimensions of these modules with the standard dimensions of the supporting elements or the structural spans to which they will be subjected.

In buildings with unidirectional slabs on walls or beams, the architect chooses a previously designed element (basically the profile of that element and the span it saves) with which he wants to work, and develops the project, taking its qualities and predispositions of use as conditioning factors. In the case of the building for the American Can Company and also in his house in East Hampton, Bunshaft organized the systems and component subsystems, taking as a module the distance between consecutive webs of the precast slabs. In buildings with perimeter supporting frames, the approach to the problem is somewhat different. The architect defines the basic interior distribution module that he deems most appropriate and, after discussing the general structural conditions, defines the design and basic dimensions of the parts, and then orders their fabrication.

In both cases, the dimensions of the structural modules organize all the elements and systems, and visually guide the interior and exterior parts of the buildings.

Internally, in buildings composed of "tee" or double "tee" slabs, the tectonic aspects of the horizontal structure are extreme. The lower faces of the slabs are fully exposed, and their webs present a pattern and frame a rhythm throughout the length and width of all the spaces. They also contain and arrange the elements of the lighting, heating, air conditioning and partitioning systems. In buildings with perimeter supporting frames, the expression of the structure in the interiors is not so evident, but it also happens. The floor slabs are cast in situ and are covered with false ceilings, which are manufactured with dimensions equivalent to those of the basic module. The internal partition walls and the glazed façade dimensions are also consistent with the general modulation.

Joints, Finishes and Unit Volumetry

The design of the pieces, the way they are joined and the finishes used on them also denote the tectonic characteristics of the architect's work.

Structural engineer Paul Weidlinger thought that the supporting elements he designed in collaboration with SOM should express the flow of stress through the buildings. These elements could be ground-floor columns, such as those found in the Beinecke Library; load-bearing walls, as with the American Republic Company; or precast units for perimeter supporting frames. The case of the precast crosses of the Lambert Bank serves well to explain this condition. The section of the vertical members tapers toward the upper and lower extremities. According to engineer Weidlinger, the "tapering" of the members helps to reduce the abruptness of the internal stress change produced by bending moment variations. The design solves three distinctive problems: constructively, meaning economy of material in the manufacture of the parts and optimum structural performance; from a business point of view, by way of giving each building an exclusive character and a unique solution; and formally, in lightening the visual weight of the structure, allowing for its multiplication along the length and height of the façades to be elegant, thereby designing a delicate three-dimensional frame.

Linkages between structural elements, whether prefabricated or cast-in-place, also play an important role. The crosses of the perimeter supporting framework of the Lambert Bank are joined with stainless steel connectors. In the same building, connectors were also placed on the ground-floor columns as capitals, joining them to the transfer beams which they support. The solution was implemented in buildings with other types of structural elements, but with the same formal and constructive logics. In the case of the Beinecke Library, there are connectors between the four large columns and the set of four steel Viereendel beams that form the façades. In the case of the American Republic building, there are large steel connectors on each of the eight large ground-floor columns that transmit the loads coming from the two lateral structural walls.

In all these cases, the function of the metal parts is the same: to show the transition between different levels of vertical structures, accentuating the conceived structural logic; to lighten the visual weight of the structure, making it more elegant; to help reinforce the tops of the columns against compressive stresses; and to stiffen the nodes between structural elements against horizontal stress.

On the left:

Detail of the joint between one of the side walls of the American Republic Insurance Company and the prestressed floor slabs.

Photo by author, 2010.

The design of the structure influences and is influenced by the other constituent subsystems; the tectonic aspect also depends on the installation systems and its routing. The latter thus acquires special significance, and requires more compromises when designing, incorporating more themes and variants into the architecture. In the case of buildings with precast horizontal structures, the air conditioning ducts are concealed and run vertically and, together with the floor slabs, take on visual prominence as they are exposed in the form of tubes within the work spaces. The architect makes an effort to establish more relationships, to arrange what is hidden and what is shown, handling new formal alternatives.

Finally, the finishes also manifest the tectonic aspects of the structural systems. In both the American Can and the American Republic buildings, the precast concrete slabs were painted white and the cast-in-place elements were treated with rough finishes, enhancing the differences in molding and fabrication of the structural members. In the case of the American Republic building, the two large bearing walls were finished with a sandblasted granite aggregate; in the case of the American Can Company, the cast-in-place reinforced concrete porches received a warm light gray granite aggregate finish, exposed by sandblasting. The precise finish of the exposed structural elements is sufficiently refined to give the buildings a luxurious and sophisticated appearance.

These basic qualities define the tectonic aspects of Gordon Bunshaft's works built with industrialized elements. As Bunshaft himself stated, "We have taken prefabrication and made a design asset of it."[78]

Gordon Bunshaft on the terrace of his home in East Hampton, September of 1970.

73 Le Corbusier. *Towards a New Architecture.* New York: Dover Publications Inc., 1986, pp. 70-72.

74 The sheet number five was updated on August 08, 1962. The update is a copy of the original plan in which there are no changes with respect to structural elements and construction indications. What was added were the projections in thick blue dotted line of the interior partitions and side walls of the house.

75 KRINSKY, Carol H. *Gordon Bunshaft of Skidmore, Owings & Merrill.* New York, The Architectural History Foundation Cambridge. The MIT Press, p. 138.

76 GENSERT, R. M. "Precast Apartment Structure Saves Cost, Shows Its Design". *Architectural Record*, New York: F. W. Dodge Corporation. May of 1962, p. 202.

77 "Building with a Future". In: *Time Magazine,* 16th of September of 1957. New York: Time Inc., p. 86.

78 "The Architects from 'Skid's Row'". In: *Fortune Magazine*, January 1958. New York: TIME INC., p. 215.

Image Credits

BAER, Morley:
56 (right photograph)

BARTOS, Adam:
62, 178, 181, 184

BLESSING, Hedrich:
18

GORDON BUNSHAFT ARCHIVES (Avery Archives - Columbia University in the City of New York):
14 (photograph by Hans Namuth), 16, 17, 18, 19 (right drawings), 20 (photograph by Robert Ficks), 34, 36 (plan photograph by Gilbert Ask), 37 (top photograph by James S. Hornbeck), 37 (bottom photograph by Torkel Korling), 103, 163, 165 (left drawing), 166, 167, 170, 186, 199.

GARRISON, Richard:
19 (left)

GEORGES, Alexandre:
164 (right photograph), 165 (right photograph)

KAUFMANN & FABRY:
22

KIRKLAND, Douglas (Look Magazine):
187

MICHALS, Duane:
162

NAMUTH, Hans:
3

SICA PALERMO, Nicolás (author):
6, 10, 13, 38, 40 (bottom photograph), 41, 42 (right drawing), 44 (right drawing), 45, 57 (middle and right photographs), 60 (midlle and right drawings), 61 (all drawings), 66 (all drawings), 67 (right drawing), 67 (right plant), 71 (right photograph), 74 (all drawings), 74-77 (all drawings), 82 (all drawings), 86, 88, 89 (all drawings), 92 (photograph and drawing), 93, 96, 97 (right photograph), 99, 100 (right drawing), 101 (left drawing), 104, 106, 109 (all drawings), 110, 112, 113, 114, 115, 116, 117, 118, 119, 122, 124, 125, 126, 127 (photograph and drawing), 129, 130, 132, 133, 134, 135, 136, 138, 139 (photograph and drawing), 140, 141, 143, 144 (left photograph), 145 (photograph and drawing), 146, 148, 149, 150, 152, 153, 154 (photograph and drawing), 155 (all photographs), 156, 157, 158, 164 (left photograph), 172, 175 (middle and bottom drawings), 176, 177 (top drawing), 179 (all drawings), 180, 181 (left drawings), 182, 183 (left drawing), 188, 189, 192, 194, 196.

SOM (Skidmore, Owings & Merrill) ARCHIVES:
12, 111, 144 (right drawing)

STURTEVANT, Roger:
62 (left photograph)

© STOLLER, Ezra/ESTO:
42 (left photograph), 44 (left photograph) 56 (left photograph), 57 (left photograph), 62 (middle photograph), 63 (all photographs), 70 (all photographs), 71 (left photograph), 83 (all photographs), 90, 91, 94, 100 (left photograph), 101 (right photograph), 102, 120, 128, 160, 169, 171, 175 (bottom photograph), 181 (right photograph).

VIRGINA MUSEUM OF FINE ARTS
107, 108

Magazines

***ARCHITECTURAL FORUM*, May of 1949:**
43

***ARCHITECTURAL FORUM*, June of 1950:**
39, 40 (top drawings)

***ARCHITECTURAL FORUM*, January of 1954:**
44 (left photograph)

***ARCHITECTURAL FORUM*, May of 1954:**
121

***ARCHITECTURAL FORUM*, July of 1961:**
97 (left drawings)

***ARCHITECTURAL RECORD*, November of 1959:**
98

***ARCHITECTURAL RECORD*, December of 1959:**
78

***ARCHITECTURAL REVIEW*, May of 1957:**
25, 26, 27

***ARTS & ARCHITECTURE*, February of 1965:**
67 (left drawing)

***BOLAFFI*, May-June 1973:**
173, 175 (top photograph),

***MoMA BULLETIN (Museum of Modern Art)*, fall of 1950:**
28, 30, 31, 32, 33

***PROGRESSIVE ARCHITECTURE*, September of 1963:**
46, 48

Books

DANZ, Ernst. *Architecture of Skidmore, Owings & Merrill, 1950 - 1962*, New York: Frederick A. Praeger, 1963:
52, 53, 60 (left drawing)

Le Corbusier. *Towards a New Architecture*. New York: Dover Publications Inc., 1986:
185